P9-DVS-509

# THEORETICAL ANXIETY AND DESIGN STRATEGIES

## IN THE WORK OF EIGHT CONTEMPORARY ARCHITECTS

For B.F., to whom I owe so much
and whose passion for architecture I know so well

RAFAEL MONEO
# THEORETICAL ANXIETY AND DESIGN STRATEGIES
## IN THE WORK OF EIGHT CONTEMPORARY ARCHITECTS

The MIT Press
Cambridge, Massachusetts
London, England

Published in association with
the Harvard University Graduate School of Design

© 2004 ACTAR, Barcelona, Spain
All rights reserved. No part of this book may be reproduced in any form
by any electronic or mechanical means (including photocopying, recording,
or information storage and retrieval) without permission in writing from
the publisher.

The images from the James Stirling chapter are used with permission of the
Fonds James Stirling, Centre Canadien d'Architecture / Canadian Centre for
Architecture, Montréal.

Robert Venturi and Denise Scott Brown, Peter Eisenman, Álvaro Siza,
Frank O. Gehry, Rem Koolhaas, and Jacques Herzog and Pierre de Meuron
have consented to the publication of those illustrations whose copyrights
belong to them.

MIT Press books may be purchased at special quantity discounts
for business or sales promotional use. For information, please email
special_sales@mitpress.mit.edu.

Printed and bound in Spain.

ISBN 0-262-13443-8

Library of Congress Control Number: 2004101376

Translated by Gina Cariño
Book design by Ramon Prat and Anja Tränkel
Collaborator: Max Weber
Production by Actar Pro, Barcelona

10    9    8    7    6    5    4    3

# Contents

# Preface

I have always held that schools of architecture must pay attention to the contemporary scene, to architects who have yet to enter the Olympus of textbooks. So it was that in the early nineties I offered students of the Harvard Graduate School of Design a course on the work of contemporary architects. I still consider some of these my elders or masters. The rest are colleagues, friends whose works I admire.

This book is a compilation of those lectures. The works of Stirling, Venturi and Scott Brown, Rossi, Eisenman, Siza, Gehry, Koolhaas, and Herzog & de Meuron are closely examined under the rubric of "Theoretical Anxiety and Design Strategies." I use the word "anxiety" because the study of architecture has in recent times been tackled in a way that is closer to reflection and critical discourse than to any desire to elaborate a systematic theory. Robert Venturi's book *Complexity and Contradiction in Architecture* would testify to that. It is a caustic examination leading to critical reflection; as such, it is a theoretical disquisition or an expression of theoretical anxiety, not a theory. In contrast, Aldo Rossi's *The Architecture of the City* shows the drama of one who, having embarked on an ambitious urbanistic treatise, ends up indulging in pure personal catharsis. At this point in history we appreciate Rossi's book not so much for its contribution to the development of theory as for its very expression of ideas, its exemplification of an architect making use of words. Theoretical anxiety is a more accurate term than theory, too, when we refer to the writings of Peter Eisenman. These are texts that reveal an intellectual capacity to transfer to architecture concepts acquired in readings of contemporary philosophers. As for Rem Koolhaas, the last to lend himself to discussion on disquisitions, it is important to understand *Delirious New York*, still to date his most valuable written work, as a book of essays, an original and very personal reflection on the principles implicit in the architecture of the city of skyscrapers. The other term needing explanation is "strategies." Here this refers to the mechanisms, procedures, paradigms, and formal devices that recur in the work of architects—the tools with which they give shape to their constructions. I speak of formal mechanisms as much when I think of the manipulation of plans and sections in the architecture of James Stirling as when I contemplate the unfolding of the shapes we associate with Frank Gehry. It may be harder to apply the term to architects like Álvaro Siza and Herzog & de Meuron, but given the former's very personal architectural calligraphy and the latter's obsessive desire to align their architecture with certain materials, I believe they can still be discussed along the same lines.

Now that I've explained the book's title, let me try to make some sense out of the grouping of such disparate architects. My intention was to make a study of those architects who have been most influential in our times, who at some time in the final quarter of the twentieth century have aroused the interest of architecture students, whose works have been most widely discussed, so much that the books they are documented in amount to tacit treatises. It seemed to me a must to begin with James Stirling. His figure invited an effort to connect what can be considered the linguistic legacy of the avant-gardes—still alive at the start of the sixties—to the penchant for complexity that came afterward. Though he is less discussed nowadays, it is obligatory to begin any study of the evolution of contemporary architecture with Stirling.

Stirling is immediately followed by Robert Venturi and Aldo Rossi. These two have often been paired, among other reasons because *Complexity and Contradiction in Architecture* and *L'architettura della città* were published in the same year (1966), but the American architect must precede the Italian. Venturi's influence was immediate and dominant in the sixties and early seventies, whereas Rossi's work, while well known in Europe, did not become "universal" until the late seventies, when his thought was disseminated in America. Each illustrated his ideas with his own works. Venturi, with the built realm as starting point, tried to explore the discipline and show how much it resists norm and tends toward the singular. In contrast, Rossi attempted to establish the discipline after having decoded the keys that explain the architecture of the city. Both influenced architectural thinking for decades, and that influence is felt to this day.

An express desire to make theory precede practice characterizes the work of an architect like Peter Eisenman. Responsible for the theory behind the work of the New Yorkers grouped together in the 1972 book *Five Architects*, he also spearheaded the Institute for Architecture and Urban Studies and *Oppositions*, thereby playing a key role in American architectural culture. Sometimes misunderstood but never ignored, his theoretical writings occupy a prominent place in the panorama of influential architects that these lectures try to describe.

Álvaro Siza and Frank Gehry dominated the architectural scene in the eighties. With them, theory seemed to give way to an architecture that was explainable through the actual building work. Although Gehry is a few years older, I present Siza first. His architecture has always been admired and he has had clout in European architectural culture since the very start of his career, when the Italian magazines discovered him. His work has always been followed with enormous interest, and one might say that he has evolved through the years without forsaking the theoretical and social commitments of his beginnings. It took Gehry some time to impose himself, but his impact on eighties architecture is unquestionable. His deliberate pragmatism, combined with his innovative way of handling materials and forms, removed from any deference to context, soon made him an undisputed reference. We will trace the incredible journey through which a provocative, quasi-marginal architect became an institutional favorite in the nineties, the decade that saw the definitive consolidation of his career through a whole chain of major works crowned by the Guggenheim of Bilbao.

Theoretical and professional interests changed radically in this decade, and the figure of Rem Koolhaas was a paradigm of this change. Koolhaas wanted architects to recover the rationality that was implicit in the architecture that developers were building, free of intellectual prejudice. There, he believed, lay the roots of an architecture that was alive, undistorted by the theoretical anxieties of the advocates of a cultured architecture. There lay the key to the architecture of a globalized world that did not regard history with the nostalgia of previous generations. *Delirious New York*, first published in 1978, had a retroactive effect in the nineties and was complemented by the very popular *S, M, L, XL*, which instituted a type of book that pays more attention to image and scheme than to text.

A counterpoint to this was the early work of Herzog & de Meuron, which proclaimed the transcendental nature of elemental solids. Contact with the figurative world of the minimalist artists was evident here, reviving the tradition that links the work of architects to that of painters. Herzog & de Meuron's influence in architecture schools was immediate, and their capacity to tackle any brief and adapt to the most diverse circumstances explains why students continue to watch their work so closely. They surely have to be included in the handful of architects I consider influential.

Having explained the choice of architects, I hasten to explain how a set of lectures became this book. As I was saying, the lectures were given as lessons at Harvard's Graduate School of Design. This was in the course of the school years 1992–1993 and 1993–1994. They resurfaced in a series of talks I delivered in November 1995 at Madrid's Círculo de Bellas Artes, at the request of José Manuel López Peláez. Without him the material presented in this publication would probably never have seen the light. The Círculo lectures, recorded in tapes, are the seed of the following texts. The book therefore preserves some of the complicity with students that occurs in a class. The colloquial tone of the classroom is maintained as much as possible, and the same images that were projected during the lectures are reproduced here. As the reader will understand, the coordination of texts and images is crucial in a book of this nature. Hence the attention given to the graphic design, achieved thanks to Ramon Prat, director of ACTAR, who has spearheaded this project.

A couple more comments are in order. First, I didn't actually talk about Venturi, nor about Herzog & de Meuron, at the Círculo. But when I thought of publishing the lectures in a book, their inclusion seemed indispensable, as both the American architect and the Swiss partners have played a vital role in contemporary architecture and I had in fact addressed them in other courses. Second, working over old lecture notes, I was tempted to stretch forward in time to works the architects built after 1995. In the end I chose to leave the lectures as they were, notwithstanding a license here and there, such as mention of a later publication of Eisenman. Neither has the cut-off date been fully respected in presenting the work of Herzog & de Meuron, the text for which is taken from a lecture I gave at the GSD some years later.

And that's about it. But I wouldn't want to end this introduction without thanking Peter Rowe, Director of the GSD, for the support he always gave to the publication of these lectures, and mentioning Carmen Díez Medina, who helped me rewrite the text. Without her talent, sensibility, and generous dedication to the project, there would be no book today.

# JAMES STIRLING

Starting this series of lectures with James Stirling is no casual thing, nor the result of any penchant for chronology. Stirling may not arouse today the interest he did in his time, but it is difficult, little less than impossible even, to think of another architect whose work illustrates an entire cycle of recent architectural history as eloquently as his. Stirling was a person who liked to come across as the instinctive, direct, spontaneous kind, the antithesis of the intellectual architect. Nevertheless he was abreast of the tendencies and interests of his contemporaries. Today his work can be considered the most complete register of architectural history spanning the years in which he practiced the profession. Hence, this lecture should serve as background for all the other lectures. [1]

Stirling earned his architecture degree in 1949. Colin Rowe has vividly described the architectural atmosphere of the school in Liverpool, a city that can be considered a paradigm of deep England. [2] Its buildings impressed upon Stirling the importance of construction in architecture, and indeed the solidness of Liverpool's docks would be a constant in his work. Stirling's experience of Liverpool was surely part and parcel of his formal education. At the same time, he became acquainted with the work of Le Corbusier, and this experience was the counterpoint he would maintain throughout his career as well. According to Rowe, Stirling's enthusiasm for Le Corbusier was a product of chance. He says that we can only attribute to coincidence the fact that during Stirling's student years, Liverpool's architecture school became a refuge for Warsaw's, whose professors were Corbusians of the strictest kind: a desire to be closer to the West than to the East reinforced the Polish professors' fervent admiration of Le Corbusier. In any case it must be noted that the precocious Stirling had by that time ceased to feed solely on academic tradition, and that the message of the Swiss master took root in him early on.

English society had in the fifties made "modern architecture" its banner and emblem. "Modern" was an accepted language, something no longer made an issue of. Those were the years of architects like Frederick Gibberd, Basil Spence, Eric Lyons, Powell & Moya, and Leslie Martin, a parade of personalities who, perhaps without manifesting the creative capacity of the modern Italian architects of the thirties, had assimilated the principles of the modern movement in architecture, using them so profusely as to be able to claim they had popularized

1 All images in this chapter are used with permission of the Fonds James Stirling, Centre Canadien d'Architecture / Canadian Centre for Architecture, Montréal

2 Colin Rowe, "James Stirling: A Highly Personal and Very Disjointed Memoir," introductory essay in James Stirling, Michael Wilford and Associates, compiled and edited by Peter Arnell and Ted Bickford (New York: Rizzoli International, 1984), pp.10–27. Also: "Eulogy: Jim Stirling" and "Jim Stirling (1923–1992)" in Colin Rowe, As I Was Saying, ed. Alexander Caragonne (Cambridge: MIT Press, 1996), vol. 3, pp. 341–358.

them. Stirling realized that the popularization of the provocative avant-garde language only served to render it banal, exhausting it altogether. A building like the new Royal Festival Hall by Robert Matthews and Leslie Martin, dated 1951, clearly showed what instrumentalization of the modern could lead to. I believe that Stirling set out to find new channels for modern architecture from the very start of his career. His attitude was shared by some of his contemporaries, and here we must remember the role played by Alison and Peter Smithson as instigators and movers within Team X. It was they who, while fully enthused with the modern, first detected fissures in it. They may not have explicitly pronounced themselves in this regard, but their thoughts were evident through the architectures they took an interest in. The architects gathered around the Smithsons admired medieval urbanism, the picturesque English architecture of the eighteenth century (which culminated with the English landscape gardeners), the industrial constructions of the nineteenth, and the projects of the Russian constructivists, among other things. Stirling was receptive to these stimuli, and we will presently see how directly he addressed them in many of his early projects. In the conviction that one had to go beyond the norms dictated by the modern, Stirling in the fifties and sixties made admirable efforts to give the language of modern architecture a new structure.

And so it was that early on in his career, Stirling discovered the potential inherent in the section and its linear shifting. If Le Corbusier had at some point said that architecture is the plan, that the architect goes about his work with the horizontal plane for a starting point, Stirling found in the sections of nineteenth-century industrial buildings the matrix of a new architecture. Moreover, he found that it was not too far removed from images that the Russian constructivists had familiarized us with. To construct, he discovered, is to master the section, and we move it over the plan, following linear structures that have the capacity to define whole precincts and "clusters," such as those his colleagues of Team X had taught him to see in the urbanism of rural England. Whereas Beaux-Arts architecture emphasized the plan, modern architecture was interested in the section. On one hand, all the technical and constructional problems of the building were reflected in the section; with it, architecture reached the degree of positive knowledge that the times called for. On the other hand, the spirit of freedom that came hand in hand with modernity was duly represented in the movement through space that the section involved.

Stirling exploited the potential of the section in the course of brilliant projects that secured widespread admiration of his work. By the late sixties, however, manipulation of the section generally gave way to mere extrusion of it, and a certain redundancy that made projects less attractive. Stirling was aware of this problem, attentive as he was to the changes of opinion that transpired in the sixties in matters of architectural theory, and he welcomed into his studio a very young Leon Krier. Krier had proven to be in total harmony with the architects of the Italian Tendenza, who endeavored to make the city architecture's raison d'être. Sure enough, Krier's arrival brought about a radical change in what up to then had been Stirling's way of thinking and doing architecture. Stirling must have read *Collage City*, a text by Colin Rowe and Fred Koetter. [3] Here, Stirling's early mentor declared his admiration of the older city. It was at this point that Stirling's projects ceased to be governed by the section and the linear structure. The plan prevailed anew, and with it the old city, the collage, the landscape. The *promenade architecturale*, a Corbusian principle, became the guiding design tool. Feeding on it, Stirling's architecture became narrative and pedagogical, and he found the opportunity to express the new attitudes in Germany, which was still remaking itself and insisting that architecture be a representation and reflection of institutions. The opportunity came in three museum projects: for

**3** Colin Rowe and Fred Koetter, *Collage City* (Cambridge: MIT Press, 1978).

10

Düsseldorf, Cologne, and Stuttgart. All three projects celebrated the triumph of the plan, and when we examine them we will see how an able architect can transform the methodological tools he has used previously and take on a totally new approach, effortlessly. This has happened frequently in the history of architecture, and here Stirling presents himself to us as a true paradigm of what an architect can be and do.

Stirling's success in Europe turned worldwide, and the final fifteen years of his career saw a wide range of projects dominated by the plan. I don't think I'm exaggerating. Just as the section had become a mere procedure, manipulation of the plan became routine. Gone was the tension that had made the Staatsgalerie of Stuttgart a definitive architectural work. There will be time to dwell on Stuttgart, so I will not discuss its excesses just yet. Stirling, an architect of exceptional instinct, realized the risks he took there, and the Braun factory in Melsungen, which can be considered his final project, bore signs of the new change that could have been. Inherent in the Braun project was an eagerness to simplify the presence of diverse elements and reinforce their autonomy, which could have led to a new liberation, this time from the tyranny of the plan. Stirling died prematurely, however, and there's no telling for sure what the next phase of his career would have been like, but there is no doubt that Stirling, attentive as he was to the winds of history, had already changed course when his life was interrupted.

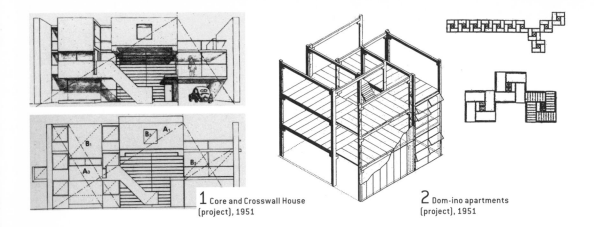

1 Core and Crosswall House
(project), 1951

2 Dom-ino apartments
(project), 1951

**1** There is a strong Corbusian presence in the Core and Crosswall House, a 1951 project, not only in the linguistic elements—such as the horizontal window and the stairs, with emphasis on the *tracés régulateurs* and the building's frontal nature—but also in the constructional elements and, in accordance with fifties Le Corbusier, in the importance given to the materials. The Core and Crosswall House has a certain propensity toward the "volumetric," as against the strictly "planimetric." This may well be its most characteristic feature.

**2** That same year, Stirling proposed this version of the Maison Dom-ino with prefabricated elements. Against the extreme freedom advocated by the Corbusian principle of the plan, geometry appears here—a centered geometry that gives rise to standardized construction (which supports the use of prefabricated elements), whether in the building structure or the envelope. Stirling's houses endeavored to be independent units that could be enlarged, in part or as a whole, through an overall change of scale. In this they differed substantially from Le Corbusier's Maison Dom-ino, which always presented itself as a definitive architectural episode. A certain pragmatism one might call very English began to make itself felt in this project of Stirling, constituting a forward step in his career that could no longer be dismissed as naive and innocent—adjectives that would rightly apply to the Core and Crosswall House.

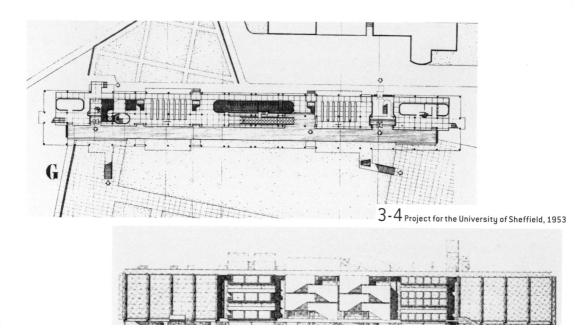

3-4 Project for the University of Sheffield, 1953

13

3-4 Here is a project of 1953 for the University of Sheffield. Notice what ensues when a floor plan is conceived as an assemblage in which compliance with syntactic guidelines is more important than the unfolding of elements serving compositional criteria. And there is no use for the *promenade architecturale*. Any kind of iconographic allusion is done away with. Neither could we begin to talk about an awareness of the picturesque: contemplating the roof, for example, we find that it is the arrangement of elements that dictates the profile. The building can be classified among what may be called translations of abstract architecture, in which prevail criteria having to do with repetition, alternation, number, etc., over and above any figurative component. This is architecture as syntax.

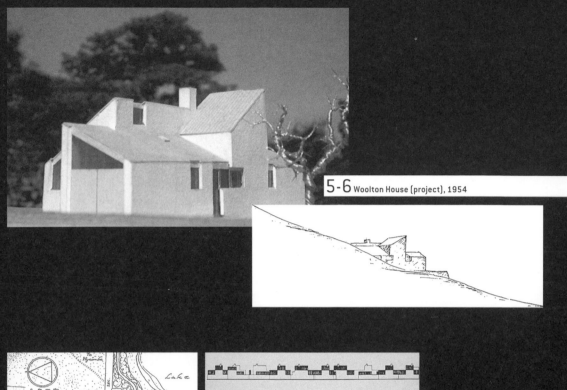

5-6 Woolton House (project), 1954

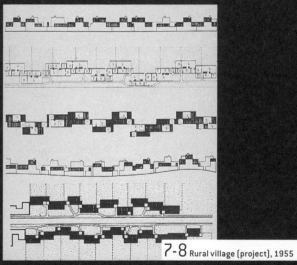

7-8 Rural village (project), 1955

**5-6** With the Woolton House of 1954, a more sophisticated project, we get an idea of Stirling's great receptiveness to stimuli. Whereas the Core and Crosswall House was dominated by an abstract volumetry that did not address building tradition, the Woolton House incorporated a whole series of elements that clearly had their origin in rural constructions. It was at this point that the first criticisms against the modern movement were heard in England—a modern movement that was being conventionalized and that had started to be consumed by the institutions. The young people of those years who formed Team X began to wonder whether architectural truth was not more present in rural architecture, which was better at addressing the specific, than in modern architecture, which was bent on defining norms. Emphasis in the Woolton House was on the richness of a picturesque profile, the result of the appearance of a higher room, a chimney, a window, a roof. On the other hand the house was attentive to its connection to the ground and sought to settle on it effortlessly, without a struggle, without promoting that dichotomy between building and place that was explicit in the Corbusian *pilotis*. This Stirling of the early fifties was beginning to explore roads that totally deviated from those that had been established by the modern tradition and absorbed into England's official architecture.

15

**7-8** These 1955 studies for the expansion of existing rural cores were carried out in tune with the work of those who formed Team X: the Smithsons, Theo Crosby, the painter Edward Wright, etc. All of them were looking for a new form, one more natural and organic and governed by the structure, and it was in anonymous architecture and earlier urbanism that they found answers. They would contemplate a medieval town like West Wycombe in Buckinghamshire and ask: can't we retrieve its sense of structure? A sense of structure, that is, that went beyond applying a series of syntactic norms to an abstract scheme, as we have seen in the University of Sheffield. Stirling's change of approach was substantial and profound. Only intense reflection on the principles governing architecture can bring about such a radical change of posture.

Though a certain hierarchy was addressed in the walls being set parallel to the street, the structure Stirling now used was more flexible. In this project, it was the shape of the structure that he was concerned with. Paying less

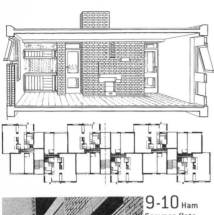

**9-10** Ham Common flats, near Richmond, Surrey, 1955–1958

**9-10** It was with the Ham Common flats of 1955–1958, near Richmond, Surrey, that Stirling, only 29, made his grand entrance into the English architectural scene. This was an extraordinarily mature project for such a young architect. The plan can be considered a fruit of his apprenticeship with Eric Lyons and is like the plans of so many other English houses of the period. The influence of the later Le Corbusier—the Le Corbusier of Ronchamp and the Madame Sarabhai house in India—is evident both inside and out. One could say that this project constituted Stirling's peculiar version of brutalism. Note the exaggeration in the autonomy given to the various elements: windows, rainspouts, chimneys. These elements become the protagonists of an architecture whose volumetric substance appears to be sustained by the terse brick fabric. Stirling tackled architecture in this way elsewhere as well, such as in the Preston housing development or the Children's Home in Putney, London.

attention to the actual houses, Stirling drew the profile of the street, a profile that reflected the topography of the place. The result was a project with an unquestionable urban flavor, its most prominent aspect being perhaps its capacity to express the notion of continuity.

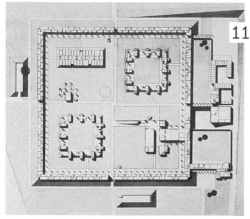

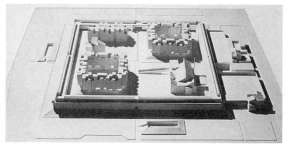

**11-12** Such was the impact of the young Stirling's incursion into British architecture that in 1958 he was invited to participate in a limited competition for Churchill College in Cambridge University. The works of Louis Kahn did not escape his notice, and were making waves among English architects in general. Issue 9 (1960) of the *Architects' Year Book*, a magazine much in line with the Team X mentality, was one of the first publications on Kahn's work to appear in Europe. The college was for Stirling a walled city where the students' rooms were the perimeter defenses. Revitalizing the interior of the premises, he built pavilions to house the various commu-

nal functions: libraries, dining rooms, clinic, and so on. The project was a summary of all his previous works, while anticipating another project of the same kind: his contribution to the "Roma Interrotta" exhibition of 1978. The two projects wrapped up two different phases of his career. Churchill College bid farewell to his youth, the years of training during which Stirling had anxiously been feeling around for the direction his architecture should take. Thereafter things were clearer to him. Selwyn College that followed can be seen as a summary of what his work would be like in the coming years.

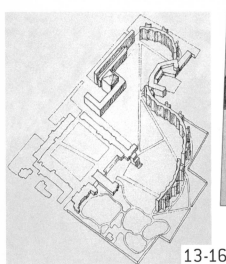

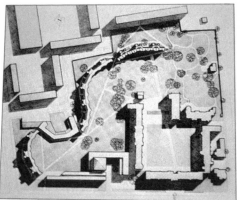

13-16 Selwyn College (project), Cambridge University, 1959

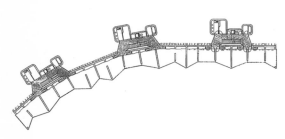

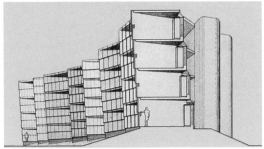

13-16 Although the 1959 project for Selwyn College, also in Cambridge, was never carried out, in my opinion it is key to an understanding of Stirling's subsequent work. On one hand, it explored the potential of linear developments and their importance in defining premises and stressing the value of boundaries. On the other hand, it initiated an investigation into the significance of the section in generating architectural form. Indeed it could be said that from Selwyn College onward, his architecture originated in the section. But above all, Selwyn College provided Stirling with the opportunity to use glass in a novel way. Glass, for Stirling, would no longer be a material with which to build a flat curtain wall whose main attribute was transparency. With the help of the fractures created by the section and the shiftings imposed by the linear scheme, he would transform it in such a way that the glazed surfaces came across as solids. The possibilities of giving glass that sense of solidness became a recurrent theme in Stirling's work. In his hands, and beginning with Selwyn College, glass was a material with which to combine the lightness required by linear developments with the solidness that allowed one to perceive architecture as volume.

The extraordinarily eloquent drawings shown here are in themselves a brief of the architecture that he would develop in the following fifteen years. We must take a close look at them if we are to understand how Stirling conceived architecture. First, the new construction engaged in a dialogue with the preexisting by acting as an undulating cordon closing the garden, thereby fencing in the space and giving the old college a new character. However, the construction of this undulating glass wall—where one easily discerns the shadow of an architect like Aalto—was an exercise in section design not too far removed from what the classical architects insisted on in their drawings of vertical sequences of moldings. Stirling pays close attention to the interior and exterior sections, and it is in this dialectic between "inside" and "outside" that glass finds its place in the front facade, in the same way as the solid wall does in the rear facade. A good look at the room shows that it, too, was drawn up with its profiles in mind: the handrail is proof of this. Otherwise, the building is very simple. The staircase, encapsulated by a tower, gives access to smaller rooms in which the plumbing and utility installations—a toilet, a shower, a small kitchen that foments communication between the four or five occupants of each flat—take on a formal presence that inevitably recalls Kahn's servant spaces. Here the floor plan is but the direct expression of the program. It is therefore minimal. It does not have the self-indulgence that we find in the section.

**17-23** The Selwyn College project was not carried out, but it led to Stirling's being commissioned for the Engineering Building at the University of Leicester. He began to work on this in 1959 and it was finished in 1963. It must be considered one of the four or five most important works of his career. Since the guiding thread of this lecture is Stirling's journey from section to plan, I want to show how the section was the matrix of the architecture of this project. But I wouldn't like this objective, above all a pedagogical one, to overshadow other issues relevant to the building. For example, there is a parallel with Hannes Meyer's 1927 project for the League of Nations. Both are abstract and volumetric, true to the idea that architecture is first and foremost a formal phenomenon. What the architect seems to have been concerned with in either case was the balance of masses, a balance achieved in a quasi-canonical manner. In the League of Nations project, the office building is a perfect counterpoint for the volume of the auditorium, and the same goes for the workshops and tower at Leicester. And in between we could situate Frank Lloyd Wright's laboratory tower for Johnson Wax, where, as in Stirling's architecture, although in a different way, glass takes on the quality of a solid material.

The plinth containing the workshops may be the project's most prominent episode—or, if you wish, the reference onto which all the other episodes are projected. We can speak in terms of geometry exercises that give architecture a sense of abstraction. Stirling started out by thinking of sheds not unlike those of nineteenth-century industrial architecture, subsequently transforming them into something more dynamic, and this through a dramatic twist that makes the diagonal of the rectangle a key element: it is the meeting of the diagonal and the perimeter that produces an unexpected profile, which in turn becomes the work's most pronounced formal feature. The architecture's abstract nature was reinforced by the lack of distinction made between vertical and slanting elements of the envelope: everything here is volume.

Awareness of a new way of manipulating glass, of its being "solidifiable" and therefore useful in the construction of an abstract architecture, is patent in the tower, where glass passes over slabs and sills, in continuity with brick slip surfaces. Whoever is interested in this should examine the tower closely, for here, indeed, is a tight design exercise where the relation

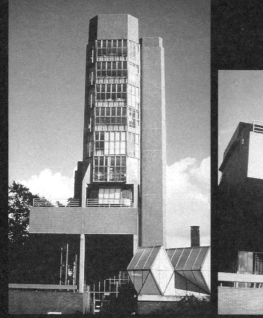

**17-23** Engineering Building, University of Leicester, 1959–1963

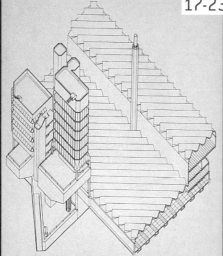

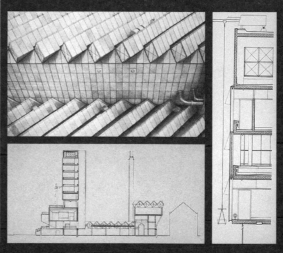

between structure and envelope reveals not so much the architect's talent as a designer, as his capacity to turn a design operation into a critical reflection. Peter Eisenman explained it in an *Oppositions* article that I would put down as recommended reading.[4]

**4** Peter Eisenman, "Real and English: The Destruction of the Box I," *Oppositions* 4 (New York, 1974), pp. 5–34.

But the formal design strategy—the dialectic between the plinth containing the workshops and the tower containing the laboratories—is always seasoned, catalyzed, by accents. Stirling always used accent—remember how he encrusted the brick wall of Ham Common with different constructive elements—and here he did so in abundance. The brick rail, the glass prism of the spiral staircase, the contour of the tower's corners, the windows that jut outward sharply, the maintenance cradle—each of these elements can be contemplated separately because it was designed autonomously. One could say that they testify to the presence of the necessary in a world of abstract forms, although it is also true that their being obligatory in terms of utility did not prevent the architect from elaborating their forms with freedom and daring. Stirling always liked the provocation involved in turning useful elements into figures with a formal value of their own. Hence the ambiguity, and the element of surprise, in his works.

Stirling's work is characterized by a wealth of episodes in which self-sufficient visions and images can be contemplated independently. But such autonomy of parts and elements did not give rise, at this stage of his career, to the collage; a more extensive, formal strategy here guaranteed a unity that would more ably address the most urgent questions implicit in the building's construction. In my opinion, it was this capacity of Stirling to maintain the unitary idea while producing a wide variety of episodes that characterizes his architecture. It also distinguishes his architecture from that of his followers, who have not always managed to keep up the double play.

On the other hand—remember that this project was contemporaneous with those of Archigram, where the exaggerated presence of mechanical installations in itself became an image—Leicester has vertical communication elements that constitute volumetric counterpoints, testifying to the Kahnian influence we noted in discussing Churchill College. These elements strike a contrast with the tilted prisms containing the classrooms, manifesting Stirling's admiration for the constructivist architects.

Returning to my thesis for this lecture, let's examine Leicester in terms of the importance here of the elaboration of the section: the importance of the outer skin in the definition of the architecture. Look at the section of the tower, for example, and observe the painstaking geometry of the windows. Or stop to examine the entrance platform, and notice how the rail is not just an instrument with a functional value, but an element with full formal value in defining the overall space. Or if we dwell on the meeting of any two surfaces, we cannot help admiring the near-artisanal attention that went into the elaboration of the joints.

Interest in the section is also perceivable in larger areas, as in the corridor with exaggerated braces appropriating the space, making for an intense architectural experience. Likewise in the main entrance, under the slanted floor of one of the lecture halls, with the glass-encased spiral staircase taking possession of the porticoed space like a huge pillar—here, once again, glass appears as a solid element. In sum, at the core of the brilliant architecture of Leicester is not so much the concept of linearity, but the section. In Leicester, the section is also the envelope, the skin. Against the neutral, inert wall of traditional building, the modern architect discovered the lure of manipulating surfaces. The Stirling who prided himself on being a primary, instinctive builder comes across at Leicester as an enthusiastic discoverer of the sensory, tactile quality of architecture.

24-27 The History Faculty building at Cambridge University (1964–1967) illustrates how the section can determine an entire construction. The strategy is simple: Stirling seemed to have had in mind the library model par excellence, the one with the reading room covered by a grand dome, as in the British Museum library. But watch the way he manipulates the typology that associates the dome with the reading room. Imagine working under a fourth of a dome in a fourth of a reading room, and picture this fourth of a reading room flanked by two built volumes. That's the History Faculty building. The dome is really not a dome, but more like a tent. You could say that the classic typology is

**24-27** History Faculty building, Cambridge University, 1964–1967

manipulated in the plan, and applied to the section immediately afterward. The development of the two volumes flanking the glazed space is carried out through control of the section, through which the vertical sequence of spaces so characteristic of Stirling's work is pursued. Such emphasis on the section reappears in the courtyard, which helps resolve the building's contact with the ground, as well as in innumerable little details, accents of the kind we mentioned when we were looking at Leicester. The dialectic between different solids comes to the fore in this work. On one hand is a glazed cover stressing the pyramidal geometry of the quarter-pseudodome. On the other are the masses of brick slip that border it, where some set-back glass planes take on the nature of solids when connected by oblique elements that, in turn, lend a sense of continuity to the facade.

**28-29** Drawn up in 1965, this is one of the projects in which Stirling's penchant for studying the section and linear development is perhaps most evident. The fact that it was a job for a steelworks company, Dorman Long, seems to have given him the pretext to make the idea of construction—section in motion—predominant. Here, too, the section presents a profile in which the higher stories have less depth, resulting in the desired inclined glass plane. But the glazed volume does not stay intact in this case. Stirling adorns it, shall we say almost *michelangelically*, with an entire outer steel frame, exalting the client's product. There is something excessive or unnecessary about the artificial order that the steel profiles create; and the manner in which these profiles come in contact with the fragile material to which the building's volumetric condition is entrusted, glass, could be described as overdramatic. A few years later, Venturi would be disdaining the efforts architecture exerted just to convey a message, and defending the rationality that was implicit in the "decorated shed." When Stirling introduced the triangulated banner with the name of the company, with its unmistakably modernist flavor (one thinks of

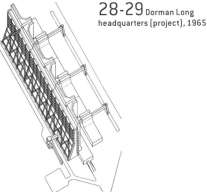

**28-29** Dorman Long headquarters (project), 1965

Asplund's banners, for example), he was actually putting the expressive capacity of architecture in question. In any case, what interests us here, which the models clearly manifest, is that this architecture was thought out in terms of the section. With the section one arrives at the formal reflection to which the project seems to allude: that produced by the encounter of vertical and slanted planes.

30-33 We are now in the late sixties and Stirling continues to put a great deal of emphasis, perhaps too much, on the previously described procedure, as we will see in Queen's College in Oxford, a project executed from 1966 to 1971. Situated on a pretty meander of a river, here the linear structure flows in a U that, like an open cloister, endeavors to be a modern version of traditional college court-yards. The dichotomy between individual cells and communal life, manifested in the open public space, finds an answer in Stirlingesque geometry. So it is that the platform, in the manner of a courtyard opening onto the river, becomes the most important element of Queen's College. Aside from being its major outdoor public space, underneath it accommodates activities so important in the life of a university residence hall, including those related to dining rooms and kitchens.

Again the section assumes command, as the U shape is made to come from the meeting of the familiar vertical and slanted glass surfaces. The U scheme produces a rather forced consciousness of communal life, as illus-trated by room interiors exposed to view, since glass is really not the "solid" material Stirling wished it to be. Users of the building have in fact reacted critically, shunning the transparency of the facade with canopies and blinds. Stirling's interest in the section is patent in the attic, where the duplex room is a paradigm for his way of interpreting space. A close look reveals numerous details in which the architect's painstaking penchant for elaborating the sec-tion comes to the fore, as in the spouts and gutters that serve to articulate the meeting of glass planes.

Unfortunately Stirling's attention to the section seems to have been one-sided, resulting in a neglected rear facade, and we can say the neglect went too far. Stirling paid too high a price to maintain a certain view of the building. Anyone who stops to look at the conflicting rear facade will understand this.

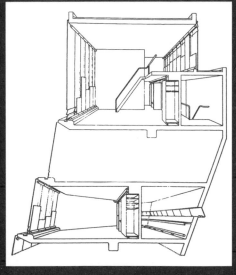

**30-33** Queen's College, Oxford, 1966–1971

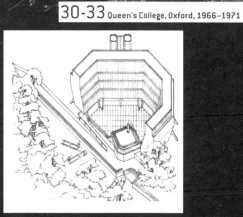

**34-35** The project for the Olivetti Training School in Haslemere, Surrey, executed from 1969 to 1972, was an important one. Here Stirling began to show signs of unease and anxiety. Although the two office wings were clearly conceived on the usual bases of linearity and the section, there were signals of an imminent change. Elements of various natures are identifiable: the two office wings, a corridor, and a divisible cruciform multipurpose hall. Here Stirling modified his strategy for relating diverse elements. The building's being interpretable as the extension of a preexisting one gives a certain collage flavor to the relation between new and old. The floor plan was now important, and the corridor, which kept alive Stirling's desire to use glass ambivalently, gave rise to a beautiful interior space that proved instrumental in organizing the building. It included the ramp, which connected the various floor levels while anticipating his interest in an architecture that can be described in terms of movement and narrative.

Elements we might consider traditional provide the counterpoint to technological materials not too frequently used at the time. Thus, the multipurpose hall presents itself as a framework constructed of plastic, and prefabricated plastic elements are used in the construction of the roof.

**34-35** Olivetti Training School, Haslemere, Surrey, 1969–1972

**36-37** A project for Siemens AG in Munich, dated 1969, is an extremely linear one where scale seems to make techniques of repetition and montage obligatory, relegating the mechanism of section shift to the background. Ever keen to bring a technological component into his work, Stirling here tried to downplay the monumentality of the complex by including a sophisticated artifice that makes giant curving screens, like mobile *brise-soleils*, surround the cylindrical buildings.

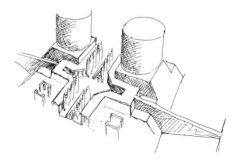

**38-41** The dormitory for the University of St. Andrews in Scotland, dated 1964–1968, is a unique project—a true island or oasis in Stirling's production of those years. Here he tackled program and landscape freely, unburdened by formal and constructive givens. The result is a complex of relaxed-looking blocks laid out on a slope. There is an artificial horizontality implicit in anything built on a slope. The familiar mechanism of making this come into conflict with the architecture is manifest here. The building is at the service of a program that seems to require a longitudinal fishbone structure, which also resolves the contact of the rooms with the exteriors and the access to them from the corridor. Stirling's skillful orientation of the blocks—avoiding any mechanical duplication and giving each a character of its own by varying the viewpoints—did not preclude the emergence of a unitary volume where interior and exterior spaces take on equal importance. The open space between the two blocks is quite memorable, and I would recommend this architectural experience to anyone traveling to Great Britain to visit Stirling's works. That the architect was aware of the importance of this space can be appreciated from the corridors, which seem to insist on impressing it upon us. Private contemplation of the landscape is reserved for the students' rooms.

38-41 Dormitory expansion, University of St. Andrews, 1964–1968

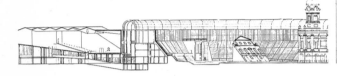

**42-45** Derby Town Centre
(project), 1970

**42-45** In 1970 Stirling worked for Derby, cradle of the Rolls Royce, which at a time of economic boom had decided to help its city by contributing to urban decor through participation in this project. It would help at this point to look at the larger panorama of the architectural scene. Many things had happened. Alternatives to Archigram's technological optimism had emerged: on one hand, studies on the city by the Italian architects of the Tendenza, grouped around the figure of Aldo Rossi; on the other hand, writings of Robert Venturi that stressed the value of the anomalous and singular in architecture. Together these created an atmosphere that expressed exhaustion with prevailing norms. Undoubtedly Stirling understood the

critique of his work that was implicit in the new direction that architecture was taking. The monumentalism of the Dorman Long project and the simplifying reductionism of Queen's College had no place in a notion of architecture that simultaneously advocated realism and complexity.

It was around this time that Leon Krier walked into Stirling's studio. Krier had already spearheaded projects that mixed elements derived from historic architecture with others taken from the vernacular. He advocated an architecture that could intervene in the old city without the trauma produced by modern architecture. I think it safe to say that Krier had a great influence on Stirling in this project. His way of thinking and his drawing hand are very much present here. The city was now at once the protagonist and the support of every architectural intervention, and Stirling explained his project with a comparison of two maps: one reflecting the current state of the city, the other representing the city which execution of the project would yield. Architecture, hence, as project for the city. Stirling proposed to "rebuild the city"—that is, the city square—through a grand arcade that on one hand became the occasion for a large parking facility, and on the other hand helped define an open space that frames a whole series of singular episodes considered characteristic of this city. Stirling thus gave Derby a gallery that had no reason to envy London's Victorian ones—never mind if the people crossing it in the drawings are dressed in Edwardian suits, as if in remembrance of the good old times of the Rolls Royce. But the public space here was more complex, and Stirling thought he might need a more Venturian argument, so to speak. In several drawings, a building that would have to be demolished was used as an architectural illustration, one not far removed from the decontextualization that pop art had familiarized us with. A market was incorporated in the plan without prejudgments about stylistic contamination. The Victory that Rolls Royce uses as an emblem was transformed, through a change of scale, into a work of art.[5] Some have wanted to interpret all these as manifestations of the British architect's penchant for irony, but in my opinion they were simply an intellectual exercise for one willing to absorb the new architectural theories and measure his capacities and strengths in territory heretofore unknown to him.

Naturally, his mastery of the section comes to the fore in this project. The profile of the plaza, the remains of the older building, the circuit of glass interrupted by the baldachin, the theater behind, the parking facility, all give rise to autonomous episodes that are integrated into a referential section, that of the arcade, that gives unity to the complex. But it is no longer just the section that generates architecture. The plan—the scheme Stirling learned to draw in a black stain, following the examples of Colin Rowe and Fred Koetter—is what dictated the project here, heralding an entire change of strategy.

**5** Stirling's emphasis on the iconic figure of Rolls Royce seems to recall studies of the same by Panofsky. See Erwin Panofsky, *Studies in Iconology: Humanistic Themes in the Art of the Renaissance* (New York: Oxford University Press, 1939).

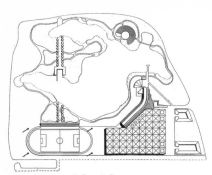

**46-48** Olivetti headquarters
(project), Milton Keynes, 1971

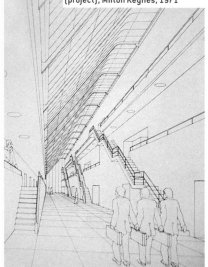

**46-48** The Milton Keynes project for Olivetti, dated 1971, was an apotheosis of the plan. Here the plan achieved an integration of architecture and landscape. This factory proposal totally ignored the tough atmosphere of nineteenth-century workplaces—those we could consider precursors of the architecture developed in the sixties—and comes across to us now as something close to the country houses of eighteenth-century English lords. The floor plan is something like a utopian proposal of a workplace, a place where, in theory, workers can take time out to read poems in the grove by the lake, and where a semicircular structure is fitted out for collective celebrations of the solstice. The project didn't overlook sports, hence the stadium, which doesn't look like something meant to keep workers healthy and fit, as it would in the project of a Russian constructivist, but rather as something for their sheer leisure. All this no longer through the section, but through the plan. The plan on its own could now integrate and incorporate an entire program and transform an architectural experience into a literary project. This was just a step away from the point where architecture would make sequential narration its prime compositional tool.

34

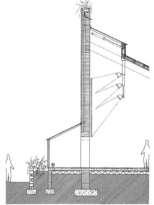

**49-50** Arts Center (project), University of St. Andrews, 1971

In the drawing, possibly by Leon Krier, we see Stirling seated on one of those neoclassical Thomas Hope armchairs that he had begun to collect during that period. Indeed, it depicts an architect more interested in setting the conditions of a pleasant life than in the formal investigations of the earlier years of his career.

**49-50** Drawn up at the same time as Milton Keynes, this unexecuted project for an Arts Center for the University of St. Andrews is a very good illustration of Stirling's interests in those years. It can be seen as an entire statement of what he would be doing in the seventies. The job was to complete and transform an existing construction where Palladianism was still much present, turning it into a student center. Stirling reinforced the presence of the modest existing construction by flanking it with two circular wings. The curved wings framed a previously open condition that included two modest structures situated along the street. The clarity and force of this enclosure allowed him to take up the entire lot and make intensive use of it, just as the program demanded. The resulting collage, a mix of ingredients of diverse origins, was henceforth a characteristic of Stirling's architecture. The impression one gets is that he would not settle for a building made by a single hand, choosing instead to construct the fiction of an architecture that was larger in time. The confident lines of the plan guarantee that this is what is to come. And Stirling's talent as an architect came forth in all its splendor in this project that, though dominated by the plan, is no less illustrative, through the galleries, of his solid experience in section design.

51-54 Stirling's proposal for the Arts Center at St. Andrews was drawn up in the seventies, in the course of a series of German projects. The first of this series, dated 1975, was for the Museum for Nordrhein-Westfalen in Düsseldorf. After the St. Andrews project, the way Stirling appropriates the Düsseldorf ruins comes as no surprise. There is in this Düsseldorf project, however, a certain exuberance not far removed from the postmodernist trend that called for a greater complexity of schemes and more freedom in bringing together diverse elements. The mission here was to complete a city block that featured remnants of the war. This was the first time in Stirling's oeuvre that the circular courtyard, the void generated by the cylinder, appeared as a key element. The cylinder would henceforth be the reference against which to measure all the autonomous episodes that, like characters of a drama, would have a bearing on the creation of something definable both as an architectural landscape and as a building. Here, the unfolding of such a landscape required the construction of a platform under which to hide the parking facility (a building element we can now consider generic, almost inevitable). In effect, thanks to cars, the old podium of classical architecture has made a comeback.

But what did I mean by "characters of a drama"? A small temple with certain Venturian echoes indicates the door. From this temple, which covers the access from the car park, one can proceed to the museum, or take a winding path to the void of the cylinder, passing under the museum and crossing the city block. What was Stirling trying to say here? In my opinion, the building performs its mission but also participates in the creation of a wider text, the city. Like Rossi, but in a different way, Stirling at this time wanted architecture and city to be one and the same thing. This may be a good moment to consider Stirling's way of intervening in the city in connection with Le Corbusier, particularly the mature Le Corbusier who was so concerned with connecting movement to architecture. But it would help to make a distinction between the *promenade architecturale* that Le Corbusier invoked early on in describing how the architecture of the Villa Savoye is perceived, and the fluid movement that determines the architecture

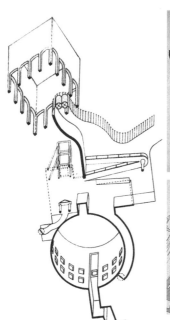

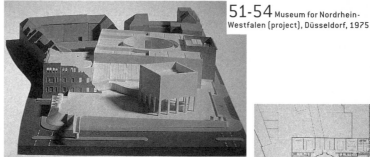

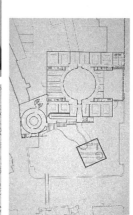

of a later building like the Olivetti offices in Lyon. I would say that this project of Stirling explores both movement and the promenade. I would associate the unfolding or arrangement of elements with the promenade idea, and find an exercise of the concept of fluid movement in the way the project solidifies forms linked, paradoxically, to the use made of a path.

The Corbusian notions of movement come into conflict with the presence of classical forms, which are static and bring us back to Schinkel, an architect surely much admired by Krier. Widely disparate ideas on how to build are thus juxtaposed, and the outcome is a highly complex architecture. The plan embodies this diversity. Symmetries and ruptures are made to coexist, as perfect figures like the circle and the square coexist with pseudo-organic undulating lines, and images of historic architecture with others linked to modern tradition. Indeed, we are talking about the plan. The plan is the focus here. It's in the plan that architecture is woven—and unwoven. The section

**55-56** Wallraf-Richartz Museum
(project), Cologne, 1975

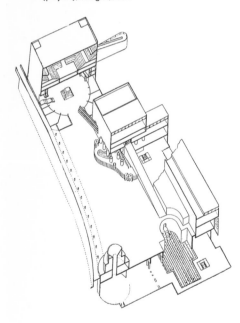

here contributes to the describing of the landscape, the city landscape that seems to have been of interest to Stirling at this time.

**55-56** Another German project of that year was the Wallraf-Richartz Museum, which was to serve to consolidate the area surrounding Cologne's cathedral. It allowed Stirling to delve further into the questions posed in Düsseldorf. The importance given to the museum's roof lighting makes us relate the project to modern tradition. The fact is that the mass of the building immediately dissolves into the autonomous episodes that Stirling liked to make use of to give life to a program. Despite their autonomy, however, the podium, the excavated church floor, the staggered tower, the mass of the assembly room, and so on are elements of a larger urban landscape dominated by the imposing volume of the cathedral.

57-64 Staatsgalerie,
Stuttgart, 1977–1983

57-64 Düsseldorf and Cologne were the prelude to the Staatsgalerie of Stuttgart (1977–1983), unquestionably the most complete project of this second phase of Stirling's career. The urban framework here is not too different from that of the Düsseldorf project. It is perhaps defined with greater precision. The lot is bordered on one side by a road that begins to descend in front of the museum, and perpendicular to this is an academic building whose morphology we are well familiar with:

symmetries, axes, entrance porticoes, corridors, regularly shaped rooms, skylights, and so on. In the competition brief, the architects were asked to address this existing building. Stirling resorted to previous experience, moving away from the road and raising a podium beneath which to place the car park. Hence he set the conditions for a reconstruction of the urban landscape that he was unable to execute in Düsseldorf. To lay out the elements needed to create this landscape he used, as

57-64 Staatsgalerie, Stuttgart, 1977–1983

before, the circle, the cylindrical void that is so full of echoes of the past. Once the circle came into play, the plan prevailed. And indeed, the Staatsgalerie project is dictated by the plan. We have often seen the circle and the inverted U in Stirling's architecture. They are what stabilize the scene here, and they are responsible for the closeness to the above-mentioned academic building, the old neoclassical gallery. Once this reference was defined, Stirling proceeded to apply a diversity of episodes to it, episodes of the kind we have so often found , in his work and of which he was such a master.

But over and above the force of these two key figures, what Stirling built here was not so much a building as an architectural landscape. The Staatsgalerie blends into the urban fabric so completely that it is not easy to distinguish between the architecture of the city on one hand and the work by Stirling on the other. An affected baldachin indicates where pedestrians can go up the podium, whether by stairs or by ramp. The enjoyment of architecture as an eminently visual formal experience makes the baldachin the threshold into the building. Everything is architecture. You cross the threshold marked by the baldachin and enter to relish the diverse world of an artificial landscape that feels altogether familiar. Decidedly enhancing this vision of architecture as landscape is the curving wall of the access way; its encounter with the slanted plane that supports the ramp penetrating the building—allowing one to relish the scene of the cylinder void—exemplifies the penchant for designing from opposite points that is so frequent in the British master's work.

This is architecture where the accidental predominates, and where the guiding thread is movement. The result is a building that, as a spectacle, is a continuous source of sensations, once the person trapped in it accepts it as such. What are the accidents? The building offers no repose. It has ramps, banisters, curving benches on the platform, steel canopies that flaunt the contrast between their vibrant pigments and the texture of the stone, skylights... all this before we've even entered the building, or passed beneath the arch that leads to the semicircular ramp inscribed within the cylinder. Without a doubt, it is in the circular courtyard that Stirling's architectural intentions reach a peak. Besides the interest that the very shape sparks, a whole series of elements invites the gaze, such as the carefully designed openings with their delicate masonry, rendered with the delicacy of an engraver working with copper, or the cornices that seem to yearn for a dome that never was. Such a tribute to architecture's repertoire of images through history is spoiled by the half-buried columns: not even an architect as consistent as Stirling was exempt from the postmodernist tide.

But there are many more architectural incidents in the Staatsgalerie. One is the window that is like a quote from Florentine Romanesque, which Stirling, understanding that he was risking being branded a historicist, stylized to an extreme that can be considered ironic; or the skillful tying-in of the courses and the voussoirs, rendered in such a way that the stone fades into the facade, much in the way a watercolorist dilutes paint into a background; or the wall from which Stirling removed a number of ashlars, making them fall to the ground, as if to give the impression that the building had already suffered the destructive effects of time.

The architectural landscape of the Staatsgalerie requires the presence of strollers, for whom Stirling created a path through the building. It is from the semicircular ramp of the courtyard that one most clearly perceives the architect's intentions. The hybridization of promenade and frozen movement that we saw in Düsseldorf is present as well in Stuttgart.

On the other hand, Stirling completed the referential scheme with an entire set of adjacent constructions through which he tried to establish contact with the surroundings, opening up a play over the road by preparing, through a broken U, for the encounter with a future enlargement. Stirling consciously reduced the presence of these subsidiary buildings, mainly a library and a the-ater, on one hand through curving forms that seem to allude to Le Corbusier, and on the other hand through a plastered finish, which has less presence than the baroque sandstone of the museum proper.

The interior of the museum is nevertheless a less attractive experience. To be sure, there is no lack of strong spatial emotions here and there, especially around the courtyard. But the galleries are rather sad, if not altogether ordinary.

And this is not the only thing that Stirling could be reproached for in this building. His friend Colin Rowe lamented the Staatsgalerie's absence of facades.[6] Though Stirling took pains to incorporate elements of classical architecture, even literally if necessary, he was unable, Rowe held, to tackle the design of a front facade in the way Renaissance architects built their palaces. We can derive pleasure from the texture of the materials, from how Stirling discovered the potential of German sandstone when handled properly; but, ever worried about being dismissed as a traditional architect, he decked the golden stone surfaces with exaggerated railings whose abuse of bright colors—blues, reds—produced an overly violent contrast.

6 Colin Rowe, "James Stirling: A Highly Personal and Very Disjointed Memoir."

As I was saying, this is an architecture that gives no respite, trapping our gaze with a multitude of incidents. The architecture emphasizes these incidents, and our eyes are necessarily drawn to them: the passage/tunnel that leads to the platform from the small plaza on the south; the angled window from which a capricious corner column, crowned by a truncated cone capital and painted a furious yellow, lords it over the scene; the brutalist balcony over the loading dock; the irregular canopy where evidence of the construction prevails, pushing all questions of form to the background; the violent cut of the surfaces. All this in a single episode. The density of the architecture is such that any attempt at precision is superfluous.

As in Düsseldorf, this building doesn't need sections. Its sections give information on how it is inscribed in the urban environment. We need the section in order to know how to move through the building. But the section here is, in a way, a mere design tool. What matters is the plan. We see Stirling's mastery in conceiving an entire building in terms of a plan. As has often been suggested, Stirling may have had Schinkel's Altes Museum or Asplund's Stockholm library in mind. It's of little importance now. Some may recognize the value of the circle as a figure from which to engender a plan. There is no doubt that Stirling intuited this, and that the Staatsgalerie provided him with the opportunity to demonstrate it.

**65-66** Stirling's mastery in the manipulation of the plan reached a peak in this 1979 project for the Wissenschaftszentrum in Berlin. To be honest, the first time I saw it, I didn't quite get the depth that lay behind the proposal. The critics presented it as yet another example of Stirling's irony. The building is anything but a joke, however. It is about the paradigm that results from exalting the significance of the plan in architecture. In the Wissenschaftszentrum, Stirling seems to have wanted to show us how the continuous structure he pursued could be achieved by linking the floor plan of a basilica to a Roman theater, a Norman castle, and a Carolingian tower, along with a longitudinal block that one might understand as a contemporary rationalist build-ing. What the project affirms is the plan's indifference to function. In the beginning there was the plan and just the plan. Consider how a postmodern architect would go about a proposal of this kind, seduced by the potential of Disney-type kitsch. The encounter of such diverse architectures would be grotesque. Stirling's resolution of this problem speaks of his powerful instinct as an architect. He eliminates the diversity of the floor plans by giving them the same windows: different plans, one same language. In this project, Stirling could have dispensed with all those accidents that he liked to spice up his works with. But he didn't, and the force of the proposal is to a degree weakened by the glazed porticoes, canopies, and other elements

**65-66** Wissenschaftszentrum (project), Berlin, 1979

**67-68** Performing Arts Center,
Cornell University, Ithaca,
New York, 1982–1987

that are gratuitously added to a building in which terms are inverted and the redundant monotony of a language reduced to the repetition of openings is made possible by the picturesqueness implicit in the plan. The plan, hence, as paradigm of any architectural operation, even those that seem most strictly visual.

**67-68** A less tense project in which Stirling demonstrates his experience in handling diverse elements and architectures is this one for Cornell University's Performing Arts Center (1982–1987), but its variety of floor plans and languages seems trivial after an examination of the Wissenschaftszentrum.

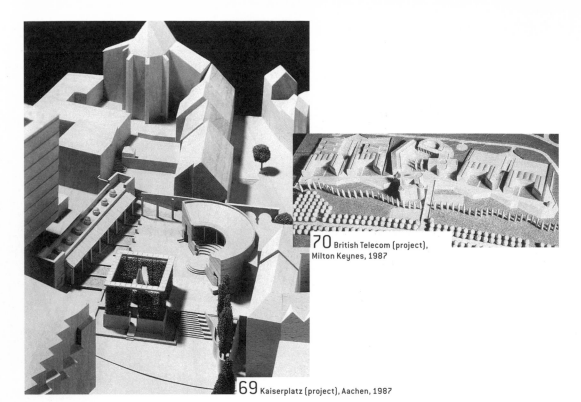

70 British Telecom (project), Milton Keynes, 1987

69 Kaiserplatz (project), Aachen, 1987

**69-70** British Telecom in Milton Keynes and Kaiserplatz in Aachen are two projects that illustrate the breadth of Stirling's professional activity in the eighties. Note how the plan becomes a predominant design tool.

**71-72** Both the model and the drawings of a project can show us how architecture can become a matter of weaving the plan. In the Science Library of the University of Southern California in Los Angeles, dated 1988, the sequence of axes unfolds an entire program. It's architecture, again, by way of the plan.

**71-72** Science Library (project),
University of Southern California, Los Angeles, 1988

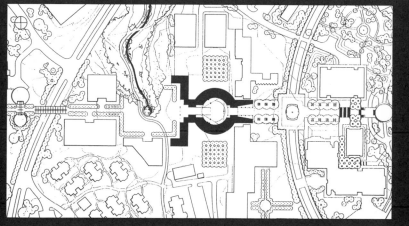

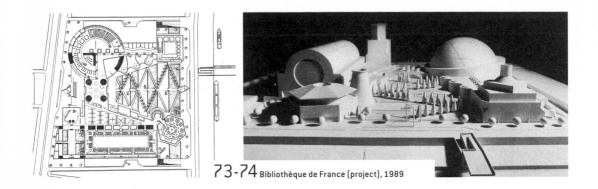

**73-74** Bibliothèque de France (project), 1989

**73-74** If the plan can generate a narrative, in the 1989 project for the Biblio-thèque de France the program turns it into an entire universal history of archi-tecture. Boullée's library is present here, as a paradigm of what is expected of a library, and with it, industrial chimneys, the towers of Albi, modern geodesic domes, and so on—an assortment of architectures coming together in a garden that, unjustifiably perhaps, recalls Versailles.

48

**75-76** Maybe Stirling grew weary of the procedure and needed a break. That's what the project that he carried out for Braun from 1986 to 1992 seems to indicate. The Braun factory in Melsungen is both interesting and disconcerting. Here we find spindle-shaped elements that could recall works of Renzo Piano or Norman Foster; large curves that seem to want to make an impact on the ter-ritory and which could bring us back to certain architectures of the seventies; monumental catwalks that, given the importance attributed to exposing the construction, seem to speak of a new radicalism. In this language is a certain hardening, a return to an architecture that puts value on autonomous elements, with the attendant forgetting of the plan that makes us suspect that Stirling was at the threshold of a new phase of his career. I'm not saying that we should reduce his legacy to the Braun factory. But this project truly opened the doors to a new era, confirming our view of Stirling—discussed at the start of the lec-ture—as an architect attentive to history and the evolution of architecture.

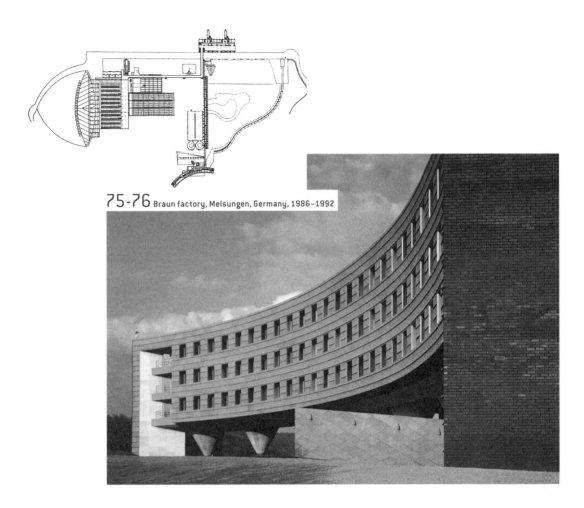

75-76 Braun factory, Melsungen, Germany, 1986–1992

49

All this is mere speculation. Stirling is not here to tell us how he sees architecture today. But he will continue to be essential to any account of the architecture of the past fifty years. In this respect, Stirling has a sure place in history.

# ROBERT VENTURI & DENISE SCOTT BROWN

The publication in the mid-sixties of Robert Venturi's book *Complexity and Contradiction in Architecture* was much welcomed by those at the time who were attentive to the development of architectural culture. And not only because the Museum of Modern Art had endorsed it with a foreword by Arthur Drexler and words of praise from Vincent Scully, perhaps the most influential American architectural critic of those years. Scully judged it "probably the most important writing on the making of architecture since Le Corbusier's *Vers une Architecture*, of 1923." [1] Readers were quick to pinpoint a critic of firm convictions, one who backed his reflections with a clear language and a whole set of examples and illustrations revealing an unusually sharp mind, and who by presenting his own work left no room for doubt as to his capabilities as an architect. That the text had such an impact is not surprising.

It wasn't common then to criticize modernity, which had become an artistic orthodoxy to be strictly complied with, and young architects took his message as a refreshing alternative. The idea of a more complex architecture that valued freedom over norm was extremely attractive. Indeed institutions and developers had "surrendered" to the modern so exhaustively that its tenets turned into an obligatory vocabulary. As a consequence, the principles of modernity were trivialized. In America, Mies's reduction of syntax was adopted by professionals indiscriminately. It was stripped of the tension that the Miesian language had had in its origins. Institutions, developers, and the building industry as a whole absorbed the experience of the avant-garde architects completely, in the process eliminating all the meaning behind it. In Europe, in turn, the cult of Le Corbusier had given rise to an institutional architecture of housing that in trying to be faithful to its principles adopted ways of living that were not always justifiable, in fact often coming into conflict with the surrounding urban context. It was natural, therefore, for critiques and alternatives to spring up. Among these were the proposals of Bruno Zevi, which tended to revive Wright's message through a messianic organic architecture where space, finally, would be the dominant aspect of architecture. There was also critique from inside the realm of the modern, such as that represented by the attempts of Team X to overcome the stiffness and stagnation that the trivialization of modernity had led to. Even the likes of Aalto and Kahn—the former through instinctive

1 Vincent Scully, introduction to Robert Venturi, *Complexity and Contradiction in Architecture* (New York: Museum of Modern Art, 1966), p. 11.

52

impulses, the latter by explaining architecture's disciplinary mechanisms in the context of history—sought to break the status quo of an architecture that had lost its energy in becoming routine and unquestionable canon. But Zevi, the theoreticians of Team X, Kahn, and Aalto all kept within the modern orthodoxy. None of them dared confess the emperor's nakedness with the energy and conviction of Venturi. At the time, that was a risky thing to do. So it was that his book aroused so much interest.

Venturi's intentions are clearly stated in the following passage:

Architects can no longer afford to be intimidated by the puritanically moral language of orthodox Modern architecture. I like elements which are hybrid rather than "pure," compromising rather than "clean," distorted rather than "straightforward," ambiguous rather than "articulated," perverse as well as impersonal, boring as well as "interesting," conventional rather than "designed," accommodating rather than excluding, redundant rather than simple, vestigial as well as innovating, inconsistent and equivocal rather than direct and clear. I am for messy vitality over obvious unity. I include the non sequitur and proclaim the duality.

I am for richness of meaning rather than clarity of meaning; for the implicit function as well as the explicit function. I prefer "both-and" to "either-or," black and white, and sometimes gray, to black or white. A valid architecture evokes many levels of meaning and combinations of focus: its space and its elements become readable and workable in several ways at once.

But an architecture of complexity and contradiction has a special obligation toward the whole: its truth must be in its totality or its implications of totality. It must embody the difficult unity of inclusion rather than the easy unity of exclusion. More is not less. [2]

Pardon the long quote, but there can hardly be a better, more precise synthesis of the book. Above all, *Complexity and Contradiction* is a denunciation of the ideological tyranny of modern architecture. Reality, architecture, is not simple. It cannot be subjected to linguistic norms established by an orthodoxy. Venturi was provoked by his colleagues, so inclined as they were to proclaiming that all means of expressing architecture had already been explored. He rose up, irate, against the defenders of an orthodoxy that had made a banner of Mies's

[2] Venturi, *Complexity and Contradiction in Architecture*, pp. 22–23.

"less is more." The architects of the modern movement were much given to simplification and reduction. This could perhaps solve problems, but it ignored the multiplicity of factors and issues that it was architecture's duty to address. The same early Venturi quoted Paul Rudolph, later a target of his diatribes, who clearly saw the limitations of his colleagues when he wrote of Mies: **"All problems can never be solved. . . Indeed it is a characteristic of the twentieth century that architects are highly selective in determining which problems they want to solve. Mies, for instance, makes wonderful buildings only because he ignores many aspects of a building. If he solved more problems, his buildings would be far less potent."** [3]

Venturi knew he could defend his stand from his vantage point of experiencing architecture as both a scholar and a practicing architect. He said as much, explicitly stating early on in the book that his being both a critic and an architect qualified him to put forward a particular **"way of seeing architecture."** The example of T. S. Eliot, who wrote about the relation between poet and critic, [4] led Venturi to call his ideas on architecture **"inevitably a by-product of the criticism which accompanied working."** [5] Having already proven himself as an architect, Venturi published his reflections, and he used his early works to illustrate his ideas. After all, it was in elaborating them, and in the evolution of his architectural work, that his ideas were forged. He said: **"Architecture is open to analysis like any other aspect of experience, and is made more vivid by comparisons."** [6] Against Le Corbusier's quasi-religious texts, Team X's voluntarist affirmations, or Kahn's pseudo-mysterious poetics, texts which architects were devouring at the time, *Complexity and Contradiction* presented itself as an exercise in analysis and reflection that didn't demand the reader's immediate surrender. On the contrary, Venturi gave readers a chance to look into the sources that he drank from. To help us understand his propositions, he offered images of the architectures that had generated his ideas, for us to think and judge for ourselves. There was room for reason and sentiment, past and present, and such an offer was bound to be well received at a time when one was expected to be true to formal principles built solely on a partial interpretation of architecture. Europeans took Venturi's writings as a new opportunity to partake of a mature architectural culture, one that didn't renounce intellectual values and in which architecture was

**3** Paul Rudolph, in *Perspecta 7* (1961), p. 51, quoted in Venturi, *Complexity and Contradiction in Architecture*, p. 24.

**4** Thomas Stearns Eliot, *The Use of Poetry and the Use of Criticism* (Cambridge: Harvard University Press, 1933).

**5** Venturi, *Complexity and Contradiction in Architecture*, p. 18.

**6** Ibid.

forged freely, not in compliance with norms. On the other side of the Atlantic the book was a puff of fresh air sweeping away architecture's dependence on the doctrines established by the avant-gardes, and giving rise to a new breed of Americanism that was direct and pragmatic.

The ever-alert Bruno Zevi deemed Venturi's work worth an entire editorial in his magazine *L'Architettura*,[7] and Vincent Scully, calling *Complexity and Contradiction* "a very American book, rigorously pluralistic and phenomenological in its method,"[8] extolled the figure of Venturi to the point of considering him "one of the few American architects whose work seems to approach tragic stature in the tradition of Furness, Louis Sullivan, Wright, and Kahn."[9]

As the book strongly expresses, Venturi felt limited by a simplistic modernity that aspired to what he considered an affected serenity, and that ignored the complexity inherent in the architectures he was drawn to. It was complexity, ambiguity, and tension that he found attractive, and that he wanted to be able to analyze and explain. Venturi related to architecture that didn't expose its workings, that wasn't obvious, that required one to feel captivated by it as a step prior to intellectualizing, that went beyond a penchant for primary and transparent forms. And he wasn't alone in this, finding support in critics like T. S. Eliot and William Empson. It was comforting for Venturi to know that Eliot considered the art of the Elizabethan poets **"an impure art,"** [10] and that Empson took Shakespeare as **"the supreme ambiguist, not so much from the confusion of his ideas and the muddle of his text, as some scholars believe, as simply from the power and complexity of his mind and art."** [11] There are more quotes, but I don't think they are necessary right now. With his book, what Venturi proposed was to look for and recapture the mechanisms that architects had used to come up with the complexity, ambiguity, and tension described by analysts of poetry. And like them, he backed his ideas with quotes and examples.

Ambiguity was manifested in the coexistence of contradictory terms. Venturi set himself the task of exploring how such contradictory terms appeared in architecture. The first phenomenon he examined was the presence of elements acting on different fronts at the same time. **"Doubles"** lent themselves to serving different functions and allowed one to speak of **"both and at once,"** of **"both-and"** elements. Venturi had no trouble coming up with examples of

**7** *L'Architettura, Cronache e Storia* 140 (June 1967), pp. 72–73.

**8** Scully, introduction to Venturi, *Complexity and Contradiction in Architecture*, p. 11.

**9** Ibid., p. 13.

**10** T. S. Eliot, *Selected Essays: 1917–1932* (New York: Harcourt, Brace, 1932), p. 18, quoted in Venturi, *Complexity and Contradiction in Architecture*, p. 28.

**11** Stanley Edgar Hyman, *The Armed Vision* (New York: Vintage Books, 1955), p. 240, quoted in Venturi, *Complexity and Contradiction in Architecture*, p. 29.

architecture where such duplicity is perceivable. He felt at ease with them. As we will recall, he preferred **"both and at once"** to **"one or the other."** Inclusion versus exclusion. Generous diversity versus uniqueness derived from exclusionary norm. Ambivalence, duplicity of meaning, uncertain interpretations, versus the obviousness of the untransferable form. Elements with double functions abound in the history of architecture: Hawksmoor, Borromini, Le Corbusier, etc. These elements enabled Venturi to explicate the **"both-and"** phenomenon that would lead to contradiction becoming a principle at the base of the architect's work.

On the other hand, in clear opposition to the inventive drive of the architects of the modern movement, he stressed the importance of accepting and making use of conventional elements. **"Through unconventional organization of conventional parts [the architect] is able to create new meanings within the whole. . . . Familiar things seen in an unfamiliar context become perceptually new as well as old."** [12] Venturi's Americanism lies not only in method, not only in accepting casuistry as a system, but also in a desire to be realistic. This is manifested in the importance he gives to actual work, and in an earnest effort to use materials provided by everyday life. The coherence and consistency vindicated by the organic architecture spearheaded by Wright excluded the everyday, equating it with the vulgar. Everything had to be unique, specific, dictated by the inevitable individuality of the particular work. Venturi's reaction to this idealism was energetic, and he extended it to the relation between architecture and the city. **"By modifying or adding conventional elements to still other conventional elements [architects] can, by a twist of context, gain a maximum of effect through a minimum of means."** [13]

In his book Venturi uses an aphorism of Kahn—**"It is the role of design to adjust to the circumstantial"** [14]—to explain how the designer must be open to possible contradictions. Then he proceeds to look for distortions and anomalies that in architecture become asymmetries and unexpected juxtapositions, fractures and ruptures, fragmentations and changes of scale, backed by a good choice of examples. He shows how in the name of coherence and consistency architects have forgotten about the desirability of naturalness. Formalism had brought about the tyranny of the orthogonal. With the reendorsement of

**12** Venturi, *Complexity and Contradiction in Architecture*, p. 50.

**13** Ibid., p. 52.

**14** Quoted in ibid., p. 54.

naturalness, architects could now inject diagonals into their floor plans. School had taught approaches based on rigid, preimposed schemes. Now there was freedom to make openings wherever the program required it. Venturi's extensive journey through the history of architecture included exploring contrasts and encounters, and he relished architectures where freedom prevails over norm. Specific architectures—such as Gothic cathedrals or Renaissance palaces— illustrate what he was trying to get across when he talked about contradiction in the process of adaptation and adjustment, or when he said that contradiction is the result of obligatory juxtapositions.

Many of the cases of contradiction that Venturi puts forward in *Complexity and Contradiction* automatically lead us to explore the categories of interior and exterior. **"Contrast between the inside and the outside can be a major manifestation of contradiction in architecture."** [15] The principle of modern orthodoxy that made continuity between interior and exterior an actual foundation of modern architecture would fall apart as soon as architects learned to contemplate architectural history without prejudice. Venturi does exactly that, citing numerous cases where there was no **"continuity of all spaces"** but, instead, a deliberate differentiation between interior architecture and exterior architecture. He takes pains to show us domes and lanterns shaping spaces that are not at all discernible from outside; buildings structured by diverse **"layers"**; **"redundant enclosures"** and **"residual spaces"** [16] that produce in us a sense of being in a complex, nonevident environment that we relate to in nonreal time. On the other hand, examining architecture in terms of interior and exterior leads to themes relating to the city. The city stakes its claim on the territory by means of defensive walls, beltways, parks, and such, and through complex schemes it appropriates the interiors of these elements. Architecture, in its capacity as the wall between interior and exterior, becomes a physical testimony of the duality and the drama it creates.

Having established the evident complexity of architecture and pointed out its numerous and continuous contradictions, Venturi moves on to more speculative ground, reminding us of the importance, in architecture, of **"the whole."** He says: **"An architecture of complexity and accommodation does not forsake the whole,"** [17] and **"I have emphasized the goal of unity rather than of**

**15** Ibid., p. 71.

**16** The terms put in quotation marks in this paragraph are taken from ibid., p. 84.

**17** Ibid., p. 89.

simplification in an art 'whose . . . truth [is] in its totality,' " completing the reflection by quoting Gertrude Stein.[18] Venturi adopts the ancient Aristotelian interest in taking reality from the viewpoint of the whole and goes on to explain how it is possible to assume this unitary condition of reality without succumbing to the reductive process of simplification and without denying the autonomy and independence of the parts. He prefers **"the difficult unity through inclusion"** to **"the easy unity through exclusion."** [19] So, resorting to casuistry, he focuses his attention on identifying the complex mechanisms that accompany the unitary condition of the work of art. Venturi is more interested in duality than in trinity—**"three is the commonest number of compositional parts making a monumental unity in architecture"** [20]—and the works of Sullivan and Piero della Francesca, of Ellsworth Kelly and Morris Louis, are eloquent illustrations of the beauty of dual compositions. Venturi later introduces the concept of "inflection." In architecture, inflection **"is the way in which the whole is implied by exploiting the nature of the individual parts, rather than their position or number."** [21] The parts—which are autonomous and free, and perform diverse functions—contribute to the whole without having to be included in its structure, without having to come across as subordinate or subsidiary elements necessary to the definition of the whole. Venturi has a stock of examples with which to defend his thesis: the English baroque architecture of Vanbrugh, Monticello, Siena's Palazzo Pubblico, the Church of the Jacobeans in Toulouse, Lutyens, Moretti. The unity of the work does not imply a hierarchy that ignores the autonomy and freedom of the integral elements.

The diversity of Venturi's examples shows just how applicable the "inflection" concept is to all architecture. He thus situates himself at the antipodes of academicism. Architecture is by nature open to the unexpected, to the unique solution that makes us appreciate the anomaly, but this is not to forget the individuality of the whole. And to exalt the whole is not to attach less value to the unresolved or incomplete: **"However, the obligation toward the whole in an architecture of complexity and contradiction does not preclude the building which is unresolved. Poets and playwrights acknowledge dilemmas without solutions. The validity of the questions and vividness of the meaning are what make their works art more than philosophy. A goal of poetry can be unity of expression**

**18** Ibid., p. 89. Venturi took the quote from A. Heckscher, *The Public Happiness* (New York: Atheneum, 1962).

**19** Venturi, *Complexity and Contradiction in Architecture*, p. 89.

**20** Ibid., p. 90.

**21** Ibid., p. 91.

over resolution of content."[22] This reflection allows him to extend his affirmations to the city, or urban design. He writes: **"The complex program which is a process, continually changing and growing in time yet at each stage at some level related to a whole, should be recognized as essential at the scale of city planning."**[23] Then, as if to confirm what he has just said: **"the building . . . is a whole at one level and a fragment of a greater whole at another level."**[24] Awareness of all these levels makes Venturi look at the city with more indulgence than the critics linked to orthodox modern architecture are capable of. **"Indeed, is not the commercial strip of a Route 66 almost all right?"**[25] Although the Venturi of the sixties didn't pronounce the declaration of populism to be found in his writings and works of the seventies, which we will be discussing later on, *Complexity and Contradiction* ends with a eulogy of Main Street. This was a premonition.

*Complexity and Contradiction* is a highly critical book. It is responsible for a good part of Venturi's success. He revolted against the interpretation of modernity that had led institutions—first schools, later sociologists and politicians—to dream of an orderly, familiar, predictable city. This interpretation, he said, is ultimately responsible for linguistic reduction and the schematic simplification of the idea of structure in so much of architecture. The proselytizing of Wright, Mies, and Le Corbusier, who disseminated slogans that served as shields for their work, was such that Venturi considered them antagonistic, and *Complexity and Contradiction* points out how the strict observance of preset formal principles leads to gross exaggeration. The three masters were the target of his critiques, which were in large part justified. To be sure, there are moments that reveal a certain inevitable respect for Wright and Le Corbusier, as when their works are used to confirm his opinions, but for Mies and his work there is little indulgence. After all, it was Mies's architecture that had brought about a proliferation, without the check and balance of critique, of the kind of constructions that transformed American cities under the banner of a necessary urban renewal. Aalto was the only modern architect whose work had the attributes that Venturi was interested in. Venturi found that the architecture of the Finnish architect admitted contradictions and responded with the complexity suited to the physical environment and programmatic requirements of each work.

22 Ibid., p. 101.

23 Ibid., pp. 101.–102.

24 Ibid., p. 102.

25 Ibid., p. 102.

Venturi also discovered possible allies among his contemporaries, resorting to the works and writings of architects like Kahn, Aldo van Eyck, or Fumihiko Maki. Much has been written about Louis Kahn's influence on Venturi, and indeed quotes from Kahn abound in *Complexity and Contradiction.* So it is that Venturi thinks that his principles, the attributes of architecture that he holds in esteem, make true the enigmatic Kahnian aphorism that says **"architecture must have bad spaces as well as good spaces."** [26] Venturi is also taken by the way Kahn interprets and uses structure as a source of **"double-function"** elements, and it pleases him that unforeseen residual spaces are to be found in his architecture. Nevertheless, as I will explain later on, Venturi and Kahn had very different approaches to the history of architecture. In Kahn there is always awe and respect toward monumental components, whereas in his quest for complexity and ambiguity Venturi has less respect for monumental architecture. In fact I would say that this is not at all the kind of architecture he identifies with. Later on we will see how much his study of Kahnian iconography bore on his work. On the other hand, however, Venturi was attentive to Team X's open critique of the architecture of their elders, and more than once cites Aldo van Eyck, with whom he shared a reticence toward conventional modern architecture.

**26** Ibid., p. 31.

**1-6** It can be said that the house Venturi built for his mother—the Vanna Venturi House in Chestnut Hill, Pennsylvania, dated 1961—was an entire manifesto of his architecture. Coinciding in time with the writing of *Complexity and Contradiction*, it was a paradigm, an illustration, of the whole Venturian body of ideas. But before we go into a detailed analysis of the project, allow me some observations of a general nature. With this house, Venturi showed us what it is to build with all of the heritage of our architectural experience. We store images, references, and episodes in our memory box, and there they stay, but they are manifested only when made part of the scheme of a new project. Our experience of and relationship with architecture in itself becomes a building material, and actually gets projected in the physical structure of the building. In Venturi's particular case, experience of architecture transcends the known and familiar to include all of history: the architect is not so much a professional, but a connoisseur who enjoys exercising his memory. In this way architecture becomes a personal, untransferable reflection. This early, not yet populist Venturi assigns full responsibility to the individual, the architect. The construction is a screen reflecting the architect's ego. This ego is intimate, interiorized, but nonetheless alert enough to glean from the entire body of existing architecture those episodes it is interested in, unfiltered and without exclusions. The procedure put forward was innovative and attractive. It implied a broken, fragmented view of the construction, and though it coincided with some of the avant-garde proposals, its view of the whole was altogether different, thereby opening a field that other colleagues would soon make use of. The result would then be very different: architecture, when carried out from the experience of individuals, leads indirectly to architecture as sensation. The avant-gardes preached the autonomy of the object; Venturi, the autonomy of the spectator. I will refrain from mentioning the user. At least in the Venturi of those years, the protagonist was the architect. Think of another emblematic house, of a different moment in time—the mature Le Corbusier's Villa Stein, for example. This work of architecture—the space it defines—imposes itself like a sensible reality. It doesn't lend itself to memory. In Venturi, architecture comes from experience. It is a continuous re-cognition operation. Whether we like it or not, we cannot escape the mesh of the known. Paradoxically, freedom is in the montage, but we will come to that later on.

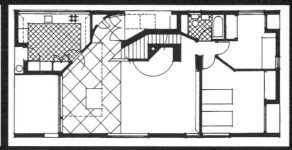

**1-6** Vanna Venturi House, Chestnut Hill, Pennsylvania, 1961

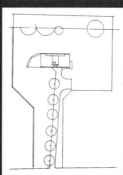

It shouldn't come as a surprise to anyone when I say that the Vanna Venturi House was conceived with the floor plan as starting point. Venturi took off from a generic shape: a rectangle slightly exceeding the dimensions of a double square. But there is no allusion whatsoever to a center. If we were to identify a center, it would have to be the fireplace, but we would have to clarify from the start that, despite its iconographical weight in the house, it is not a structural piece. The rectangle in itself does seem to allude to a conventional construction. Its dimensions are deliberately domestic and they anticipate the overall orthogonality of the house. The floor plan admits a double frontality: that produced in the vertical plane of the entrance, and that which corresponds to the private sphere of a back garden. It's a floor plan that can be interpreted as the transition from one facade to the other. On the side of the public facade are the kitchen, a closet, the more or less centrally positioned entrance, a bathroom, and a second bedroom; along the private facade are the dining room, the living room, and the main bedroom. The pseudo-bay along the public facade is dense and tight, whereas the spaces along the private facade are wide and open. The passage from one facade to the other forms a geometry that allows the inclusion of an arch, which in turn serves to give direction to the diagonals. Everything is rendered in such a way that the floor plan can be read as an episode taking off from the virtual entrance portico and unfolding undulatingly until it is violently interrupted by the frontality of the rear facade over the garden.

Let us now explore how "**architectural experiences**" are accommodated in the geometric mesh created by the rectangle, as well as in the virtual arch. Surely when we try to pinpoint the attributes of this architecture—the porch, the main door, the staircase, and the fireplace, all contained within the rectangle— they come across as the episodes that most lend themselves to discussions on "**density**." The porch, key to an understanding of the house's public facade, does not frame a central entrance. Venturi reckons that the door, as in old fortifications, must be handled only by the owners. Each element can now be associated with a particular "**experience**." The door connects with the closet and gives the visitor a full view of the living room area, where the staircase embracing the fireplace comes across as an architectural element with a value of its own. In effect, it is not hard to see that the counterpoint to the diaphragm-facade that facade that connects us to the exterior world of American suburbia is the entire scenography that the staircase and the fireplace create. The plan of the house seems to push the most familiar or more standardized activities to the edges. The kitchen and the bedrooms appropriate three of the rectangle's corners. The cubists taught us elaborate mechanisms of manipulating surfaces; Venturi did none of the overlapping and superposing of the architects influenced by them. In his determination to maintain the independence and autonomy of individual elements, Venturi found himself making adjustments and resolving accesses through cuts and diagonals. The virtual arch that transports us from one frontal vertical plane to another becomes an efficient ally in resolving the program. Venturi looked at the pieces of the whole as diverse scenes. The architect's skill lay in bringing them together and maintaining a certain unity that gives the work a clear identity.

But though the project takes off from the floor plan, it is in the facades that the architecture is most interesting, and this is what we will dwell on now. Of course the facade through which you enter is the more attractive one. It has a clear frontality. The allusion to classical architecture—pediments, symmetries, centrality, etc.—is only apparent. The balance dictated by the forceful axis of symmetry that determines the formal order of the facade is, on the whole, a virtual balance: appearances prevail. The architecture **"densifies"** around the axis. The austere portico is accompanied by a molding that curves over the lintel, provocatively ignoring it. In accumulating all these elements, which continue to spread over the strict volume of the chimney, a presumptuous verticality is produced that has little to do with the building's modest program. But when we stop to examine the facade, we find a deliberate asymmetry, naturally in the arrangement of the openings, which in accordance with the tradition of modernism reflect the diverse purposes of the spaces they serve. Horizontal windows for the kitchen, a single central one for the bedroom, and the square window which the arch ignores all blend into the scene easily. The divided pediment—which inevitably recalls Moretti's Palazzina Girasole, so admired by Venturi—reinforces the virtual symmetry, which comes across clearly when the chimney moves off the axis defined by the gap. On the other hand, the frontality seems to explore the flatness that the building systems used here lead to:

the superposition of formal patterns derived from traditional architecture, and a definition of these formal patterns through moldings, which do not conceal their nature but actually present themselves as added elements independent of structure that contribute to the creation of an ambiguous image. Venturi had so perceptively encountered all these mechanisms and ingredients in his studies of architectural history, and no doubt he wanted them present in his building work. Through the years, the facade has not lost the architectural energy that so impressed critics and professionals when the house was first published, back in the sixties. The rear, private facade is less interesting. The modern way of making openings simply reflect the interior spaces isn't as efficient when the "figure" that accommodates them has lost value. The opening of the porch, that of the living room, and the one shared by the living room and bedroom do not manage to revitalize a controversial—and hardly convincing—horizontal cut in the facade that gives way, on a second plane, to the pseudothermal window of the upstairs bedroom. The system of horizontal moldings that we contemplate in the access facade is repeated here, hence a certain continuity in the elevations that other common elements seem to ignore deliberately.

It is interesting to examine a case like this because it illustrates what Venturi understands architecture to be: an end in itself, even at the cost of forgetting the setting, a typical American suburb. Deliberately ambiguous, the house ignores both its social and its physical environment. Just look at the site plan. The front facade makes no reference to context whatsoever. It mattered more to the early Venturi to make a manifesto than to address the demands of place and program, and he was obsessed with making this house a spectacular unfolding of architectural episodes not far removed from the architectural experiences that were much alive in his memory.

**7-12** Coinciding in time with the Vanna Venturi House, Guild House on Spring Garden Street in Philadelphia, dated 1961, initiated a new programmatic approach. This approach involved realism: an architecture that maintained its attributes without ceasing to be **"normal and everyday,"** that didn't surprise, didn't provoke, and wasn't anxious to be novel. At a time when European architects were still trying to apply the duplex schemes of Le Corbusier's Unité d'Habitation and

**7-12** Guild House, Friends Housing for the Elderly, Philadelphia, 1961

7-12 Guild House, Friends Housing for the Elderly, Philadelphia, 1961

the experiments carried out by Team X in its search for an autonomous urban dimension for housing, Venturi was bent on using the elements of unsophisticated construction, in the hope that the presence of architecture would redeem them from ordinariness. But architecture, with its bona fide disciplinary mechanisms, doesn't in the least demand the invention of new elements. In other words, there is always room for architecture, even in the tight margins of commercial architecture. Guild House is quasi-symmetrical, frontal. There is not much distance between the Vanna Venturi House and these Philadelphia apartments for senior citizens. In both cases we can talk about fronts and rears, and so on. The floor plan strategy in Guild House is to put as many apartments as possible on the street side. This brings about a staggered formation that speaks of

Venturi's longtime admiration of Alvar Aalto. But the diagonals reveal the inward orientation of the encounters of planes, leading us to a hypothetical center that speaks of a dense and solid residential building, and the ring of bathrooms and kitchens that are laid out along the corridors serving the apartments testifies to this. Speaking of Aalto, it would help to remember how carefully such corridors—which are public spaces—are rendered in the residential projects of the Finnish master, and compare his attitude toward them with Venturi's. In Aalto the corridors are often unique spaces, entities in their own right. In Guild House Venturi chooses not to waste a single square foot on public space, thereby sticking to the governing geometry of the strictest commercial architecture. Private spaces predominate, but do not come across as unique. On the contrary, they are designed to maximize regularity and optimize measurements: regular spaces and right sizes.

What, then, is so interesting about Guild House? For one, Venturi's clever way of reducing the dimensions of the facade, which made it possible to focus the design on a plane and give it a dense iconographic content. On the conventional brick plane of the facade, Venturi deployed an entire sequence of icons that begins at the cylindrical pillar of the entrance portico and ends all the way up in the TV antenna, a crowning element that with a tinge of humor bordering on sarcasm is a reminder of how television is central to the lives of so many people. This sequence, which gives a certain monumentality to the series of concave-convex ruptures in the facade, could be considered ambiguous and contradictory. For example, the smooth glass surface of the high arching window above the balconies is a gesture that is radically at odds with the depth of said balconies. The cylindrical support hardly dialogues with the wall perpendicular to the facade, and only the gigantic "Guild House" sign reconciles them. The juxtaposition of colored textures is entrusted to a single material, brick, without the use of orthodox constructive mechanisms. The figure, its profiles, its contour, could be seen as Kahnian, but Kahn's tectonic treatment is so different that such an affiliation has to be discarded.

Venturi attached a lot of importance to the entrance, and this is evident in the three preliminary sketches. Guild House and the Vanna Venturi House anticipated the importance he would later attach to announcing the access, which in his design strategy would often be the starting point of an entire project.

**13-16** In this 1965 project for the small city of North Canton, Ohio, Venturi and Rauch had the opportunity to demonstrate their ability to apply their principles to any kind of environment. They were tasked to build a town hall and a youth center (the YMCA) and to enlarge an existing library. Unintimidated by the disparate nature of the program, the architects responded by stressing the autonomy and independence of the buildings which "float" in an urban ambit where they relate to one another through a system of voids, unchained to any geometry that might otherwise condition them. The buildings **"watch"** each other while performing their respective functions, freed as they are from any pressure to form a **"whole."**

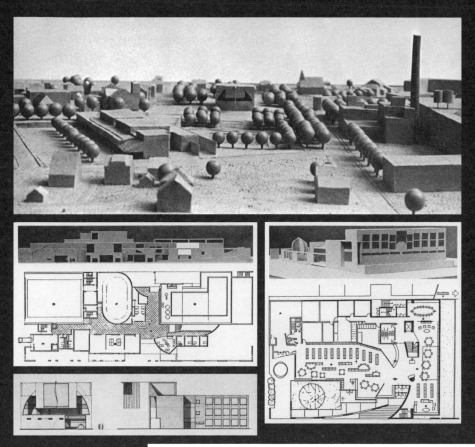

13-16 Town hall, YMCA, and library expansion (project), North Canton, Ohio, 1965

Let's begin with the town hall. This is what Venturi tells us: "**The town hall is like a Roman temple in its general proportions, and also because it is freestanding, but—in contrast with a Greek temple—a directional building whose front is more important than its back. . . . I like Louis Sullivan's use of the giant arch to give image, unity, and monumental scale to some of his late banks, which are important but small buildings on the main streets of mid-Western towns.**" [27] Without a doubt, the words of Venturi help us understand the drawings. The building has a facade, a front, a public image. All the administrative

**27** Stanislaus von Moos, *Venturi, Rauch & Scott Brown: Buildings and Projects*, trans. David Antal (New York: Rizzoli, 1987), p. 154.

areas hang from this facade, accommodated in a cubic volume with square holes we can consider conventional. The architects don't complicate their lives analyzing the program. What they set themselves to do instead is design an expressive facade. The element that gives **"image, unity, and monumental scale"** is a free, isolated facade that features an arch broken by a plaque. This gives rise to a geometric solution with echoes of Kahn. The symmetry established by the arch breaks where the axis of the entrance fades. A huge flag eliminates any possible confusion as to the function of the building. Segregated from the volume, the facade is a clear reference to the separate missions of plane and volume, and it is there that the architects have concentrated their efforts. There is no style. The image suffices, and it is what gives that unity and monumental scale that the architects believe buildings of this kind should have.

The YMCA and the library extension are, for their part, like the Vanna Venturi House: buildings derived from the floor plan. The strategy is based on differentiating the large spaces—gyms, courts, swimming pools, etc.—from the administrative area. Of help here is a corridor which the architects seem to have taken great delight in designing. What's important is the interstitial space of the corridor. The rest is eventually regularized, ending in a rectangle that floats in the neutral urban space of downtown North Canton.

Venturi and Rauch went about the library extension project very differently. Here, diverse scales are made to coexist without creating discontinuity. The preexisting conventional building explodes, diffusing its contours, which now delimit a space that is at once a reading room and a book depository. What makes the work of Venturi and Rauch interesting is not so much the interstitial spaces, but the contiguities created by the elements that divide the space. Observe how the diagonals help both to define the reading room/book depository and to shape the reception area. Again a remembrance of Aalto, in the free manipulation of the perimeter. But the rectangle opens with an arc that generates the entrance, and opens up within through courtyards that actually define the character of the building, stressing its autonomy. The project was never carried out, unfortunately, but it had a considerable impact. Venturi included it among the examples of his architecture presented in *Complexity and Contradiction in Architecture*. As far as urban design is concerned, the lesson is clear. So are the clues that the project gives with regard to linguistic development: broken symmetries, regularity as base to later ignore, coexistence of different dimensional orders, and so on. North Canton was already the project of a mature architect.

**17-19** The same criteria used by Venturi and Rauch to draw up the North Canton Town Hall project would be applied to another project the following year: Fire Station No. 4 in Columbus, Indiana, dated 1966. This one was carried out. The floor plan here is simple. It reflects the geometry of the site, and the oblique character of the rear facade is used as a pretext to introduce a pseudo-symmetry that produces the project's most interesting and complex space: the small kitchen incorporating the potent solid of the hose tower. With the floor plan resolved, the architects turned to the facades. Here again, the matrix of the project is the idea of a building that is both right side and wrong side, front and rear. Again, the main facade explores frontality and incorporates different scales: large scale for the garage for the fire trucks, small scale for the domestic part of the fire station program (kitchen, living room, locker

© David Hirsch

© David Hirsch

**17-19** Fire Station No. 4, Columbus, Indiana, 1966

room, etc.). Hence, horizontal windows (kitchens) coexist with square-shaped windows (living rooms), and monumental openings (access to garages) coexist with more strictly domestic openings. Every opening maintains its autonomy, the openings don't interrelate. On the other hand, the surface of the facade, alternating between conventional brick and glazed white brick, is character-ized by the discontinuity that comes from combining two different textures. It is a facade whose aim is to render imperceptible the formal criteria it was built upon. We could simplify things and take it as functionalist to an extreme. But we could also consider that the diversity has brought about a picturesqueness that eliminates the emphasis put on the building's public character. The fire station of Columbus was a commendable effort to construct a building from facades, which are deliberately interpreted as independent, autonomous episodes. The facade—quintessence of the vertical plane—here anticipates something that would be a constant in Venturi's work: flat surfaces for building envelopes. So it is that cladding as a field of architectural work is important in this early work of his. How far we are from the architecture of his masters! The fire station of Columbus has little to do with Louis Kahn's architecture of solids, or with the "shells" that Eero Saarinen used profusely in the latter part of his career.

**20-23** The Venturi of *Complexity and Contradiction in Architecture* gradually gave way to the Venturi of *Learning from Las Vegas*. We will discuss this at length later, but the National Football Hall of Fame at Rutgers University, New Bruns-wick, New Jersey, dated 1967, is a good illustration of that evolution. The Venturi who had discovered in Rome and older architecture the joy of dispensing with norms was now attracted to the logic that lay behind spontaneous architecture, declaring himself an ardent admirer of the commercial architecture of American cities. A project like Venturi and Rauch's National Football Hall of Fame tries to incorporate elements derived from fields that are not strictly architectural, such as billboards. The result is one of those **"encounters"** that Venturi liked to stumble upon in his travels through Europe's older architecture. The huge screen is a mobile, active facade, a facade that doesn't indulge in the static, ritual con-dition of traditional facades, but which, like them (like the facades of Venetian mansions, for instance), generates a vertical plane that becomes the building's

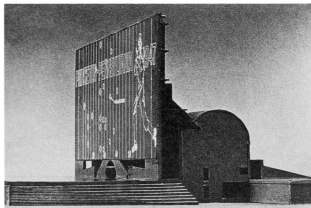

20-23 National Football Hall of Fame (project), New Brunswick, New Jersey, 1967

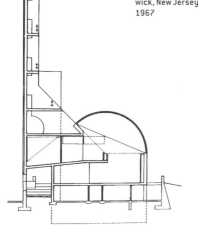

image. Although Venturi mentions Tintoretto when he talks about the vault to which the **"paraphernalia"** of football players extends, the section reminds me of an architect like James Stirling. The screen's connection to the long vault demonstrates the architects' mastery, based as it is on a complex system of diagonals. The model followed by Venturi and Rauch here seems to be that of the architect as guiding thread, as a professional able to assess problems without succumbing to formal prejudgments.

**24-27** The Trubek House and the Wislocki House on Nantucket Island, Massachusetts, both dated 1970, can serve to illustrate Venturi, Rauch and Scott Brown's attitude toward the concept of architectural type. This attitude is not critical—or theoretical, if you wish—like that of Muratori, Argan, Rossi, Colquhoun, or the Krier brothers. Venturi, Rauch and Scott Brown tried to recuperate the traditional American balloon frame house through building systems and images, altogether ignoring its formal structure. While they took extreme care to respect the exterior appearance of the popular housing typology, they didn't seem to have too many qualms about taking liberties inside. Only the popular exterior image persisted, and the architects introduced as many elements as they desired, whether windows or staircases, again without overworrying about violating the original model they were working on. Defined by image, these houses contain many disparate elements, which, though largely standard, are stripped of any possible relation to the formal structure of the buildings. The architecture uses them as familiar material, as episodes with an end of their own, and the houses come across as unique and precise events that can be seen neither as expressions of a known type nor as new prototypes.

For Venturi, Rauch and Scott Brown here, type is reduced to image. Better still, the image is the type, following the idea that communication occurs through images. The type/image is more likely to be recognized than the very structure of the house. The result is an architecture in which image is responsible for producing unity, even while the elements present belong, indiscriminately, to the history of architecture. But the interdependence between elements and whole that characterized architectures of the past is done away with completely. The internal formal structure of the type disappears, and because the simple architectural elements take on the role of images/types, they can be considered independent, autonomous fragments.

Indeed we have before us a fragmented, undone architecture. Venturi, Rauch and Scott Brown have deliberately dispensed with the idea of typological unity that dominated architecture for centuries, in the process finding—a bit to their surprise—that the image of architecture reappears in the broken mirror. If architecture in the past was an art of imitation, a description of nature, it is so once again, but this time with architecture itself as the model. Architecture thus

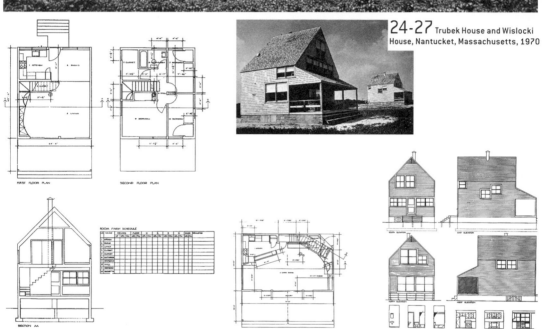

**24-27** Trubek House and Wislocki House, Nantucket, Massachusetts, 1970

returned to mimicry, but of itself, reflecting the reality of history, a history that is not in the least broken and fragmented.

Some years after the very successful *Complexity and Contradiction*, specifically in 1972, Venturi followed up with a second book, this one written with Denise Scott Brown and Steven Izenour. In *Learning from Las Vegas* they ventured into a provocative analysis of the city of images **"where fiction reigns."** Critical reflections on modernity accompany this analysis, and, like *Complexity and Contradiction*, the book uses Venturi's own body of work as an example and a paradigm of the attitude he advocates. His purposes are manifested with extreme clarity from the very first pages, beginning with the heading **"Symbol in Space Before Form in Space: Las Vegas as a Communication System."** [28] In effect, what Venturi, Scott Brown, and Izenour want to get across to us here is that modern architecture has forgotten about the importance of symbol, and that, paradoxically, it's a city like Las Vegas that retrieves it. They take us on a ride through the Strip and show us how its architecture of apparently banal hotels and casinos manipulates signs, how the constructions along it are then perceived by drivers as artistic models. The point, for the authors, is that Las Vegas is a city where architecture has recovered the power of persuasion it had in the past. As we know, the end of the sixties witnessed a tendency to turn architectural theory into a specific case of a general theory of language, giving rise to a confrontation between those who gave priority to syntax and those who were simply interested in semantics. It is clear in the book that Venturi, Scott Brown, and Izenour are inclined to uphold the communicative, rather than the structural, aspects of architecture. Las Vegas is the paradigm of an architecture whose raison d'être is communication, and the book begins with a eulogy thereof. Influenced by linguistics, they use the terms **"denotative"** and **"connotative"** very beautifully in commenting on Guild House: **"the sign saying GUILD HOUSE denotes meaning through its words; as such, it is the heraldic element par excellence. The character of the graphics, however, connotes institutional dignity, while contradictorily, the size of the graphics connotes commercialism."** [29] Umberto Eco, who dedicated a whole chapter to architecture in his manual of linguistics *La struttura assente*, [30] could not have found a better way to explain the meaning of the concepts of denotation and connotation.

  Once the cards were dealt, Venturi, Scott Brown, and Izenour went on to attack head-on what in those years was still understood as avant-garde architecture. They declared war on architecture that sought to communicate only through form. Modern architecture dispensed with symbolism, choosing instead to **"[promote] expressionism, concentrating on the expression of archi-**

**28** Robert Venturi, Denise Scott Brown and Steven Izenour, *Learning from Las Vegas* (Cambridge: MIT Press, 1972), p. 4.

**29** Ibid., p. 71.

**30** Umberto Eco, *La struttura assente* (Milan: Bompiani, 1968).

tectural elements themselves: on the expression of structure and function." [31] A little further on we read: **"The substitution of expression for representation through disdain for symbolism and ornament has resulted in an architecture where expression has become expressionism."** [32] For Venturi, Scott Brown, and Izenour, the modern architects' overemphasis on form had resulted in a style, hence their own efforts to come up with a language that was free of formalisms and removed from expressionism. Throughout the text, they severely lambasted the obsessive determination to understand architecture as an **"art of space"**— an attitude frequented by the critics who followed the Wölfflinian categories. **"Perhaps the most tyrannical element in our architecture now is space. Space has been contrived by architects and deified by critics, filling the vacuum created by fugitive symbolism."** [33] Modern architects had shunned the complexity that comes from assuming the many obligations of architecture, and the result was an abstract quest for spatial values. *Learning from Las Vegas* rejected this attitude energetically. In its view, the city could not be taken as a concatenation of spaces, nor was a building a mere manifestation of the spaces it offered. Venturi, Scott Brown, and Izenour clamored for the retrieval of everything that had fallen into oblivion: **"A second generation of modern architects acknowledged only the 'constituent facts' of history, as extracted by Sigfried Giedion, who abstracted the historical building and its piazza as pure form and space in light. These architects' preoccupation with space as the architectural quality caused them to read the buildings as forms, the piazzas as space, and the graphics and sculpture as color, texture, and scale."** [34] Venturi, Scott Brown, and Izenour set themselves the task of toppling such an interpretation: modern architecture had been **"totalitarian,"** abstract; by aspiring as well to manifest the obligations that society expected of it, through a language capable of reflecting the whole, it had confused the limits within which it must operate as a discipline.

To make clear to us what architecture had become, *Learning from Las Vegas* speaks highly of the **"decorated shed"** in contrast to the **"duck"** that the moderns wished to build. What did Venturi mean by **"ducks"**? He meant the artifacts that architects would offer in the belief that they were symbolic forms capable of performing the tasks traditionally expected of constructions. Form prevailed and had a synthetic, organic, and overall value. According to Venturi,

**31** Venturi, Scott Brown, and Izenour, *Learning from Las Vegas*, p. 72.

**32** Ibid., p. 97.

**33** Ibid., p. 99.

**34** Ibid., p. 73.

we can say **"duck"** in cases where **"the architectural systems of space, structure, and program are submerged and distorted by an overall symbolic form.
This kind of building-becoming-sculpture we call the duck in honor of the duck-
shaped drive-in, 'The Long Island Duckling,' illustrated in God's Own Junkyard
by Peter Blake."** [35] In dramatic contrast, a **"decorated shed"** is present where
**"systems of space and structure are directly at the service of program, and
ornament is applied independently of them."** [36] According to Venturi, the history
of architecture is full of **"decorated sheds."** Las Vegas is an update on an age-old
architectural mechanism. The cathedral of Amiens is a billboard, an advertise-
ment with a building behind. The Italian palazzo is the **"decorated shed"** par
excellence: Strozzi, Rucellai, and Farnese are buildings whose facades have
a life of their own, hiding behind them a conventional typological mechanism.
The eclectic architecture of the nineteenth century is a sampling of **"decorated
sheds,"** and its tendency to mix up aesthetics and function exemplifies what
architects aspire to. Modern architecture dispenses with ornament, and sin
leads to penitence: the Vitruvian *venustas* does not come from making *firmitas*
and *commoditas* coincide. Venturi clamors for *venustas*, for a concept that he
associates, like Ruskin, with **"ornament."** It is an attribute with a value of its own,
the loss of which makes itself felt in the vacuous formal deployment that Venturi
so passionately attacks.

It has often happened in the history of art that the new is the result
of an acritical reaction to what predominates. Venturi sees the targets of his
darts clearly. He rebels against the architecture of his **"academic"** colleagues,

**35** Ibid., p. 64.

**36** Ibid., p. 64.

78

meaning the academy of the avant-gardes, as backed by works like Paul Rudolph's Yale School of Architecture or Kallmann & McKinnell's Boston City Hall. Venturi, Scott Brown, and Izenour think that the semantic condition of a building can be tackled with economy in the facades without affecting the structure, and thus without compromising the program. Paradoxically, what is taken for vulgar architecture—the spontaneous architecture of the Strip—is the heir of ancient architecture, the architecture that Venturi had learned from masters like Labatut and Paul Cret, seen in Rome, and so energetically and brilliantly shown in *Complexity and Contradiction*. Whereas Venturi's first book attacks modernity by using the Academy, *Learning from Las Vegas* does so through the arguments and works of populists, those who defend the silent majority in the face of the elitist excesses of the intellectuals. So it is that Venturi became a champion of Americanism, of society generated by capitalism, of a mass culture more in touch with ancient culture than one would think.

Venturi, Scott Brown, and Izenour's eulogy of Las Vegas, the Strip, or the **"decorated shed"** cannot be dismissed as pure polemicizing. Venturi could not accept that architects should continue to design **"dead ducks"** [37] in the interests of a heroism and an originality that only served to inflate their vanity. From an ethical position that made him identify with the **"silent majority,"** he opted for the ugly and ordinary. There lay the real life, and paradoxically, architecture.

**37** Ibid., p. 109.

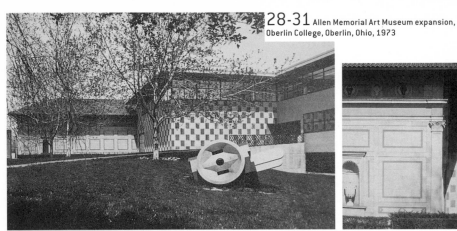

**28-31** Enlarging a building always carries a profound reflection on its architecture. We feel the passage of time when we have to deal with an architecture that was built on formulas we are unaccustomed to. What to do? One option is to stick to those formulas and carry out a literal repetition of the preexisting, with all the risks that using current resources and means brings with it. Another is to respect and maintain the scale but use a language in accord with current interests. This seems to have been the approach of the architects who in 1937 enlarged the Allen Art Museum at Oberlin College, in Ohio, built by Cass Gilbert twenty years before, in 1917. The courtyard building that Gilbert built in emulation

of the Renaissance architecture he so admired was linked up with two new courtyards that, however, forgot about the cloister scheme. The first one keeps two open walkways, while the second one turns them into corridors. The result is a building that takes off from Gilbert's original museum, preserving the cloister structure. Any further enlargement operation could be understood as a project without a future of its own, as an intervention in an area whose potential had been exhausted. Venturi, Rauch and Scott Brown were therefore faced with a true challenge. Without exaggerating the worth of Cass Gilbert's architecture, their 1973 enlargement was respectful toward it, keeping its own volume

80

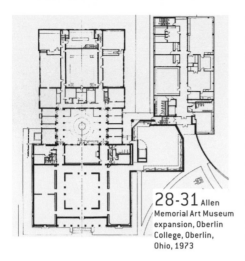

**28-31** Allen
Memorial Art Museum
expansion, Oberlin
College, Oberlin,
Ohio, 1973

that the neutral and schematic figure of the square is transformed by two operations: subtraction and cutting. The removal of one of the corners provides the desired opportunity to introduce the provocative pop image of the Ionic column. The cutting out of the corner allows the visitor a view of the framework in which the intervention took place. Removing another of the corners in turn leads to the introduction, on plan, of those slants that Venturi, Rauch and Scott Brown are so fond of and that they use here to define the character of the entrance. Proof of their talent is the skill with which different scales are handled, thanks to which the two buildings are nicely woven together.

within certain bounds while sticking to orthogonal systems of composition. They were certainly also aware that in adopting such an approach they would have to be subtle. Better still, cunning. So they leaned on strictly functional criteria when they packaged, in a building anyone would tag as conventional, all those parts of the program that did not require special attributes. In the construction of a neutral element that allowed them to connect the old structures with the new exhibition pavilion, they found the key to adding the more characteristic volume. An interplay of three instead of two.

If you like to examine the cunning arguments of an architect, study the floor plan of the pavilion and notice

But it is above all in the exterior finishes that the effort to stay close to the preexisting architecture is most manifest. Venturi, Rauch and Scott Brown insisted on decorating the walls, enriching them where they meet the roof. Naturally, they covered/decorated the walls in their own way. Whereas Cass Gilbert made use of modular alternation and framed panels, Venturi, Rauch and Scott Brown opted for a checkerboard pattern that for some hidden reason recalls fifties decor. Venturi, Rauch and Scott Brown make a show of adjusting to Gilbert's architecture, and it is perhaps this deliberate, ostentatious presentation of the differences between one architecture and the other, and the difficulties these differences cause, that their project is all about. But can the exhibition of anomalies and differences be called a procedure? Isn't there something hidden at the heart of the anomaly that is lost on us once it is exhibited? Or once it becomes an intellectual loot of the architects? Examination of said pattern leads to this reflection. The pattern, the most characteristic element of the architecture of the permanent exhibition hall, is all the more lost in the services building. Taking the pattern as a reference, the openings are installed in it. Their vulgarity is compensated for by their arrangement. Once again Venturi, Rauch and Scott Brown indulge in anomaly. They shift around the openings as soon as they can, depriving them of all possible criteria of order.

The extension of the Oberlin museum is definitely one of the most interesting of their works. It invites multiple readings and reflections. In it, to conclude, the architects connect their work to the figurative aspect of the pop artists. A proof of that is the image of the corner window that

**28-31** Allen Memorial Art Museum expansion, Oberlin College, Oberlin, Ohio, 1973

becomes the frame for the **"simulacrum"** of an Ionic column. The Ionic column could well be a sculpture by Oldenburg, and it's quite probable that that's where it comes from. But at the same time, the column is a load-bearing element. The ambiguity Venturi talks about in *Complexity and Contradiction* here becomes an entire manifesto, perhaps an overly explicit one, for the making of architecture.

**32-33** Venturi, Rauch and Scott Brown considered that spontaneous architecture was where architects would find the true rationality they should use as
professionals. In their eagerness to incorporate methods of spontaneous architecture, they tried in these next buildings to address one of the most urgent
questions posed by contemporary construction: how to resolve the cladding
with which the structures are sealed up, whether in concrete or in steel. This
was a problem that modern architects had already paid a lot of attention to,
solving it in strictly constructional terms, at least in appearance. But whereas
Mies indulged in results that manifested a congruence between structure and
cladding, doing away with ornamentation, Venturi, Rauch and Scott Brown dispensed with such a relation and, given the preference for the epithelial condition
of claddings, found the opportunity to reintroduce ornament.

In the Institute for Scientific Information (ISI) headquarters in Philadelphia, dated 1978, the volumetric composition and the fenestration are strictly
conventional, even vulgar I would say, and the architects seem to have focused
on defining the pattern that enriches the brickwork. The facade emphasizes the
flatness of the cladding, expressing that there is no choice but to enrich it with
ornament, in this case in the form of the bond. As in Guild House, the building
accepts symmetry, even if this is broken in the plinth. The Venturi of *Complexity
and Contradiction* reappears in the one who, at first glance, seems to live only
in *Learning from Las Vegas*.

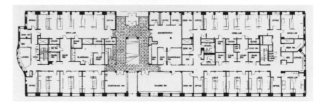

84

**34-35** The procedure was applied again to projects like the Khulafa Street Residential and Commercial Building in Baghdad, Iraq, dated 1981, where the liberties taken by Venturi, Rauch and Scott Brown around the plinth do not seem to justify the literal adoption of traditional ornamental forms. Proposals of this kind cast doubt on the idea of the "decorated shed." In my opinion, if this building on Khulafa Street had been carried out, it would have cut a figure especially for its volume, its structure, and it would therefore have fallen under the kind of conventional architecture that is inspired by modern architecture and that tends to drown all signs of local identity.

**36-37** The problems that Venturi, Rauch and Scott Brown tried to solve in the Institute for Scientific Information headquarters reappear in the 1983 project for the Lewis Thomas Laboratory for Molecular Biology in Princeton, New Jersey. The solution adopted is not very different, but the program, being more complex, allowed the architects to unleash their design skills further. The floor plan asserts their interest in putting the laboratories along the perimeter, reserving the center for ancillary services. Note, too, how the building's freestanding condition in the campus made the architects pay special attention to its rear.

The neutrality of the scheme, established by the structure, the windows, and the pattern, subtly exploits the joints, thereby favoring both a partial and an overall reading of the parameters. The access is situated on an off-center axis and the modular scheme breaks up, giving rise to a virtual facade that is absorbed by the whole. As in the 1981 project for Khulafa Street in Baghdad, the moldings of the main door are suspended and cut, dissolving into a pattern through a subtle checkerboard that inevitably recalls Oberlin. Once again, the "decorated shed" as standard operating procedure.

**38-39** Basco showroom, Philadelphia, 1979

**38-39** Consistent with their proposals, Venturi, Rauch and Scott Brown set about to "formulate" a problem. They resorted to "graphics" and color. The photograph of the monumental O with which they liked to present the Basco Showroom in Philadelphia, dated 1979, shows how far this kind of architecture can go. It would be difficult to use this work to illustrate the principles put forward in Venturi's first book. Here the architects pass the test as professionals, and gracefully, without having to contrive a unique or subtle architecture. By defining a whole series of obligations that hardly give rise to the anomaly he so effectively taught us to spot in *Complexity and Contradiction*, Venturi, Rauch and Scott Brown were once again caught in the web they themselves had woven.

40-41 Best Projects Catalog Showroom, Langhorne, Pennsylvania, 1977

40-41 The foregoing commentary on the Basco showroom can be applied to the Best Products Catalog Showroom in Langhorne, Pennsylvania, of 1977. This project is perhaps of greater interest because it highlights the architects' graphic design skills.

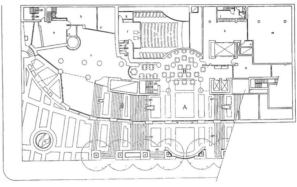

**42-48** Seattle Art Museum, 1984–1991

**42-48** Let us pay close attention to this museum in Seattle, which could be said to be a precursor of a major work in the career of Venturi and Scott Brown, the Sainsbury Wing of London's National Gallery. The project for the Seattle Art Museum (1984–1991) is yet another illustration of Venturi and Scott Brown's confidence in the floor plan and the importance they give to working on a right fitting of a building into its site. The Seattle project tries to exploit the corner condition of the site. Situating the access at the corner produced a linear structure that enabled the architects to distribute the rooms on the upper floor with extreme clarity. The exhibition spaces are arranged on the two upper floors, while the two lower ones accommodate all other museum services. Venturi and Scott Brown here seem to indulge in the superposing of uses and functions. One gets to the galleries above from a mezzanine level in which access to the elevators is in the same area as the restaurant. Perspective views of elements like the staircase are mixed with false hexahedrons and columns, displaying that admirable capacity of the architects to bring together architectural episodes having nothing to do with one another. Indeed, the eclectic, nineteenth-

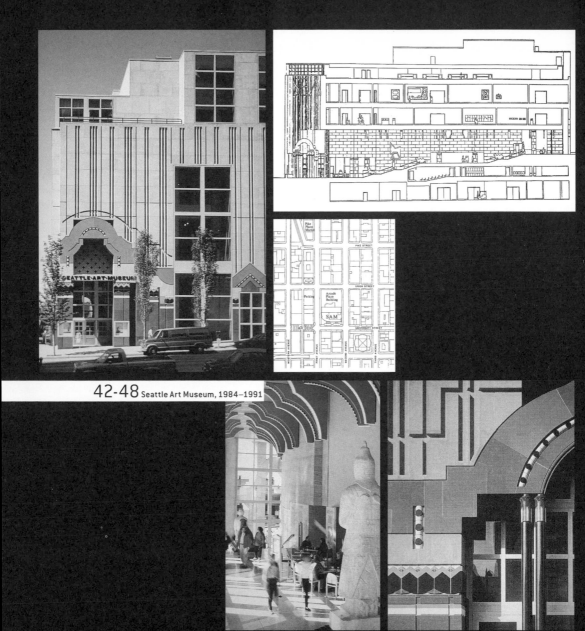

**42-48** Seattle Art Museum, 1984–1991

century-like aroma that seems to emanate from the architecture has little to do with the order and structure of the floor plan. It can be said that it is the elements—a staircase, a corridor, a series of lined-up columns, etc.—that are made responsible for creating a visual order. To appreciate the full extent of Venturi and Scott Brown's work as architects, observe how skillfully they have tackled the entrance.

The image of the Seattle museum's rear facade provides an opportunity to analyze how Venturi and Scott Brown went about the project. First let us establish that at the origins is the texture of the stone surface, with its unique striated rhythm. This panel, which seems to want to stress the frontal value of the facade, is made to include all those elements that are considered necessary. These elements are inlaid in it, flaunting a freedom of action not too different from that of a child cutting pieces of paper and pasting them to a cardboard. Let's look now at the series of doorways that, in the manner of Russian dolls, each give access to the next through a conventional oak door. The facade exfoliates in two planes. Inlaid in one of them is a complex opening where lintels are mixed up with arches and moldings gashed in it. A medium-height lintel bears the sign reading "Seattle Art Museum." Encrusted in the two jambs

that now respect the symmetrical order—as a counterpoint to the asymmetric rhythm of the stone facade and the glazed structure that includes the doors—are colorful elements that bring to mind nonexistent capitals. Asymmetries and decoration. Historic architectures and vulgar elements. Natural materials and painting. Carved stone in contrast with polished stone. Cuts made in the manner of moldings that are interrupted at will, without any apparent pattern. The corner of Second Avenue and University Street is another good illustration of Venturi and Scott Brown's working procedure. We could think of the corner as the result of superimposing planes with different formal purposes. In the generic plane textured in carved stone is encrusted an arch of polished granite, and left behind—off the axis—is a glazed gridded structure into which the doors are inlaid. Each of these virtual, abstract planes has a material texture of its own, and the result is an intricate overlapping of autonomous structures that prevents us from identifying any dominant form: a deliberate complexity far removed from any supposed solution to a conflict. The architecture of Venturi and Scott Brown is complex, but not spontaneous. It is more the result of a method than the answer to a need. Things didn't happen this way in the examples Venturi presented to us in *Complexity and Contradiction in Architecture*.

**49-58** The competition for the new enlargement of London's National Gallery through the construction of the Sainsbury Wing (1986–1991) presented Venturi and Scott Brown with the opportunity to prove the validity of their theories in an architectural problem that raised not only strictly disciplinary questions but also urbanistic and symbolic ones. At first sight it seemed a mere matter of attaching a new building to the well-defined volume that William Wilkins built. As the floor plan reveals, Wilkins's building had undergone two enlargements along the rear facade. The new extension would then have to be on Trafalgar Square. A close look at the floor plan shows that the architects of the previous extensions paid little attention to Wilkins's building, and that their constructions

are mere protuberances. Venturi and Scott Brown's winning project contemplated the construction of a more sensitive new building at the point where Pall Mall East begins, at the northwest corner of Trafalgar Square. The project obviously sought to approach the architecture of the National Gallery in a literal way, as in **"vibration through affinity."** How did Venturi and Scott Brown go about it? The first step was to accept the order of measurements established by the halls of the original National Gallery. In accordance with a well-known museum typology, the new building was to be understood as a set of rooms. But unlike the rooms in the old building, those of the new building do not follow a pattern. Venturi and Scott Brown here connect the cruciform schemes of the old building to the new bays by means of an axis that establishes a continuity with the preexisting while facilitating the colonization of the new lot. They follow the axis. But the minute they've reached the area on which they are to build, they dispense with the orthogonal order defined by Wilkins, and introduce a slanting line that alludes to the orientation of Whitcomb Street. This orientation is at the origin of the three bays in which the galleries are laid out, responsible for a generic order that the architects themselves soon set about to make us forget. One room leads to another, but in a way that is removed from any order imposed by the bays. Only the central bay is allowed to maintain some kind of an order, namely the axis of perspective. In the other two bays, bay-imposed order breaks down entirely, deliberately, resulting in rooms with a high degree of autonomy. Finally, the perimeter is determined more by preexisting circumstances of an urbanistic nature than by any say that the bays might have with regard to form. This interior/exterior contrast, so much to the liking of Venturi and Scott Brown, results in a high diversity of rooms, which is something the architects give a lot of importance to. Significantly, whereas in Wilkins's building the *poché* takes place at the very heart of the building, deep inside, in the Sainsbury Wing it appears in the perimeter. We will address this question further when we talk about the articulation and encounter of the two buildings.

And now let's see how this system of bays—which as we have said is at the origin of the building—affects the lower floors. On the entrance level the bays come to constitute systems of columns that the architects took good care to manipulate in some way, whether by associating them with the facade or by pairing them up in a manner that plainly had nothing to do with the severe parallel walls. The same can be said of the mezzanine level. Only on the basement level do the walls reappear, however timidly. The desire to mark distances between the (top) floor that generated the building and all the others is all the more manifest if we interpret the intricate profile separating public from private as a game through which the architects arbitrarily created profiles evoking the moldings of the grandest moment of the Beaux-Arts manner. One could say that the architects indulged in this game to reverify the arbitrariness of the discipline.

It is surely of interest to acknowledge the importance Venturi and Scott Brown gave to such aspects of architecture as the articulation (juxtaposition) of volumes, the choice of materials, and the language of sealings and facades. Here the articulation of two volumes is resolved through a floor plan device that could be considered quasi-conventional. The rotunda that functions as a joint connecting the last room of Wilkins's building to the landing of the new staircase is key to the transition. True, the transition seems better thought-out in the main floor than in the intermediate levels, where the construction of the rotunda has given rise to an ambiguous space—ambiguous this time in a negative sense, not in the Venturian sense that invites praise. But there is more to the transition. Between the oblique positioning of the new spaces and the orthogonal alignment of Wilkins's building rises a transition bay, parallel to neither. This is where the staircase goes. A good look at the floor plan reveals that the staircase uses the effect of inverse perspective—inverse to the perspective one might consider canonical in traditional examples of the baroque, such as Bernini's Scala Regia. Plans hence once again show us Venturi and Scott Brown's deliberate use of contradiction: when used, the modest side access to the staircase offers a magnificent, spectacular panorama.

So far I've talked about articula-

tion only in terms of the floor plan. We should put it in a broader scheme of things and address volume as well as cladding textures. In volumetric terms, continuity between Wilkins's building and the new construction—visual articulation—is achieved through near-literal respect for the former's horizontal order. The rigid Wilkinsian pilasters are made responsible for creating continuity between the two volumes. However, the symmetrical order of Wilkins's building gives way to a syncopated manipulation of the pilasters, which whirl around a point that marks the encounter between a wall that is still parallel to Wilkins's building on one hand, and on the other hand the free curve that marks the transition which, in turn, makes the new volume respect the alignments of Pall Mall East. The

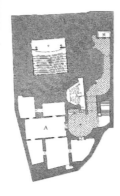

**49-58** Sainsbury Wing of the National Gallery, London, 1986–1991

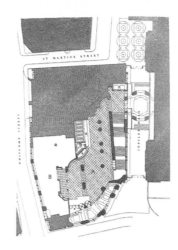

series of pilasters—manipulated more as iconographic elements than as referential signs of an internal order—is applied to the broken wall, ending the iconographic sequence with a column that, like an echo or a shadow, is still accompanied by a half-pilaster, making the traditional physical elements blend into a flat wall that reveals a certain influence of Edwardian architecture. The cornice protects the face and makes the transition imperceptible. Again, Venturi and Scott Brown demonstrate the eminently visual nature of the discipline. Once the visual impact is taken care of, there is license for everything. And so it is that, in a further search for controversial dissonance, the volume beneath the building is resolved by means of radical cuts that forcefully show how the architects have deliberately dispensed with any design element that might have made the operation less painful. The exhibitionism of freedom as standard operating procedure.

Venturi and Scott Brown take it that each one of the facades—all of which are in any case situated in very different urban conditions—demands a different architecture. The building's formal consistency doesn't come from its internal structure. Quite the contrary; as the Sainsbury Wing clearly illustrates, Venturi and Scott Brown think of architecture as the result of addressing specific, unique demands. Hence a building with the capacity to assume a diversity similar to that of a collage. Circle the Sainsbury Wing

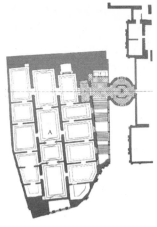

**49-58** Sainsbury Wing of the National Gallery, London, 1986–1991

and you come across a facade that respects Wilkins, a curtain wall, a symmetrical facade over the small square facing St. Martin's Street that incorporates typography and ventilation grilles as plastic elements, and so on. In short, the taming of contradiction.

Let's go inside. As we said, Venturi and Scott Brown insist on an architecture that uses the old mechanism of perspective axes to give structure, at least visual structure, to a building. There are two axes. The first one, which prolongs the axis of Wilkins's building, diagonally cuts the walls that define the bays. Venturi and Scott Brown

avoid the effect of the diagonal by cutting the bays with an opening that recalls the Serlian window and that makes it possible for the arch to bear upon the walls totally free of prejudgments, leading again to the so-called contradictions. All the interior spaces have contradictions, and a look at the proportions and the moldings of the supposed Tuscan order being used by Venturi and Scott Brown suffices to reveal the obstinacy of the procedure. The breathtaking Cima da Conegliano painting we find at the end of the itinerary justifies all the trouble taken in composing the spaces.

The axes that are parallel to the walls take on different forms. The axis of the central bay has a continuous and symmetrical composition, stressing the perspective that is ever present in the paintings hung within it. The other two are discontinuous, giving the rooms a high degree of autonomy. As the floor plan shows, the walls that shape them have nothing to do with those that mark the divisions of the central bay. The side bays recognize the irregularity of the perimeter and explain the efficiency of the strategy employed: the discontinuity of the axes is endorsed by the irregularity. Only in the bay along Whitcomb Street is there an attempt to produce a more continuous episode, with the three last rooms using the axis that the bisection of the walls gives rise to.

Venturi and Scott Brown's belief in a simplified iconography—as if we lived on exaggerated images alone—is manifest in the arches they use to cover the staircase. The manipulated structure presents itself as the mere amplification of a cardboard model, with distant echoes of both the arcades of traditional architecture and the assimilation of the arch by early nineteenth-century engineers. Note how the structural elements are attached to the walls and you will agree with me about the predominance of the iconographic. On the other hand, the lack of respect for order that the windows impose enables Venturi and Scott Brown to display how freely they go about things, their lack of prejudgments, and the inevitability of "**contradictions.**"

Again a section suffices to explain how Venturi and Scott Brown operate. One might say that it tries to flaunt its pragmatism, hence the emphasis it puts on the treatment of the skylights. If the interior volumes of the rooms are solved with a high degree of independence, this translates into an asymmetrical roof where what counts is the regularity of the interior spaces. But since all the elements of the outline are drawn up alike, the regularity is not evident in the drawing. What matters to the architects is the "**action.**" The building is presented to us with the paintings in their places, with people moving toward the cloakroom or going up the staircase. In Venturi and Scott Brown, the section doesn't have the same importance as it has in the work of some contemporaries of theirs, such as Stirling. In their work, it's not the section that structures the building. The section of the National Gallery clearly shows that the project took off from the floor plan—specifically the upper-level floor plan. The monumental stair-

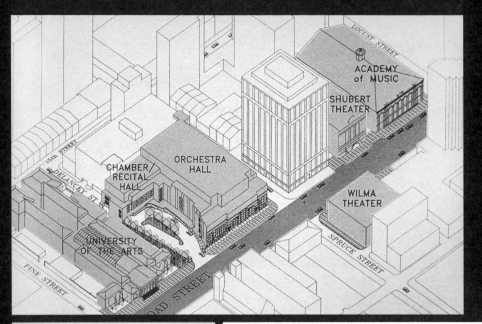

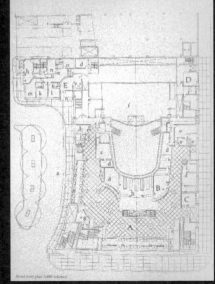

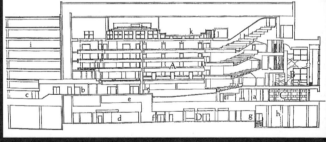

**59-65** Philadelphia Orchestra Hall, 1987–1996

case leads to this level, as if it had no other purpose than to serve this level. The entrance level, the mezzanine, and the basement are simply horizontal planes that help knit the program together.

**59-65** Venturi and Scott Brown must have felt very flattered when an institution like the Philadelphia Orchestra commissioned them to build its concert hall. True to their principles, they began by accepting the concert hall as a known type of building, and proceeded to follow models that were on everybody's mind. Echoes of the nineteenth-century architecture that had consolidated the concert hall as a typology appear as much in the geometry of the auditorium as in the series of superposed amphitheaters. The objective of the architects seemed to be to fit a generic and universal building into a set of very specific urban conditions. Venturi and Scott Brown are extraordinarily sensitive to Philadelphia's urban fabric. They are very familiar with the city and know well how its buildings act within the fabric. For the Philadelphia Orchestra Hall (1987–1996) they chose to maintain the perimeter of the city block, but on one side—on Delancey Street, where the building faces the University of the Arts—they took the presence of another institional building as reason to create a more peaceful atmosphere, one more secluded than one would expect of a street, a space that would allow access to the auditorium by car while avoiding conflicts with the traffic of Broad Street. Meanwhile, one can also enter the building from Broad Street. In sum, Delancey Street provides comfortable access by car, whereas it's on Broad Street that a facade rises and speaks of an institution's importance to the city. With this project Venturi and Scott Brown showed us how respect for a well-known urban structure, the city block, is not at odds with creating something specific. Indeed, this project must be seen more as a skillful shaping of the volume of a city block than as a freestanding building. And once they had defined the volume by addressing urbanistic conditions, the architects shifted their attention to the problem of fitting the predetermined auditorium into it. And so we have a perfectly symmetrical hall, but the symmetry is not that of a nineteenth-century concert hall. The design of the foyer shows how the symmetry of the hall doesn't apply indiscriminately to the adjacent spaces. It is maintained in the development of the program, but any anomalies produced

**59-65** Philadelphia Orchestra Hall, 1987–1996

in adjusting to the strictly established perimeter, or to building guidelines, are willingly assumed and accommodated. Notice how the emergency stairs maintain a symmetrical composition, as if safe in the knowledge that the grand staircase connecting the lower and upper foyers will completely upset any preliminary symmetrical reading of the whole. Venturi and Scott Brown seem keen to create the ambiguity that leads one at first sight to interpret the building as a symmetrical space. The pillars play a key role in destroying such an impression, varying in diameter and dotting the void unpredictably, erratically.

This Philadelphia project is yet another good illustration of how Venturi and Scott Brown understand architectural composition. First they accept the building systems in use. Then they proceed to project on them the particular iconography they are interested in, depending on the case. The serious, institutional character of this project seems to warrant the use of traditional architectural elements. Hence the pediment and the columns. But standard construction calls for a curtain wall. This is made to absorb the pediment, the columns, and in addition, the modern grids. The axes fade out, the symmetries break up, the corner of the pediment coincides neither with the axes of the virtual pilasters nor with those of the openings. Again and again, Venturi and Scott Brown indulge in contradiction, and here we may call it a tamed contradiction. The easygoingness that the times seem to demand takes the form of a gigantic frieze on the facade that is, literally, an amplified musical staff. All too obvious. Gone is the freshness of the examples we appreciated in *Complexity and Contradiction in Architecture*. Professional practice

**59-65** Philadelphia Orchestra Hall, 1987–1996

seems eventually to have led Venturi and Scott Brown to take up set formulas.

It's instructive to trace the origin of the facade. The transformation of the veneer facade into a curtain wall is simply an exercise with no effect on the iconographic content, so it's important to see how the facade evolved. The 1990 scheme still has echoes of the Seattle project. The strict symmetry of the entrances fades at the far edges. Venturi and Scott Brown would have us believe that the facade perforated in the stone face is symmetrical, when actually a close look reveals that they have tried not to make it so. The same goes for the 1995 scheme, where the system created by the superposition of orthogonal grids is disrupted by the slants of a virtual pediment. Venturi and Scott Brown took care not to make the corner of the pediment coincide with any of the grid's axes. There is a very patent effort to find unique forms of expression for what are really conventional building techniques. Whereas the first version of the elevation explores the possibilities of a veneer facade, the second is a sample of what can be done with a curtain wall. The desire to be professionally competent—which in this case calls for the acceptance of current building methods—doesn't preclude the presence of architecture, which makes its appearance by making use of a formal world with direct references to architecture of the past. The project seems to have been nurtured by the fantasy of reconciling the interpretation of historical architecture put forward by *Complexity and Contradiction*, the use of iconography advocated by *Learning from Las Vegas*, and conventional building techniques.

# ALDO ROSSI

The task that Aldo Rossi embarked on at the start of the sixties was enormously ambitious. Trained in the circle of Ernesto Rogers and other editors of the magazine *Casabella*—people like Vittorio Gregotti, Carlo Aymonino, Francesco Tentori, and Marco Zanuso—young Rossi was alert to the first criticisms of modern tradition that were being formulated at the time. To situate ourselves, suffice it to remember the controversy between Reyner Banham and the Turin architects who defended *neoliberty* such as the then very young Roberto Gabetti and Aimaro Isola. [1]

Rogers was mentor to all those Milanese who had finished their studies in the second half of the fifties. With extensive professional practice behind him—the famous BBPR of G.L. Banfi, L. Di Belgiojoso, E. Peressutti, and E.N. Rogers was without a doubt Milan's most active studio in the fifties—Rogers was the leader of Milan's architectural culture through his work as professor and critic. His *Casabella* editorials and other writings are compiled in a 1958 book entitled *Esperienza dell'architettura*, of immense value for a feel of the architectural climate of those years. [2]

Educated in the strict modern tradition and a rationalist architect in the thirties, Rogers had actively participated in the architectural competitions organized by the administration in Mussolini's Italy. His Jewish origins sent him underground during the war and he collaborated with the *resistenza*. As editor of *Casabella* he became a figure who was crucial to an understanding of Milanese culture of the time. *Casabella* initiated a critical revision of the history of modern architecture and published monographic issues on architects like Hoffmann and Loos. These were inspired by Rogers, though responsibility for producing them landed in the hands of his young collaborators, who thus had the opportunity to demonstrate their talents.

Responsive to the first criticisms being formulated against the modern movement, Rossi reacted with particular intensity to the historians who were triumphantly chronicling its ongoing development. Among these was Bruno Zevi, the most belligerent historian and critic of forties and fifties Italy. Zevi preached a modern movement where intentions of sociological progressivism coincided with a continuous evolution in purely visual and figurative terms. Above all, he was interested in establishing a continuity between architecture and other

1 La Bottega d'Erasmo can be considered the first work ever carried out with the express purpose of presenting an alternative to the dominant "modern" aesthetic. This early project of Gabetti and Isola sought to recuperate aspects of architecture that the modern movement deliberately ignored. Renewed interest in ornament and the specific are perhaps the most characteristic features of a work that surprised the architects' contemporaries and can be said to be the seed of the revisionism of subsequent years. For more information see Reyner Banham, "Neoliberty: The Italian Retreat from Modern Architecture," *Architectural Review*, April 1959.

2 For more information on the figure of Ernesto Nathan Rogers see Ezio Bonfanti [and M. Porta], *Città, museo e architettura. Il gruppo BBPR nella cultura architettonica italiana 1932–1970* (Florence: Vallecchi, 1973).

artistic pursuits. To simplify things, in Zevi's view architecture had to do with the history of manners and styles. To him, architecture was not removed from an evolutionist belief in progress that still had Wölfflinian roots. Such an attitude led him to think that its history could only reach fullness in modern architecture, as it was only in modern architecture that space was what prevailed. In this Zevi saw the architecture of Wright as the paradigm of modern architecture: it was in Wright's work that architecture had succeeded, through a long evolution, in becoming what Zevi considered to be its essence: an art of space.

Rossi placed himself in the opposition. He was not so much interested in connecting architecture to the more advanced arts as he was in finding for architecture a specific base of its own. I wouldn't think it an exaggeration to speak of the lure that Marxism had for Italians then under thirty, and to say that their devotion to it made them think it important to set some positive foundation for any science or discipline. For Rossi, architecture didn't end in the mere satisfaction of an artistic vocation, nor therefore in linguistic exploration, in questions that then still mattered to Zevi. From the very start of his career, Rossi wished architecture to be a positive science and wanted the work of architects to be seen as something not removed from that of scientists. If the natural and human sciences had been been able to explain and arrange the territory in which they moved, there was no reason to think that architecture couldn't do likewise. There was in Rossi's attitude a desire for objectivity much to the liking of the Marxists of the period. And neither would it be too daring to say that when Rossi spoke of a theory of architecture, he was thinking of a body of doctrine not too different from that which Lukács had established when talking about a theory of the novel. For architecture to become a positive science at the service of a more conscientious and responsible society, one had to see how it could break away from its traditional attachment to the artistic.

In sum, the ambitious task proposed by Rossi led him to believe that architecture should be thought of in the same way as the natural and human sciences. For this to happen, the first step was to pinpoint *where* architecture was, to determine the territory it could call its own. Rossi had no doubts here: architecture's territory was the city. Now, if architecture was in the city, it was necessary to know how the city was built, what principles had guided its development, how the different zones and quarters comprising it had been formed. Hence, it was important to begin by describing the city, that reality which was for Rossi "the most complete representation of the human condition." Rossi was convinced that describing the city would help him find the keys to explaining architecture.

In 1966 he published *L'architettura della città*, elaborated with material taken from previous articles. In this book he endeavored to define concepts that would give a "scientific" view of the city. The book is in accord with the ideology of the structuralists who were in vogue at the time, but we have to admit that it doesn't nowadays make one see the principles Rossi established as invested with "scientific objectivity." The concepts presented are vague, imprecise, diffuse. But it was enormously attractive to my generation. So influential was it that by the close of the sixties, concepts like "place," "type," "monument," and "urban form" had become household terms.

Rossi also stressed the idea of the permanence or timelessness of architecture. This soon led him to abstract it from its functional obligations. He actually spoke of functional indifference, giving architectural form a value of its own and eliminating any determinist relation between form and use. For him, the notion of the type went beyond the instrumental and became the image—and note that I'm talking about image, not structure—of a house, a school, a hospital. It was with these set images—Platonic shadows?—that a city came to be. These were the types that conferred value on architectural form. Through them, architecture took on an objectivity that transcended the individual creativity of the avant-gardes. Which was not to ignore the efforts that the avant-gardes had exerted in the process of linguistic revision.

Rossi's words: **"Ultimately, we can say that type is the very idea of architecture, that which is closest to its essence. In spite of changes, it has always imposed itself on the 'feelings and reason' as the principle of architecture and of the city."** [3] Type over reason and sentiment. Type as origin and beginning of architecture and the city. Type guaranteed the continuity that was, perhaps, its most valuable attribute. But there must be room left for the singular, the unique, and the exclusive: that reality which at a given moment catalyzes and gives meaning to a specific event/place. Rossi then spoke of "monuments,"

3 Aldo Rossi, *The Architecture of the City*, trans. Diane Ghirardo and Joan Ockman (Cambridge: MIT Press, 1982), p. 41.

those architectural events that we store in our memory and of which we learn in histories of architecture. They were, in Rossi's words, **"physical signs of the past"** [4] that contain the substance that society has given them—which is not to say that they have lost control of their lives and destinies.

4 Ibid., p. 59.

5 Ibid., p. 101.

Analysis of the city then led Rossi to explore larger spheres, beyond type and place. Spheres that flowed into the territory and, in time, geography. So it is that his book rests more on geographical treatises than on his colleagues' investigations of history and architectural criticism. Again, his determination to align himself with the work of scientists made him shun, and perhaps aggressively disdain, that of his colleagues. But, having analyzed the city and the territory, it was necessary to find a norm by which to construct the city. And it is at this point that the book introduces us to the concept of "construction." "Construction" was crucial to Rossi because through it his ideas could be materialized. To make architecture is to "construct." It is to be able to form those *fatti architettonici* of which the city is made. An entire phase of Rossi's career was dedicated to learning how to construct. It constitutes a narrative of how to graduate from analysis to facts by way of construction.

Type is a diffuse concept that contains a constructive solution—one that gives rise to a space and is resolved in a given iconography—but it also speaks of a capacity to grasp, protect, and make sense of those contents that are implicit in its use. Because of this, the images through which types ultimately manifest themselves are impregnated with sentiment. So it is that Rossi can muse: **"When one goes to a charitable institution, the sadness is almost something concrete. It is in the walls, the courtyards, the rooms."** [5]

To know and to feel. An imaginary line divides this lecture into two parts: one that shows Rossi as a slave of knowledge, and one where he is a victim of feeling. A good part of this lecture will examine how our architect learned to build. The other part will explain how his thirst for knowledge became an imperious expression of feeling. Feeling prevails at the surprising conclusion that one is more capable of feeling than of knowing. In sum, in examining the architectural work of Rossi, we will witness a shift from knowledge to feeling.

Let us start with the beginnings of his career—a career marked, as often happens, by relationships and affinities. At the start of his career, Rossi was close to Gianugo Polesello, with whom he drew up one of his early projects. It is always risky to make simplifications, but there was in the early Rossi projects a true obsession with analysis and the objective, and this was manifested in the use of primary shapes. It was an objectivity not far removed from that of the Russian constructivists. The project for the Centro Direzionale in Turin serves to illustrate this. A certain change is observable in the Poligono di San Rocco in Monza or the school in San Sabba, Trieste, indicating perhaps the influence of another architect Rossi was close to in those years: Giorgio Grassi. These projects, which we could consider illustrations of *L'architettura della città*, were characterized by an anxious pursuit of architectural forms that would make the characteristic features of a given type appear more forcefully. Rossi's apogee — manifested in the respect and admiration of his contemporaries — was achieved with the Modena Cemetery, a project that won a 1971 competition but was executed later in the eighties. The Gallaratese housing may be the project most in line with the cemetery, ideologically, and I would say that these dwellings are more representative than the cemetery of Rossi's thoughts at the time. Remember that the cemetery was carried out fifteen years after it was drawn up.

In 1976, Aldo Rossi traveled to America. The trip constituted a fall on the road to Damascus because, in a way, it was this trip that dismounted him from his scientific zeal and led him to realize that one could only work with images. Let us follow this journey in a run-through of his oeuvre.

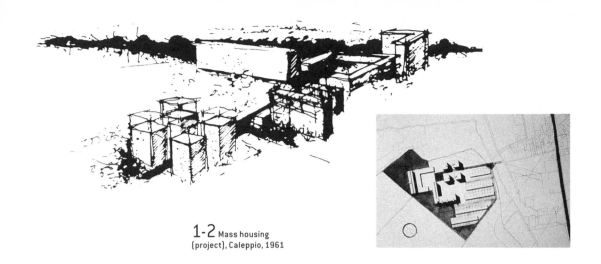

1-2 Mass housing
(project), Caleppio, 1961

1-2 The 1961 project for mass housing in Caleppio gave no hint of Aldo Rossi's future. It was a project like so many others of the time, not only in Italy but also, say, in Spain. A polygon—with everything that signifies in the urbanistic jargon of the seventies—takes in a set of blocks that are rather forceful. The grouping of the four volumes gives rise to an urban episode that goes a bit beyond the mere grammar of blocks or the simple play of volumes with which other architects of the time would have resolved an architectural problem of this kind. Though loaded with commitments to function or use, we can perceive in this project a desire to make a connection between the old city and a new fragment of city. It speaks of the architect's endeavor to endow the modern city with all the characteristics and attributes of the old city.

3-4 But Caleppio is a lukewarm project compared to an entry from 1962, in collaboration with Gianugo Polesello and under the motto Locomotiva 2, to the competition for Turin's Centro Direzionale. This was a radical project in which Rossi and Polesello's devotion to societies embodying ideals of solidarity and community translated into categorical architectural forms. It is easy to take a critical stance and dismiss the project as totalitarian, but we have to acknowledge and admire the architects' intentions. As far as they were concerned, archi-

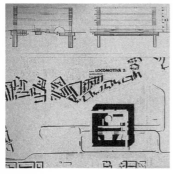
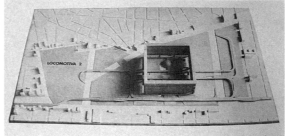

3-4 Centro Direzionale
(project), Turin, 1962

tecture could not be reduced to mere volumetry. It had to have a symbolic content. This, it seems, was the project's main intention. The social energy of community life is manifested in the hemisphere around which the entire urban design revolves.

This powerful fragment of city was to connect with Turin through a complex system of thoroughfares that had nothing to do with the architects' proposed abstract volumes, and which speak of a vision in which enlightened components are mixed with mechanistic and technological ones, so alien to Rossi's future architecture. As we said, the Rossi we are looking at now was attentive to the idealistic architecture of the Russian constructivists, however difficult it is to establish similarities in their formal criteria.

5-6 Another 1962 project was the Monument to the Resistance in Cuneo, a small city north of Milan. In this project Rossi delved further into issues he had addressed in Turin. He explored the formal possibilities of an abstract architecture, which he would nevertheless endow, when possible, with symbolic content. Hence the cube as a categorical figure with the capacity to contain all the attributes of the planet. One could work on the cube by means of basic geometrical operations, operations totally removed from any condescension to the visual. And yet the tangible world we perceive with our eyes manifests itself here in a framework that is at once theatrical and subtle. We are asked to enter the cube through the inclined plane of the stairs, and go up without knowing where to. The exercise is symmetrical to Dante's descent to hell, because only when we've reached the unexpected platform does the space open, and we find ourselves alone before the heavens. But once we've reached it, we become aware of the crack that reestablishes contact with the outer world, that has something to do with bunker architectures, and that subtly speaks to us of resistance, of defending oneself from inside a citadel.

The cube of Cuneo forces us to cut all ties with the outer world, and hence a sense of relief when we come across the horizontal that puts us in touch with the mountains where the guerrillas being honored fought. In this project, where the work of an artist such as Max Bill may be present, there is a vision that assumes freedom with respect to what we understand as historical memory. Because of this, we have spoken of an abstract architecture. But at the heart of Rossi's thought is also something very dramatic, very theatrical, when suddenly the whole world, all of life, all of history, comes to us panoramically in the horizon. All this, nevertheless, through a geometrical manipulation of form that makes no reference to the representational whatsoever, and which seems to nourish the fantasy that a pure, essential architecture is possible, one totally abstracted from any kind of indulgence with language.

Rossi had been responsible for an important *Casabella* issue on Adolf Loos,[6] and Loos's impact would be ever present in his work. It can be said that the spatial investigation in Cuneo is more in line with the interests of the Viennese architect than it is with Corbusian linguistic explorations.

6 Aldo Rossi, "Adolf Loos, 1870–1930," *Casabella Continuità* 233 (1959).

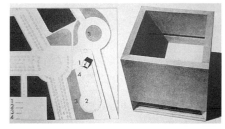

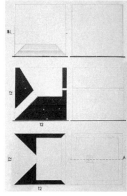

5-6 Monument to the Resistance (project), Cuneo, 1962

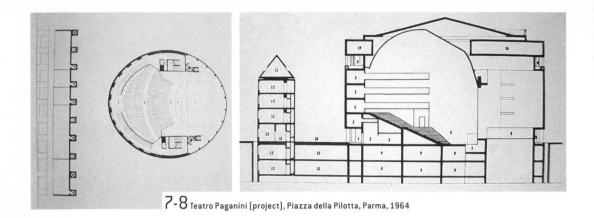

7-8 Teatro Paganini (project), Piazza della Pilotta, Parma, 1964

7-8 But history would soon come into the picture, and through a project like the Teatro Paganini in Parma's Piazza della Pilotta, dated 1964, Rossi's architecture began to incorporate traditional figurative elements. Though a project for a new building, it accepted the traditional understanding of an Italian theater. At the same time, the use of categorical basic shapes suggests a close link between architecture and the discovery of polyhedrons and simple, pure forms: comparison between the cylinder and the prism becomes the substance of the space that the architect here took pleasure in creating.

The space of the plaza does not enter the drawing. One might surmise that the void, the interstitial space, is not designed; it is simply felt. And the experience is physical, free of any kind of linguistic pressure. Architecture is reduced to an exploration of space with elemental figures. If in the Cuneo monument we found a hollow cube, here we find a prism that, as a roof with a triangular interior that unexpectedly results from the cube being emptied, becomes a lookout from which to contemplate the whole new architectural world that Rossi offers. Henceforth the prism-turned-roof of the Piazza della Pilotta would be a canonical element of his iconographic world.

9-12 What we have just seen in the Piazza della Pilotta was consolidated in the 1965 project for the town square of Segrate. Here, Rossi went one step further in the search for the theoreti-

Il movimento di
Segrate 1965
AR

a Nate 20/2

AR
DSC
N30
79

9-12 Town square, Segrate, 1965

cal principles that would lead him to the construction of the city. He was inspired by the architecture of the Enlightenment. This was for obvious reasons, including what we could call ideological affinity. Rossi was of the belief that the late eighteenth century was a time when humanity managed to free itself of many of its atavistic features, and that in that commendable period of ideological passion, more clearly than in any other point of history, architects were capable of discerning what architecture really was. Boullée spoke of what the space of a library should be, proclaiming that it should represent all knowledge, all the wisdom that books contain; the library as paradigm of human knowledge. In the same way, the town square of Segrate, a modest proletarian district of Milan, was to exemplify public space, be a paradigm of community life. The Segrate town square, hence, as one of those Greek agoras drawn by the architects of the Enlightenment. So it is that the pavement was planted with drums of columns, in the manner of witnesses of a painstakingly achieved social life. The highlight is the fountain, where the cylinder that comes across as a contemporary version of Trajan's column is crowned with the triangulated prism we first saw in the project for Parma. To Rossi, public space was not so much about celebrating community life visually, but about creating a scene that was conducive to reflection, meditation.

Architecture, hence, as a venue for thought. This makes us establish connections between Rossi's work and that of some conceptual artists who were his contemporaries. Both are hard, severe. Naturally there is provocation. Never mind that what to him was almost sacred took on a new dimension with the public making such diverse use of it. It didn't matter that the column, which he relished as a fresh fountain, was now a support for posters. Maybe he even approved. When Rossi published the Segrate square with the column sullied by posters, he had no laments. He did not think that such use degraded it. On the contrary. It served as a framework for the wonder of the child passing by on his bicycle, the child who must get used early on to living in a world of phantoms. In the final analysis, architecture did nothing but collaborate in the creation of such phantoms, these new monuments. Segrate was at that time, to Rossi, a monument.

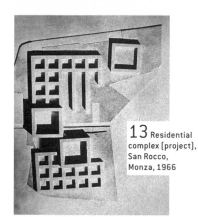

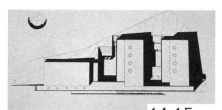

**14-15** School, San Sabba, Trieste, 1968–1969

**13** Residential complex (project), San Rocco, Monza, 1966

SCUOLA MEDIA SAN SABBA TRIESTE

**13** This hard, almost abstract architecture that would consolidate in the mid-seventies became somewhat less severe, and closer to the models that had seemingly inspired it, in the 1966 project for San Rocco in Monza. Rossi worked on this project with Giorgio Grassi, and the changes discernible in it may be attributable to the latter. Whether or not we need Grassi to explain this project, San Rocco diverges much from the collection of geometric figures on the pavement that gave rise to the Segrate square. A place like San Rocco also has to do with the feel of communal space constituting the different courtyards, the contrast of different scales, the changing sensations produced in the open and closed spaces, and so on. Mechanisms like segregation, repetition, and shifting are placed at the service of a deliberate individualization of spaces that should yield the desired variety and diversity. There is a world of difference between the San Rocco and Segrate projects.

**14-15** The spirit of San Rocco continues in the 1968–1969 project for the school in San Sabba, Trieste, even if allusions to historic architecture are more evident here. The school is conceived, first and foremost, as a public space that begins—as in the earliest stirrings of Mediterranean architecture, such as the palaces of the Cretan kings—with a platform from which to contemplate, in this case the city. Subsequently Rossi delights in imagining children getting there by proceeding through a series of porticoes, arriving in the classrooms and the open spaces that are for them an initiation to civic life. San Sabba illustrates the usefulness of the analysis of historic architecture that he had undertaken in *L'architettura della città*. The mechanisms he had detected in the city came in handy, and the principles by which it was built remained valid. Rossi was aware of the value of his analysis in decoding the construction of the city, and endeavored to apply this knowledge to his projects through contemplation and examination.

**16-17** The section of the 1968 Scandicci town hall project is a lesson in how to build. In Rossi's view, building was a simple matter of being familiar with the elements of architecture and establishing a sequence. Because of this sequential character of architecture, an architect's work was

not unlike that of a storyteller. After all, a town hall was but a courtyard for dignified entrance—befitting a public space—into diverse spaces for assembly and the performance of administrative functions. Here, an entire series of spaces strung together by a corridor culminates in a hall where politicians can meet and discuss public issues. I would say that the whole sequence of spaces has no other object than to manifest the presence of this hall—public space par excellence dominating the whole. This, to Rossi, is what a town hall was all about. For him, architecture possessed that quality of transparency that makes it a self-evident chain of elements made meaningful by the functions they are destined to serve, a chain of elements differing little from

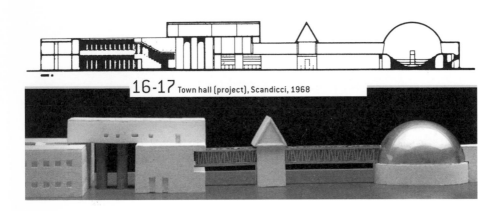

**16-17** Town hall (project), Scandicci, 1968

that first encounter with architectural order that children experience when they play with wooden blocks.

Building was just that: a matter of manipulating elements. It was a matter of having the courage to accept the reality of architecture without fear of identifying it with those images through which we learned to distinguish the differences of diverse types. As simple as that. Despite Rossi's respect for the traditional architecture nearby, nothing is farther from a Beaux-Arts *parti* than the Scandicci town hall.

**18-19** Rossi had no major commissions in this period. In 1969–1970 he found himself with projects like this one for a school in Broni. In the conviction that architecture was something independent of time and place, he had no scruples about simply changing the scale of the Segrate fountain. The photographs of the Broni school show a cruel scenography, one provocatively divorced from everything that has to do with a sense of comfort or with indulgence in the perception of space. It's as if Rossi were trying to instruct a very young child on the toughness of institutional life: truth is the best school, and children must not be deluded with regard to what awaits them in life.

**18-19** De Amicis school, Broni, 1969–1970

One can't help comparing this attitude with the ideas held in a Nordic country. What's a Scandinavian school like? Architects of those countries are preoccupied with questions such as where to put a window, or with choosing a warm wood for the floor. But as far as Rossi was concerned, architecture should not deceive. The child should not be confused with regard to institutions. Rossi advocated honesty, even at the cost of cruelty. Life is a court of tears, so the courtyard of the Broni school is precisely that. The fountain offers nothing but pain and misery.

**20-24** And so it goes, too, for a work like the Gallaratese quarter in Milan (1969–1973). Rossi, who was interested in a pseudoscientific (or "scientific") approach to architecture, found that in proletarian district housing the norm was an architecture where dwellings could be taken for military barracks. Once again, his courage lay in adopting the toughness with which architecture addressed programs, as against hiding reality. Hence the ordinariness of the masonry, where the only questions that matter are those having to do with repetition and scale. Such ordinariness tries to balance itself against a space like the portico, where the scenographic predominates and one expects a figure like Monica Vitti to appear—she of old Antonioni movies. Rossi's bare spaces seem to have the sole mission of anticipating that singular moment that will rescue them from total nondescriptness. They become the frame of an unexpected situation. Only then does the complex light up and acquire the quality of uniqueness, just as the architect's mind had planned. The singular moment justifies the sordidness of the everyday. Perhaps in the Gallaratese case, the unique moment is intensified by the pilgrims who have traveled to see the site for many years now.

**20-24** Gallaratese quarter, Milan, 1969–1973

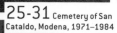
**25-31** Cemetery of San Cataldo, Modena, 1971–1984

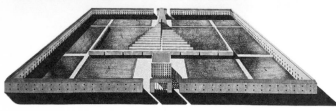

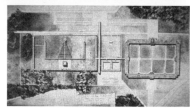

**25-31** When the career of an architect is examined in retrospect, some projects—or a single one—may constitute a showcase of all his interests and sentiments. In Rossi's case, that representative work is unquestionably the Cemetery of San Cataldo in Modena (1971–1984). San Cataldo once and for all convinced his contemporaries of his stature as an architect.

The competition brief called for the enlargement of a cemetery, but Rossi did not take the project as a mere question of adding elements. What he puts here is a building in itself, complete and unsusceptible to any future enlargement. Rossi proposes to duplicate it, and does so in a truly subtle and complex way, through an entire series of intermediary constructions situated on an axis that allows such virtual reflection. It's a clever duplication that dissimulates the symmetry. To Rossi, the Modena cemetery building is not the result of a duplication. On the contrary, it invites a unitary reading. And this reading leads to the presentation of a visual drama. One enters through the ambiguous double access to find a house stripped of all the elements that once made it inhabitable: a desolate, roofless cube that recalls the Cuneo project. But the house doesn't hide the path. The path stretches

between gaps that speak of the infinitude of eternity, of the loss of the value of time that death implies. This presence of death leads us to the denouement of the drama: the truncated cone that follows us so obsessively, like a ghost. Was it the memory of the Mole Antonelliana of Turin that took permanent control of Rossi's mind? Or the impact of one day finding himself inside one of those industrial chimneys that give us an irresistible sensation of vertigo? Or these images, the intellectual reflection of those brick ovens that evoke death, like a phenomenon invariably linked to cremation? All we know is that this architecture is drawn onto the blue of the sky, as expressed in the motto of Rossi's competition entry.

The building is of a hair-raising toughness. The project was publicized worldwide and both admired and criticized. When carried out fifteen years later, in the mid-eighties, Rossi still managed to manipulate the ordinariness of the constructive mechanisms, using them even more provocatively than his drawings had insinuated. And since a cemetery is but a house for the dead, it was built with the idea of storage as the only preoccupation—storage for forgotten lives, spent lives, history. This is what visitors feel at the sight of those enameled photographs, testimony of the loving devotion to and respect for the dead that is common in Italy.

32-35 It is difficult to build a type when there is a set geometrical scheme that simplifies it. A case in point is the school in Fagnano Olona (1972–1976). The canonical scheme of Beaux-Arts buildings appears here in a system of orthogonal axes. This allows a perspective view and the unfolding of subsidiary spaces through corridors. And that's about it. The subsidiary spaces enclose a central area that is emphasized by the cylinder containing the multipurpose hall. The cylinder also gives rise to a series of exterior spaces that Rossi goes on to exploit. The iconographic power of the cylinder alludes to the authoritarianism of institutions.

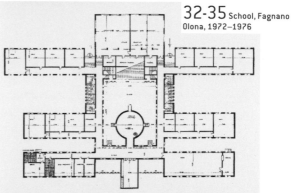

32-35 School, Fagnano Olona, 1972–1976

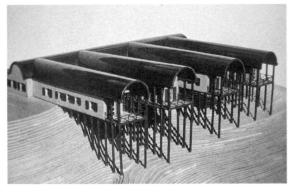

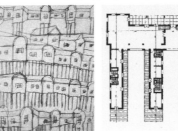

**36-38** Villa (project), Borgo Ticino, 1973

**36-38** Geometry of type left a provocative stamp on architecture. This is clear in the 1973 project for a house and pavilion in Borgo Ticino. A weekend home for a busy Milanese, it is a lakeshore dwelling on piles. Rossi relishes making one project assume the following: (1) the geometry of an architecture of rationalist blocks; (2) the symmetry that characterizes so many architectures whose origins lie in the academy; and (3) the nostalgia of the rational construction of vernacular architecture. He is aware of the contradictions that come from confronting opposites, showing it through the indifference with which the blocks admit the uses that their diverse spaces are assigned. Dining room, living room, and kitchen come together in one same block, while the corridors interact with each other in the other blocks, producing new and unexpected symmetry patterns. The house loses its unitary character, and one surmises that the people who move through those corridors are not parents and children, but members of an odd community of occupants of a house that is used only on weekends.

All the contradiction that the house withstands is transferred to the sphere of the constructional. So walls are sustained by fragile *pilotis* and the light roof of corrugated sheet metal is related to the solid walls. Contradiction ends in constructive violence. The Borgo Ticino villa efficiently illustrates the deliberate toughness that characterized Rossi's architecture of that period.

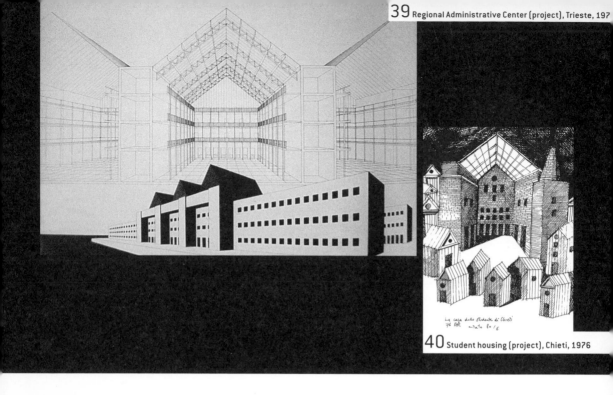

40 Student housing (project), Chieti, 1976

**39-40** Tough, too, are Rossi's entries in the competitions for the Regional Administrative Center in Trieste (1974) and the student residence in Chieti (1976). The insights of the preceding paragraph apply to these as well.

In 1976 Rossi traveled to America, summoned by the Institute for Architecture and Urban Studies. The IAUS welcomed him warmly. Rossi was well known by then, and his work was closely followed by the architectural world. While there he prepared the translation of *L'architettura della città*, exhibited his drawings, and lectured in schools. The stint in the United States brought about a substantial change in both Rossi's work and the way it was perceived. America made him realize that his architecture consisted first and foremost of his drawings, that it was his drawings that best expressed his feelings, and that they were his sole legacy, what could be passed on to others. The Lukácsian reality that he had pursued so anxiously was now unacceptable. His goal now would be to materialize his sentiments and propose "another" reality that would result from actually executing the drawings. So much for the idealist mechanism he had put forward in his book, leading from type to urban form to territory, from uses to construction, and which had yielded such works as the Gallaratese quarter or the Borgo Ticino villa. The only thing left was the iconography. The drawing would become that "other" reality, and this had little to do with the city that had been at the origin of his reflections. The drawing would dictate what the new reality would be. In the final analysis, the new reality would be taken for architecture. Rossi was fully aware of this at the close of the seventies.

Rossi, who had "announced his glad tidings" in Europe and had important groups of followers not only in his own country but also in Switzerland, Germany, and Spain, now began to have fans in America, and in some schools there his principles were becoming norms. In Miami, for example, students were being taught to build a city "according to Rossi," and the resulting manifestos were occasionally excessive. Paradoxically, or perhaps because he now saw the dangers of generalization, Rossi realized that he was more in control with feelings than he was with the instrumentalization of knowledge that had been the slogan of the start of his career. He realized he was more capable of building what he felt than he was of defining a series of links leading hierarchically from type to monument. So much so that while in America he began to work on a new book. In *A Scientific Autobiography*, he clearly made the leap from knowledge to feeling. If the early Rossi had endeavored above all to be objective, the Rossi returning from America was convinced that all he could explain was himself, that only the subject counted.

The following are particularly eloquent extracts from the book, exposing Rossi's thoughts in a highly transparent way.

Around 1960 I wrote *The Architecture of the City*, a successful book. At that time, I was not yet thirty years old, and as I have said, I wanted to write a definitive work: it seemed to me that everything, once clarified, could be defined. I believed that the Renaissance treatise had to become an apparatus which could be translated into objects. I scorned memories, and at the same time, I made use of urban impressions: behind feelings I searched for the fixed laws of a timeless typology. I saw courts and galleries, the elements of urban morphology, distributed in the city with the purity of mineralogy. I read books on urban geography, topography, and history, like a general who wishes to know every possible battlefield—the high grounds, the passages, the woods. I walked the cities of Europe to understand their plans and classify them according to types. Like a lover sustained by my egotism, I often ignored the secret feelings I had for those cities; it was enough to know the system that governed them. Perhaps I simply wanted to free myself of the city. Actually, I was discovering my own architecture *[This is a curious jump from the general to the specific. As for his own architecture. Why? What is one's own architecture?]*—A confusion of courtyards, suburban houses, roofs, gas storage drums, comprised my first exploration of a Milan that seemed fantastic to me. The bourgeois world of villas by lakes, the corridors of the boarding school, the huge kitchens in country houses—these were memories of a landscape out of Manzoni which disintegrated in the city. Yet their insistence on things revealed a craft to me. [7]

After quoting Melville in a paragraph about lighthouses, capes, ships, etc., Rossi says:

I could ask myself what "the real" signifies in architecture. For example, might it be a dimensional, functional, stylistic, or technological fact? I could certainly write a treatise based on such facts. But instead I think of a lighthouse, of a memory and of a summer. How does one establish the dimensions of these things, and indeed, what dimensions do they have? [8]

## 12

**7** Aldo Rossi, *A Scientific Autobiography* (Cambridge: MIT Press, 1981), pp. 15–16. Asides in italics are Rafael Moneo's.

**8** Ibid., p. 24.

For Rossi, vague memories are what matter. More:

Markets, cathedrals, public buildings, display a complex history of the city and man. The sales booths inside markets and the confessionals and chapels inside cathedrals display this relation between the individual and the universal, translating it into a relation between the interior and exterior in architecture. Markets—especially those in France, in Barcelona, and also the Rialto in Venice—have always had a particular fascination for me, which is only partly linked to architecture. They are the things that I remember; the quantity of food on display never fails to impress me. Meat, fruit, fish, vegetables appear again and again at the various stalls or sections into which the market is divided, and the fish are particularly striking: they have such varied forms and appearances that they always seem fantastic in our world. Perhaps this architecture of the street and of things, of people and food, of the flux of life, is fixed forever in the *vuzzeria* at Palermo. . . . When I think of markets, however, I always draw an analogy with the theater, and particularly the eighteenth-century theater, with its relation between stages as isolated places and the total space of the theater. [9]

The project is fixed in time and space. [10]

The theater, in which the architecture serves as a possible background, a setting, a building that can be calculated and transformed into the measurements and concrete materials of an often elusive feeling, has been one of my passions. [11]

Today if I were to talk about architecture, I would say that it is a ritual rather than a creative process. I say this fully understanding the bitterness and the comfort of the ritual. Rituals give us the comfort of continuity, of repetition, compelling us to an oblique forgetfulness, allowing us to live with every change which, because of its inability to evolve, constitutes a destruction. [12]

Thus, at the Politecnico in Milan, I believe that I was one of the worst students, although today I think that the criticisms addressed to me then are among the best compliments I have ever received. Professor Sabbioni, whom I particularly admired, discouraged me from making architecture, saying that

**9** Ibid., p. 26.

**10** Ibid., p. 29.

**11** Ibid., p. 33.

**12** Ibid., p. 37.

my drawings looked like those of a bricklayer or a rural contractor who threw a stone to indicate approximately where a window was to be placed. This observation, which made my friends laugh, filled me with joy, and today I try to recover that felicity of drawing which was confused with inexperience and stupidity [felicity as naive stupidity], and which has subsequently character-ized my work. In other words, a great part of the meaning and evolution of time escaped me and still does so today, as if time were a material which I observe only from the outside. The lack of evolution in my work has been the source of some misunderstanding, but it also brings me joy. [13]

And on Loos:

Loos made this great architectural discovery by identifying himself with the object through observation and description—without changing, with-out yielding, and finally, without creative passion, or rather with his sense of being frozen in time. . . . Loos's kind of frozen description also appears in the great Renaissance theorists, in the categories of Alberti, in Dürer's letters; but the practice, craft, and technique they had followed vanished, because from the beginning it was not important enough to transmit or translate. [14]

Description was very important to Rossi. And now a passage of crucial importance:

In order to be significant, architecture must be forgotten, or must pre-sent only an image for reverence which subsequently becomes confounded with memories. [15]

I have always claimed that places are stronger than people, the fixed scene stronger than the transitory succession of events. This is the theoreti-cal basis not of my architecture, but of architecture itself. In substance, it is one possibility of living. I liken this idea to the theater: people are like actors; when the footlights go up, they become involved in an event with which they are probably unfamiliar, and ultimately they will always be so. The lights, the music, are no different from a fleeting summer thunderstorm, a pass-ing conversation, a face. But at times the theater is closed; and cities, like vast theaters, sometimes are empty. While it may be touching that everyone acts out his little part, in the end, neither the mediocre actor nor the sublime

[13] Ibid., p. 39.

[14] Ibid., p. 44.

[15] Ibid., p. 45.

**41** Houses in Mira, northern Portugal

**42** Convento de las Pelayas,
Santiago de Compostela

**41** Houses in Mira, northern Portugal: Above all, these Portuguese houses talk about the people who inhabit them. These people have accomplished much in building a floor that keeps them free of ground humidity. Still they are able to give importance to the door, distinguishing it with concrete blocks that provide a certain symmetry. The builders take pains to expose the logic behind the basic construction techniques that are implicit in the overlapping of wooden boarding—techniques, to be sure, that easily adjust to the topography and that just as easily include any accidents that may suddenly give rise to a known, substantially everyday scene.

**42** Convento de las Pelayas, Santiago de Compostela: What better representation of life in a monastic community subjected to the tyranny of repetition and regulation than this convent facade? The meters transpiring between the windows and the pavement of the square speak of the distance imposed between those living in conventual seclusion and those who, not having abandoned the world, continue to enjoy all that a city like Santiago de Compostela has to offer.

**16** Ibid., pp. 50–51.

actress is able to alter the course of events. [16]

Rossi gives much importance to awareness of history, history as a happening of peoples and a fixed frame of an architecture to whose heritage we would like to contribute. Some examples:

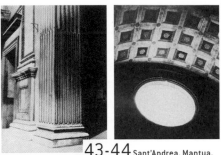

**43-44** Sant'Andrea, Mantua, by Leon Battista Alberti

**45** Filarete's column, Venice

**46** Lichthof, University of Zurich

**43-45** Alberti's Sant'Andrea, Mantua: It is hard to think of an image that more effectively illustrates the linguistic effort of so many generations to explain how a column settles on the ground, or how to make two super-posed stone blocks indistinguishable from one another by way of flutes. Likewise, what bigger challenge for the architect than to dissimulate the differences between elements as diverse as the coffered vault, the wall-diaphragm, and the oculus in such a way that they form a whole?

**46** University courtyard, Zurich: The efficient ordinariness of architecture that accepts set conventions through common languages is exemplified in this building of the University of Zurich, where the Italian portico is given an air of distinction through a facade that, once again, insists on the image of a temple. This is architecture at the service of institutions, to the point of representing them. It is a minor architecture in its endeavor to be a personal expression of the architect, yet a major architecture in being a direct manifestation of the structure of its own language.

**47** Courtyard in Seville

**48** Houses on the delta of the Po

**47-48** Courtyard in Seville and houses on the delta of the Po: Rossi's true love was anonymous architecture, the architecture that belongs to collective knowledge. He contaminated us with an enthusiasm and respect for it, for which we should be grateful. Painting a plinth olive-green on a narrow Seville street is an architectural gesture par excellence. It speaks of the decorum desired for a public space that is to be a venue of much social life. As for the houses on stilts connected by nets, they suggest the collective colonization of the waterway. Through the communal fishing activity that the architecture foments, they address the desire to transform nature into a source of production. The ability of architecture to participate in the reinforcement of community life was, for Rossi, its most valuable attribute.

Here the feel of the unfinished, of the fragment, has little to do with the work concept discussed by Eco, or with the satisfaction that the establishing of unexpected connections produces, as in collages by Schwitters. What amazes Rossi is the contemplation of the moment at which the work as a whole is interrupted in time, giving rise to a fragment that renders itself visible.

**49** Lighthouse in New England

**50** San Carlone, Arona

**51** Interior of a farmhouse near Parma

**49-50** Lighthouse in New England and the San Carlone, Arona: There are times when architecture is literarily confused with what we call figures. A case in point is the lighthouse of New England, so full of literary resonances and inclined to unleash our fantasies. The statue of San Carlo, for its part, seems to embody the phantom we have so often seen in our dreams and tried to suppress. To our dismay, by becoming a paradigm of the arbitrariness that is intrinsic to any construction, the dream comes true. Anything can be built. Ancient civilizations built the Colossus of Alexandria, immigrants built the Statue of Liberty. The logic of construction cannot make the phantoms of our lives vanish forever in the manner expected when we pray to St. Charles Borromeo.

**51** Interior of a farmhouse near Parma: This interior shows us architecture's ability to provide respite to people who spend the whole day tilling the land. Presiding over it, the table speaks of the moment when a family comes together. Farming implements are the mute witnesses of that moment. The order of the house, as manifested in the way the construction unfolds, speaks to us of a communal sphere in which work, tools, and persons are one, totally abstracted from specialization. The private sphere of intimate relations is suggested by the staircase, up which the occupants retire to a dark room. The dignified character of the carved wooden banisters keeps alive a remembrance of the achievements of city dwellers.

These images, so painstakingly selected by Rossi, transport us to what he believed to be the essence of architecture—architecture based on feeling which, with his help, we have been able to approach. I believe this is what he wanted to get across to us in his drawings. He wanted to show us the depositories of those feelings that, as we saw in the preceding images, he had discovered in the city and its architectures.

After the trip to America, Rossi was inspired to take on a quasi-heroic role and had no qualms about presenting himself, and his drawings, in the manner of classical treatise writers. If Palladio had dared to engrave images of his buildings on wood so that they might serve as examples to his colleagues, Rossi didn't see why he shouldn't proceed likewise, and so it is that he offered his works—which, as we've said, were drawings—as models for anyone interested in his message. His drawings became increasingly intelligible and beautiful.

52-55 In 1979, Rossi was so convinced of the importance of such an architecture of sensitive images that when Paolo Portoghesi offered him the job of building a small, ephemeral theater for the Venice Biennale, he magnified it and presented it as a descendant of all Venetian architectures. Hence we see the *piccolo Teatro del Mondo* blend into the tangle of domes of Longhena, in La Salute, where we also discern the Mercury of the Punta della Dogana. The architect left no room for doubt that the ephemeral structure afloat on the canal is as valuable as the timeless architecture Venice is famous for. There is a good distance between the scientifically oriented architecture advocated in *The Architecture of the City* and this new procedure that dwells on iconography as a support for sentiment. Rossi condensed his whole view of Venice into this small theater, invoking everything that the city evoked for him. In his opinion, the floating wooden construction did not differ much from the city's fifteenth-century bridges so masterfully painted by the Bellinis

52-55 Piccolo Teatro del Mondo, Venice, 1979

**56** Dwellings in Goito, 1979

**57** Dwellings in Pegognaga, 1979

and Carpaccio. The spirit of Venice was captured in those paintings, and so was it captured in his theater. An architect could aspire to leave such a testimony of his feelings. When the Mercury of the Dogana and the sphere of the Teatro del Mondo appear together in photographs, Rossi's message is that the image of architecture that the sphere synthesizes has the same value, architecturally, as the construction punctuating the Grand Canal which the gilded Mercury has inhabited for centuries.

**56-57** There is a cruel contrast between the Venetian theater and the houses for cooperatives in Goito and Pegognaga, both projects of 1979. It explains Rossi's withdrawal to some winter barracks in which there was room only for image. There can be no other positive reading of this architecture than as a provocative denunciation of the crude character of the housing to which citizens of modest incomes had access. The severeness of such housing called for rebellion, and only if rebellion was the architect's intention would this architecture of expressionist minimalism be justifiable. If we think of the optimism behind the German *Siedlungen* of the thirties, a deep sorrow comes over us, because this architecture of Rossi can only be understood as an escape forward, whereby he tells us that the city cannot be built in terms of housing and that, therefore, architecture only makes sense serving institutions and representing these through images. Rossi's awareness of this phenomenon at the start of the eighties explains his future work, characterized by an apparent willingness to accept any kind of commission with heroic serenity, with no other arguments to use than those that reduce architecture to sentiment and image.

**58-59** Still in 1979, this Australian competition is a good illustration of the foregoing. Melbourne is a city "known" for the mere fact that it is "a city": a city drawn by Rossi. Though it is situated in the antipodes, Rossi ever so naturally includes a skyscraper.

**58-59** Office building (project), Melbourne, Australia, 1979

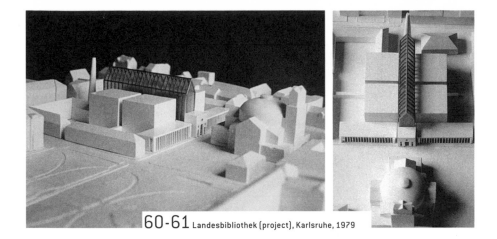

60-61 Landesbibliothek (project), Karlsruhe, 1979

60-61 And likewise for the entry to the 1979 competition for the Landesbibliothek in Karlsruhe. There is little difference between this library and the Modena cemetery. Place does not count. When we design, we simply manifest our knowledge of what a building is. Not coincidentally situated behind a church with a dome, the building competes with it through a facade that is not altogether unlike a church's. Like a church, a library has a nave that has to be cut short by a facade. There is the strange appearance of a chimney, as if to be used for censorship. Whether or not this is the case, chimneys seem to have been an obsession for Rossi. With or without justification, they appear continuously in his work. It is one of those images that, in the Platonic view he had of architecture, were glued to Rossi's retina so strongly that he couldn't rid himself of them. So it is that his drawings trap that imagery that he considered to be the essence and material of architecture.

62-63 Fiera Catena (project), Mantua, 1982

62-63 Sometimes there were happier projects. Here is a most brilliant, beautiful drawing submitted for the 1982 competition for Mantua's Fiera Catena. This may be the moment to mention how much Rossi was indebted, in drawing techniques, to the Italian painters of the twenties and thirties. Definitely present in this drawing, hence obligatory to mention, are de Chirico and Sironi. The territorial scale here allowed him to include the lake and the wall, as well as his memories, translated to images, of other institutions. One easily identifies elements of the Parma theater, or the Fagnano Olona school courtyard. A trade fair precinct that eventually scatters, as in a garden city, into a series of pavilions that make us appreciate the northern Italian plain.

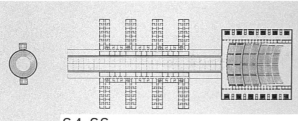

**64-66** Convention center (project), Milan, 1982

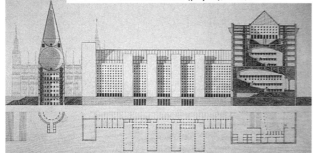

**64-66** To me, the drawings that show how Rossi envisioned the profile of Milan's convention center of 1982, and how this profile would be assimilated by the city, are more attractive than the floor plans. Before the architectures of his repertoire were subjected to the tyranny of the floor plan, his proposals were very clear and reassuring. Such clarity generally disappeared when programmatic obligations gave rise to floor plans reflecting architectural structures governed by indiscriminate repetition. Rossi's drawings began to be redundant and obsessive. It seems he couldn't go beyond repeating the images coined by the architects of the Enlightenment. This explains the virtual superposition of images that translates into anguished architectural monsters that seem to have lost all relation to the dimensions and scales of the original forms we are familiar with. There is a moment when one asks if it would have made sense to build these giant spaces, once stripped of their sacred content, in which all authentic and genuine links with reality Rossi himself demanded would have been lost. Rossi claimed an *auctoritas* for his architecture that, if accepted, would have obliged us to live in the strange world it generated.

67 Apartment building (project), Südliche Friedrichstadt, Berlin, 1981

68-69 Casa Aurora, Turin, 1987

67 The 1981 project for Südliche Friedrichstadt in Berlin warrants similar reflections. The generic values of residential architecture are shifted here in order to achieve an urban aura, with no regard for the costs of such translation.

68-69 The Aurora building in Turin, dated 1987, is in my opinion one of Rossi's finest works of that period. An iconographic element we are by now familiar with is used to resolve a corner, which becomes the core of this office building that occupies a block in the city's nineteenth-century enlargement. Changes in scale, the emphasis placed on the exhibition of different constructive elements, the painstaking brick masonry, and other aspects result in a building that speaks of other known architectures and the capacity of these to accommodate everyday work. Despite a certain modesty in the elements we consider definers of standards, the building has an urban presence that tells us that the Rossian project of the seventies had not been in vain.

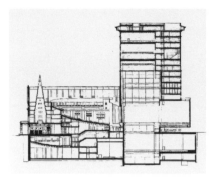

## 13

**70-72** Teatro Carlo Felice, Genoa, 1982

**70-72** With the Teatro Carlo Felice in Genoa, of 1982, Rossi once again showed us what results mechanisms like iconographic decontextualization and the exaggeration of scale could lead to. An example of excess scale is the monumental cornice which, far from simply crowning the building and performing articulatory functions, is an iconographic element with a value of its own. Here the architect indulged in iconography, dispensing with considerations relating to construction or use. Remembering an exemplary cornice of history—that of Rome's Palazzo Farnese immediately comes to mind—suffices to show that a world of difference separates Rossi's work from the architecture that inspired him.

The idea that architecture is in itself an expression of the theatrical nature of life is present in the decoration of the hall. The side walls of the theater, which throughout history have given architects many a headache, are transformed here into images of a street in which box seats give rise to a surrealist experience. Once again, Rossi relishes ambiguity and provocation. However, the exterior porticos show his mastery, and they give rise to a building that fits into the urban fabric of Genoa with great ease.

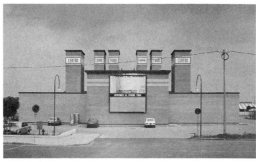

73 Civic Center, Perugia, 1982 74 Commercial center, Parma, 1985
75 Apartment building, Paris, 1986 76 School of Architecture, Miami, 1986

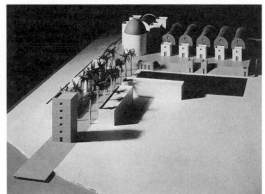

73-76 Projects like the Civic Center in Perugia (1982), commercial center in Parma (1985), apartment building in Paris (1986), and the School of Architecture in Miami (1986) reaffirm the readings that have been heretofore made of Rossi's work. Rigor was expected of him, but it seems he indulged in iconographic clichés: Miami's palm trees, Perugian pediments, Parma's false spontaneity, Parisian attics.

77-79 Let us now look at what I believe to be one of Rossi's best projects of the period: the hotel in Fukuoka, Japan, dated 1987, with its simple typological arrangement that has little to do with the powerful facade. One can't help thinking of the New York buildings of cast iron that surely inspired this project. But knowing the precedents doesn't prevent us from acknowledging the force of this facade, largely attributable to the solidness of the construction and the intelligent choice of materials. In the midst of the chaos of the Japanese city, this absurd traveler's temple keeps alive the promise of an early Rossi interested in exploring the origins of architecture. Delight at the sight of unexpected spaces is not something one should look for in this building. Manifest here is a rejection—or forgetting—of an architecture born of the control of spaces. The static form prevails, and the building, as if an architectural meteorite, presents itself as a fragment of the history of architecture, indifferent to place, like something that has happened and been constructed in compliance with the norms established by a discipline that endeavors to be removed from circumstances. Once again, type has dissolved, if not altogether been ignored, in the powerful image yielded by a wisely rendered construction of the facade.

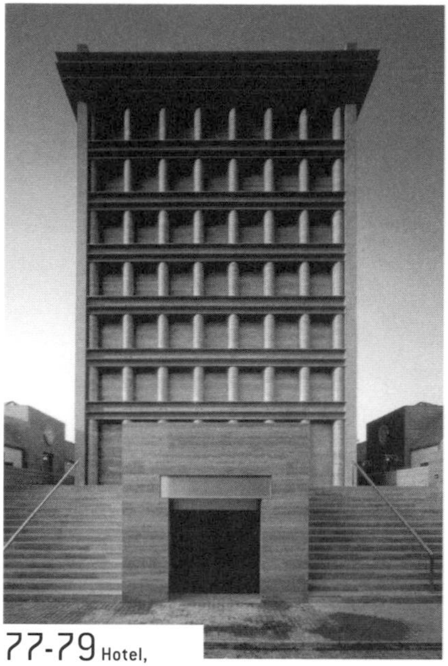

77-79 Hotel, Fukuoka, Japan, 1987

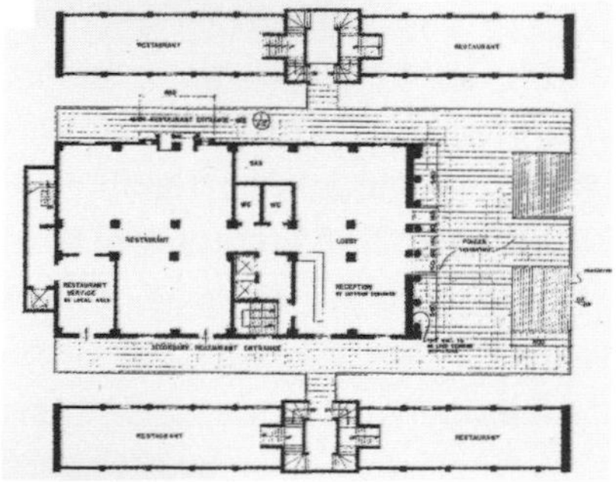

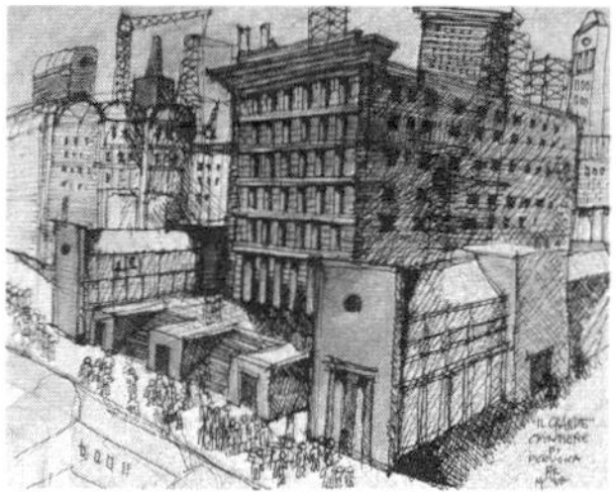

**80-87** Finally, these images of the building of Maastricht's Bonnefanten Museum of 1993 show to what degree Rossi's last works were not so much a reflection of the construction, but a reflection of images. If at the start of his career construction was a metaphor that helped him understand the city and architecture, by the start of the nineties Rossi had gotten us accustomed to seeing the world as a set of images. His architecture then contained images racked by sentiment. At some time, Rossi drew his room: a drawing in which the world of objects that accompanied him in life, his things, coexists with the world that unfolds in the architecture we see through the window, the city of Milan that he loved so much. Paradoxically, Rossi became a master of constructing objects. He was capable of putting his feelings into an object without harming its construction, completely satisfying the use expected of it. Think of his furniture pieces, his watches, his coffee makers. In the object lives the iconography, the image, but freed of all the demands that come with architecture. The building was something much more complex. It resisted the process of simplification that Rossi had subjected it to in those years. An object admits the tyranny of form. A building can't.

There's no telling to what degree he was aware of the profound changes that had taken place in the course of his career. He always claimed to be the same. To be sure, the architectural world he had seen in his youth remained the same in terms of image. But I wouldn't say that his approach was the same when he left us. The attachment to knowledge that attracted my generation so much gave way to the expression of sentiment, which, as Rossi said, finds refuge in objects and resists being translated into architecture.

A Bonnefanten Museum, Maastricht, 1993

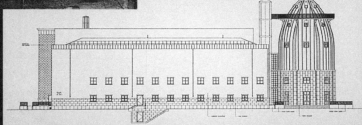

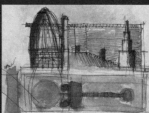

B Aldo Rossi's designs for everyday objects

# PETER EISENMAN

Peter Eisenman has played a crucial role in the architecture of the past quarter-century. A constant catalyst of architectural culture, his work as a publicist has been influential all these years in widely diverse places within the field. His ideas and opinions have been omnipresent both in the schools and in the profession of architecture.

Since he is a leading figure in the architectural scene of the final third of the twentieth century, a review of Eisenman's career guides us through the shifts in direction that architectural culture has taken during this period, just as a run-through of Stirling's helps us trace the changes of orientation that took place at an earlier time. Stirling, however, endeavored to go unnoticed as a persona, preferring to be judged on his works, whereas Eisenman likes his work to be taken as biography. For this reason we will have to look into personal biographical notes, however briefly. It simply isn't possible to examine his work without touching on his persona. Peter Eisenman the person, the man who invents architectures, is as important as his architecture, inseparable from it. Let us begin with Eisenman's efforts to enter the profession. Everything in his work as a cultural agitator and an advocate of the study of architectural theory has been ultimately aimed at getting himself respected as an architect. That is, his activities as a theoretician, as a critic, as a publicist, as a lecturer, and even as a corporate figure have all been directed at earning respectability as an architect and, with this, access to actual professional work. He has finally earned such access, and so it is that, behind the person so anxiously committed to the theoretical study and promotion of architecture, there is also an architect.

Peter Eisenman is one of many American architects who have been attracted to Europe. After finishing his undergraduate studies in Cornell, he took a master's degree, and subsequently a doctorate, in Cambridge, England. There he came in contact with people like Leslie Martin, Colin St. John Wilson, and Colin Rowe, and was initiated into modern architecture. It may have been at Cambridge, perhaps in response to Rowe's teachings, that he first perceived that modern architecture fell short of being fully realized. It would thereafter be his goal to carry out the objectives of the modern movement and bring modern architecture to its fullness. If Rossi's program aimed to make architecture a positive science, just like biology or geology—thus his penchant for describing and interpreting the city as a step prior to building—Eisenman's mission was to recover for architecture the ideals of modernity. Modern architecture had never been fully executed, it had never come to incarnate the true spirit of modernity, because of distractions with questions of style and because it had made functionalism its banner. True to an attitude toward life that I won't hesitate to call messianic, Eisenman embarked on the intellectual adventure of rescuing from oblivion the true spirit of modernity.

This all came to the fore during his years as a professor at Princeton. Also there at that time was a young Michael Graves, who shared Eisenman's enthusiasm for the work of the cubist painters. Together they studied the work of Le Corbusier and the writings of Giuseppe Terragni. In 1967, Eisenman founded the Institute for Architecture and Urban Studies in New York. Its program was imprecise but it was extraordinarily active and efficient, and the IAUS soon became a compulsory point of reference for anyone in the city who was interested in architecture. It organized a wide range of activities—lectures, exhibitions, courses, presentations, etc. But above all, it became the launching pad of a view of architecture in which theoretical thought took priority over pure professional practice. The IAUS published *Oppositions*, a magazine that became an emblematic medium for the manifestos of its members. Above all, it was a publication that was attentive to theoretical questions, over and above pure information. At this distance of time, we can say that *Oppositions* was open and eclectic, less dogmatic than one would have supposed. It was free of the programmatic manifestos of the older avant-garde magazines. Instead it published essays, historical studies, critical analyses. The editors were keen to stimulate theoretical discussion. True to its desire to offer the American public the latest tendencies of architectural thought, *Oppositions* was instrumental in acquainting American culture with European theoreticians like Manfredo Tafuri, Anthony Vidler, Jean-Louis Cohen, and Francesco Dal Co.

Why didn't the modern spirit come to full term? For Peter Eisenman the reasons are many, but none as definitive as the commitment to functionalism that modern architecture acquired in the process of its gestation. This, he believes, is what most distracted modern architects from modern architecture's most genuine, original objectives. Eisenman's obsession was to free architecture of all shackles and allow it to unfold without contaminations, whether of place, function, or building systems. The goal was architecture at its purest: an architecture that, by adopting the new and unfortunately already forgotten formal principles of modernity, aspired to the same thing as physicists did when discovering the world through new (and not forgotten) formulas derived from the theory of relativity, or as those involved in knowledge of the human psyche did through the use of new (and not forgotten) psychoanalytic techniques. The change clamored for by the modern spirit could not be a mere change of style but a change of substance and, with this, a change of language. Architecture was on the right track when, attentive to the work of the cubist painters, it set about to explore new formal principles. In the same way as painters had managed to do away with the dependence on content that had long characterized the visual arts, architecture should cleanse itself of all obligations dictated by function, place, technique, or program, and address only those formal principles that helped solve the constructional problem in question. Indeed, an architecture willing to go back to its original principles, which were, first and foremost, formal principles. It couldn't be any other way for one trained under the wings of Colin Rowe, who himself had so much respect for the formalist critique of the first half of the century.

Attentive as he was to the trend of thinking of architecture as just one more manifestation of language theory, Eisenman naturally took to Noam Chomsky. The development of language as something subject to immanent structural laws that could explain its evolution—the so-called deep structures—was an idea he believed could be applied to architecture. All his efforts as a theoretician of architecture in those years were aimed at finding structures, laws, or principles that would explain the appearance of form. Eisenman was therefore a formalist/structuralist, and hence his constant show of disdain for any possible interpretation of architecture in visual terms. He clearly situated himself in a syntactic position, ignoring or, better still, rejecting any attempt to semanticize architecture. The view of architectural theory as something not far removed from syntax theory becomes clear with Charles Morris's definition of syntax as "the study of the . . . relations of signs to one another in abstraction from the relations of signs to objects or to interpreters." [1] Eisenman thus put himself in a position that was diametrically opposed to Venturi, who, advocating the com-

**1** Charles Morris, *Foundations of the Theory of Signs* (Chicago: University of Chicago Press, 1938, 12th ed. 1970), quoted in Mario Gandelsonas, "On Reading Architecture: Peter Eisenman, the Syntactic Dimension," *Progressive Architecture*, March 1972, p. 71.

municative nature of architecture, suggested that it was capable of expressing the cultural values that are latent in the spirit of a social group. Eisenman didn't want to hear about the symbolic. He wanted to define the norms and behavior of architectural language as something self-explanatory. For Eisenman, architecture was a mental operation based on the use of such norms. From what's been said so far we can deduce that his project bore a promise of autonomy. This explains why Eisenman took so much interest in Aldo Rossi's arrival in America, despite the profound difference in the way they viewed autonomy. For Rossi, autonomy found its confirmation in history, whereas for Eisenman, autonomy lay in the elaboration of a self-sufficient language.

Eisenman's work as an architect during the decade 1968–1978 was scanty but intense. He designed and built several houses, numbering them chronologically the way a composer would number his symphonies and thereby asserting the abstract character of his work. But Eisenman's limited work as a practicing architect was accompanied by heavy work as a critic, and this led him to choose and interpret those moments of architectural history that were most closely in line with his view of it. He was especially interested in formal questions. When he wrote on Stirling's Leicester School of Engineering, he emphasized how its use of materials was determined by formal principles. [2] But it was in his readings of Terragni that Eisenman found the perfect context for showing us his real objectives. Terragni's writings allowed Eisenman to offer a view of the modern movement that we could call alternative and complementary to the classical version of it—the version supplied by historians like Giedion, for whom Le Corbusier's architecture was a prime reference. Eisenman's view of Terragni gave us an understanding of the meaning of syntactic mechanisms in architecture. This was something he would diligently pursue in the course of his career.

A sentence from a text on Terragni should serve as a framework for studying Eisenman's architectural project, as well as for understanding his belief that Chomsky's deep structures can be used in architecture: "Terragni's process of developing forms can be understood as an attempt to suppress the object or the reading of the surface structure, in favor of a visible presence of the conceptual or deep structure." [3]

[2] Peter Eisenman, "Real and English: The Destruction of the Box I," *Oppositions* 4 (1974).

[3] Peter Eisenman, "Dall'oggetto alla relazionalità: la Casa del Fascio di Terragni," *Casabella* 344 (January 1970), pp. 38–39.

So it is that Eisenman would distinguish between superficial aspects of architecture that are manifested through sensorial perception of the object, such as texture, color, and form, and deeper aspects that are not perceived sensorially, such as frontality, obliquity, setbacks, elongations, compressions, and shifts, which we perceive with the mind. Once again a Manichaean view of blacks and whites, manifested in the confrontation of mental and sensorial. Eisenman advocated an architecture that could be read, understood, and judged in the manner of a strictly mental operation. Paradoxically, the categories or attributes that he puts in his architecture are of a purely visual nature. Don't concepts like frontality, obliquity, shifts have a strongly sensorial, perceptual component? It wouldn't be difficult to connect the principles and mechanisms used by Eisenman to those used by critics like Wölfflin or von Hildebrand, who explored the work of art in general, and the work of architecture in particular, in purely visual, abstract terms. This is natural if we consider that in establishing such categories, Eisenman doesn't stray far from the concepts handled by Colin Rowe and Robert Slutzky in their famous article "Transparency: Literal and Phenomenal," [4] less read today but a must fifteen years ago, which examined formal mechanisms for understanding cubist painting and, therefore too, cubist architectures.

To define the categories—frontality, obliquity, shifts, transfers, etc.—Eisenman rejected all figurative supports associated with elements of traditional building. There was in this early Eisenman, therefore, a resistance to the representational that must be stressed: instead, geometry as an alternative to figure, to image, a geometry where the abstract elements of the grid—the point, the line, the plane—are notational minimums that yield the mentioned categories. These categories, incidentally, soon become design mechanisms, thereby taking on an instrumental and operational character. The abstract space being worked on is still a Cartesian space, one that can be activated by the mentioned operations. The abstract space that the grid generates is a backdrop, a screen on which to project the architectural invention. Over the ideal grid, which really speaks of the neutrality of the space that serves as support, concepts like addition and subtraction, solids and voids, rotation and transfer, coatings and levels, and strata and shiftings give rise to an architecture that,

**4** Colin Rowe and Robert Slutzky, "Transparency: Literal and Phenomenal," in Rowe, *The Mathematics of the Ideal Villa and Other Essays* (Cambridge: MIT Press, 1976). Written in 1955–1956 and first published in *Perspecta* 8 (1964).

by making use of the elements described, endeavors to be abstract, removed from all possible external references, free of contamination to a greater or lesser extent. As Eisenman noticed early on in his career, this architectural proposal that leads to an abstract and distant object—by object I mean something that is not the result of personal expression, but speaks instead of a near-ontological "sameness" that keeps the final construction close to the person responsible for its materialization—does not produce a built reality that is identifiable, visible, and thus nameable. Of course knowing this was most disturbing, and Eisenman felt obliged to introduce the concept of "process," the idea being that a project must be read in terms of the sequence in time that has made it possible. On its own, the object doesn't reveal the architect's intentions—or ideas, if you will. For them to be perceptible, it is necessary to give evidence of process. Representing the architecture is not a mere matter of defining the object, but of taking stock of the process behind it. And so we see how the ideal grid on which the architect is to work is activated by a first, formal impulse that gives rise to a series of transformations and inventions, and these are documented at every single phase of the work. The process is made visible by documenting it. Registering its different stages helps us understand the development of the formal operations dictated by the mind through time. This is something that the object, which we only see in its final state, does not lend itself to. Eisenman's desire to put on record what he calls the "ideas" that generated the architecture makes him confuse them with the process. Only by knowing about the process can we have access to the essence of his architecture.

The importance of the concept of process in establishing a theory of project design has been magnified in recent times. Anyone who has been involved in architecture schools for twenty-five or thirty years, like myself, can testify to the increased emphasis on process in project presentation, by architects and students alike. We have so often heard that the important thing is to register the process, the whole succession of formal stages that endeavors to justify a final or definitive stage. Of greater interest than the architectural work itself is the "biography" of the project, hence the eagerness to preserve all testimonies of its gestation. Just as in a chess game or a painting, if the movements of the pieces or characters—or the successive moments of the development of the image, in the case of the painting—can be kept visible or transparent, a work of architecture should preserve and document the various stages of the project. Curiously, Eisenman had vindicated the architectural work's condition as object, distancing the architect from the construction. By now stressing process as the essence of architecture, he was making the architect fully responsible for it. Despite the desired abstraction, despite the desire for the prevalence of the object, the important thing is to relate how the architect has gone about the job. What matters is a description of the development of the project, the adventure of its gestation. For Rossi, architecture lived and appeared in type—that stable Platonic image or shadow that he would suddenly capture with a scratch of his pen and the colors provided by his paintbrushes. For Eisenman, architecture is manifested in its gestation.

What counts is production, the production of the project. Rossi versus Eisenman: contemplation on one hand, action on the other; architecture that is received versus architecture that is invented. Again we succumb to the temptation to confront Europeans and Americans. In any case, a focus on process gives architecture didactic substance. In the past, architecture had been an opportunity to indulge in pleasure or address a need. An occasion for delight, that is, and thus a mental operation or one involving protection and refuge in the face of adversity. Now, the architectural experience was didactic material. Process shows "how." Architecture as process is the architecture of the schools, places where we learn "how to."

The importance of process for Eisenman was detected by those who wrote on his work early on. So Mario Gandelsonas:

**Eisenman has introduced an important idea from generative, or transformational grammar, in which language is seen as a generative activity rather than as a description of semantic and syntactic relationships. In this view of language, syntactics takes on a new meaning where syntactic structure itself is seen as the primary generator of language. Eisenman incorporates this concept into architecture because it helps him to account for what he sees as a similar process of synthesis in architecture, the process of the generation of architectural form. [5]**

**5** Gandelsonas, "On Reading Architecture," p. 82.

The process through which an architectural form is generated would not be very different from that described by linguists when they established the norms of the generative grammar immanent in language.

Naturally, the idea of architecture as a process soon makes us wonder where the reality of architecture comes from. From the built work? From the model? From the drawing? From an understanding of the process? Since Eisenman considered process the substance of architecture, in his view the finished work was irrelevant. To describe his work, he coined the provocative term "cardboard architecture." Of cardboard are the models that tell the story of the projects. In the final analysis, his architecture resides in those models. The term "cardboard architecture" is not to be taken pejoratively, but as a provocative acknowledgment of the material through which the process is described.

Eisenman's program, as ambitious as Rossi's but opposed to it, is clearly present in the eleven houses that constituted his work from the late sixties to the early eighties. These were obscure years of generous dedication to architecture, years of determination to make others take the same passionate interest in it that he did. Let us now examine the eleven houses and expound on the concepts so far presented.

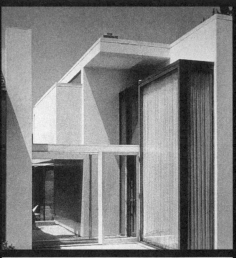

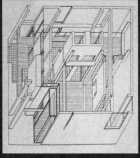

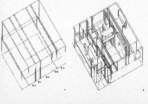

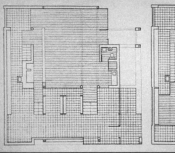

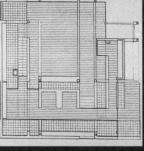

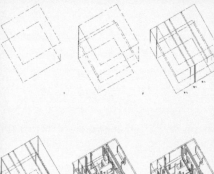

**1-6** House I of 1968, Peter Eisenman's first work, was an enlargement of a small house owned by a toy collector in Princeton. Eisenman's admiration of Terragni is evident here. Like Terragni, he breaks the cube apart, associating it with a scheme that inevitably transports us to the diagrams that Wittkower drew to explore Palladio. The project's elements of columns and windows are placed over this ideal scheme. But the columns and windows are stripped of the traditional images by which we identify them as such. More than a structural, load-bearing piece, the column is either the result of the intersection of two planes (when it still is to perform its old static mission), or a simple void that ensures the continued validity of the grid (when we are to understand that there is such a thing as a virtual column that supports no loads). And the window is no longer the precise architectural element it has been in the course of years of evolution, but a new stretch of space—"negative" space that appears on the surface and assumes an identity of its own. The windows are not at all isolated, autonomous elements, but integral parts of a broader, general formal strategy that is neccesary to explain the formal structure, the formal invention that made the birth of a specific cube we call House I possible.

Through voids, Eisenman introduces the possibility of virtual elements. He introduces the notion of absence, a notion ever present in his architecture. Even in this first work, Eisenman's architecture tries to rub out anything that makes the definition of formal elements coincide with the definition of structural ones. For example, traditional architecture took pains to resolve the encounter of wall with cladding materials, perhaps through a molding or cornice. Here it suffices to think up solutions to a practical problem. The architect assumes that the problem exists but wishes it didn't, and proceeds to do something about it. Since it isn't possible to eliminate all physical (and also formal) features of the construction, one has to admit a certain degree of inconsistency in the house. We detect it as soon as a constructive detail becomes necessary. Nevertheless, given the house's density of formal episodes, such inconsistencies can be overlooked. If we pay attention to Eisenman's formal strategy, we are able to discern an ideal cube and, over this, the impulses that give rise to and activate the architectural episode that is the engine of this project: the phenomenon of superposition (the term *overlapping* frequently appears in the writings of Eisenman) which allows us to see the intersection of abstract elements—planes, columns, floors, ceilings, etc.— that the architect manipulates.

The house seems to want to have a clear front. Therefore, the wall—which here can be called the facade—presents itself as very diverse. We perceive shiftings giving rise to numerous plastic episodes, whether encounters or overlappings. For Eisenman, the essence of the architecture lies in the shifting that has produced a whole chain of diverse formal episodes. He doesn't dwell on reliefs or textures, nor on the final plasticity of the wall. Instead he pays attention to the movements that constitute the strategic game of architecture he is interested in. Two columns help shape a staircase. A kitchen and a toilet are anomalies that become part of the surge of forms.

Some of this is discernible in the floor plan. We see the facade wall, as well as the skylight it incorporates. Later we see that the "detached," autonomous element reinforces the house's frontality, being a series of determinant transverse episodes in the expression of that frontality. The abstract structural grid that holds up the house is rarefied. So would it be in Terragni, where there is no discretional use of the Corbusian frame. Instead, the plane is subjected to a painstaking, complex elaboration of the grids that generate and structure it, which are originally simple and homogeneous. They are not indifferent grids. On the contrary, they are grids activated by the initial movements—shiftings, transfers—that get the process going. Eisenman speaks of "architectural strategy" when referring to them.

One of the images here illustrates the intersection of planes mentioned above. A close look reveals that an abstract plane stretching along the double bay interferes with another alignment. A mechanism of subtraction is discerned when the columns that function like solid spaces are put in relation to the voids that, as if reflecting an absence, are produced in the wall. It is the hypothetical and abstract shifting that generates columns and voids, and gives rise to the movement that unleashes the process.

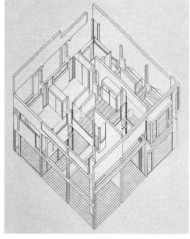

**7-13** House II,
Hardwick, Vermont, 1970

**7-13** In this first group of Eisenman projects, the best may be House II in Hardwick, Vermont, dated 1969–1970. The blanket of snow definitely helps give it a reality completely removed from the ground it rises on. With its white surfaces superposed on the snow, House II reaches that abstract condition that Eisenman wants his architecture to have. The snow eliminates all possible references to the surrounding landscape, so that House II is pure architectural form.

A superficial examination of the project may give us the idea that the architecture of House II comes from models of De Stijl or Terragni. Terragni is in fact present here. But it is also true that Eisenman has his very own,

peculiar way of working on the grid, and the way the walls seem to serve as infill for the structure confirms this. There is an explicit desire to emphasize the interdependence of infill and structure, which are assertively presented as entities on their own. On the other hand, the initial movement—where the diagonal of the cube coincides with the shifting—is manifested both on plan and in the elevations and sections. The diagonal shift that gives rise to the formal process of House II draws along every single one of the elements, creating fissures and reliefs in which the shift is easily discerned.

Eisenman regulates the grammar he uses in the building of these houses with extraordinary consis-

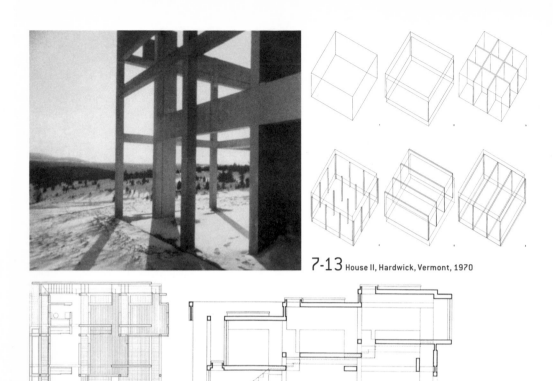

7-13 House II, Hardwick, Vermont, 1970

tency. They are not subjected to caprices of the eye. The formal structure generated by the movement that is at the origin is reflected in the rigor of the final built work. Contemplation of these houses requires an exercise involving the discovery of norms that have been complied with very strictly. These norms have a bearing on the clearly identifiable elements of the construction—the grid of columns, for instance—as well as on the virtual elements that Eisenman's drawings show, such as interior spaces treated as solids. The process helps us understand the norms. Architecture as process implies that the resultant form will to a certain degree be something unexpected. One might say that Eisenman doesn't care much about results.

The thing pursued is not a predetermined architecture, not something pre-imagined or subject to a given model. Here, architecture is simply the end of the process. Indeed it can be said that in the designing of the house, no facades or sections were "drawn." Or they could have been drawn, but without an intention of pursuing any given image. Eisenman uses the conventional floor plan, section, and elevation to represent his architecture, not as starting points of the project.

More on process. After all, without it the building becomes pure delight in final spaces, and as we've said before, this is something Eisenman simply takes for granted but has no real interest in. We should begin by establishing a frame of reference from which to proceed. First we have to identify the minimal notational elements. In this case it's the grid of columns. The grid can be formed by isolated elements, or as the result of the intersection of orthogonal planes. The base of the grid is the square. Now imagine that the grid shifts, and in such a way that it gives rise to a chain of operations. These operations must be taken as stages of the process that lies at the origin of the form. House II builds on a shift along the diagonal. The movement is carried out over it, and its influence continues to be manifested in the shapes of both the floor plan and the section. Implicit in any process is a continuous overlapping of readings. The tripartite structure of the cube sometimes presents itself as a solid—the void solidifies—and at other times we are shown the linear condition of the columns. The distinction between vertical linear elements (columns) and infill (vertical planes) is ever present and becomes one of the more prominent of the building's formal conventions. The final result always carries traces of the process: fissures in the infill, repeated columns in the scheme. It is a difficult but not impossible task to remake the norms that have dictated the process. This has to be done with calm. The drawings help us understand the process.

Some of the formal elements that lay at the origin of the referential grid when the process began are maintained. The gaps produced by the shift are occupied by building elements, such as the staircase, or spaces with less momentary uses, such as kitchens and bathrooms. That such easily identifiable, conventional elements come into play seems somewhat anomalous. The abstraction Eisenman aspires to in his work is threatened by the presence of specific, ordinary uses. Our experience of architecture makes us consider only the final spaces, the premise being that the process led us to them. Is sensorial delight in the final result what Eisenman wants in the first place? Let's say we are to speak only in terms of "sensations." Certainly House II provides a vivid architectural picture. The complexity of the formal operations carried out has yielded a lively and diverse space bordering on the picturesque. But was this what Eisenman wanted? I'm afraid not. His insistence on the importance of process seems to tell us that what House II calls for is a reading that invites a retracing of its process: the intellectuality of process versus pure sensorial emotion. Instead of feeling captivated by the space, we are encouraged to discern that at the origin of the architecture lay a grid of columns that later underwent a shift. The space ought to manifest to us the same tension that the shift provoked in it. For Eisenman, the shift is ultimately responsible for an intellectual and spatial experience, of the kind he wants us to go through when we study House II.

In Eisenman's view, anything that lies outside of the formal process has no real value for architecture. The construction, the program, the place, and other concrete things are there for us to see, but can be ignored. What matters are the architect's invention and use of a syntax and the initial movement that got the ball (process) rolling. The house addresses its function. It contains all the necessary programmatic elements—kitchen, fireplace, stairs, baths, etc. But these are trapped in the interstitial spaces. They are mere anecdotes, coincidences that have no value architecturally. The need to incorporate conventional practice into the architectural exercise comes to the fore all throughout the project—in the roof, in the arrangement of the terraces, the skylights, and so on. A desire for consistency makes Eisenman complement the planar shift with a sectional shift, and this double movement that is the source of the overall form is reflected in the roof.

Hence House II is an object that, by materializing them, incorporates all the geometric operations comprising the process. The result is pure form that ignores all the circumstances surrounding it. Proof of this is the way the house relates to the ground: a simple horizontal plane with no references whatsoever, either to the topography, to building techniques, or to tough climatic conditions that would in theory call for a foundation.

## 16

14-17 House III, Lakeville, Connecticut, 1971

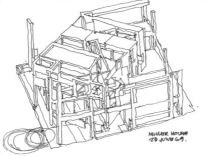

**14-17** If House II was the result of shaking a cube through a series of shifts, in House III in Lakeville, Connecticut, dated 1971, Eisenman applied a mechanism of rotation. The drawings clearly show how the form is the result of turning the tripartite cube and interlocking the result with the original three-dimensional form. Of course syntactic mechanisms of this kind are common and no longer surprising nowadays. Such rotations have been around for twenty or twenty-five years, and they are still very much on the drawing boards of architects and students alike, so we are by now immune to surprise. But in the early seventies they were a novelty. Eisenman's drawing of House III is very clear about the rotation. Where did the rotate-and-interlock idea come from? We could look to nature—the interlocking of crystals, for example. We could look to the work of artists. Or we could read in it a desire to condense time, ascribing to architects the power to write history by making different fictional moments coincide in a single architectural form. Chances are that Eisenman didn't have any of this in mind when he designed this house. It's more likely that he was simply thinking of formal mechanisms.

**18-19** House IV (project), Falls Village, Connecticut, 1971

**18-19** If in the first three houses the cube was the object of a tripartite division that gave rise to a preferentially frontal orientation, in House IV for Falls Village, Connecticut, also dated 1971, Eisenman began to show an interest in the possibilities of a cubic figure's nucleus or core. This is evident in the series of drawings illustrating the project. The nucleus explodes inside, and the result is something more intricate and complex than the two previous houses. House IV was never materialized.

**20** House V (project), 1972

**20** I'll skip the less elaborated and therefore more uncertain project for House V of 1972.

**21-25** House VI, Cornwall, Connecticut, 1975

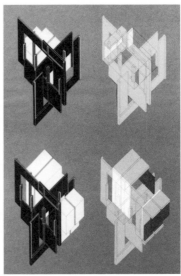

**21-25** House VI in Cornwall, Connecticut, dated 1975, was designed as a vacation house for friends of Eisenman. The tripartite division of the cube is more complex here. And because of the virtual erosion of the exterior faces, elements of the structure appear here and there, becoming autonomous iconographic features with a value of their own. Eisenman's interest in asserting the autonomy of the architectural form, its lack of obligations to function and use, is manifested in an architecturally canonical element, namely the staircase. Proof of this autonomy is the staircase's formal ambivalence. Eisenman manifests this through the paint colors, which confer on the upper end of the staircase a value identical to that of the lower, while preventing it from being confined between two vertical planes. House VI emphatically asserts the importance of the nucleus, hence the loss of interest in the periphery, which has less energy and vibrancy than we saw in the facades of House II. In other words, the cube loses its value as such when the nucleus becomes the basis for defining it.

Over the years, Eisenman elaborated a language in which superposing, shifting, symmetries and asymmetries, cuts, the distinction between solids and voids, etc., mixed to become formal mechanisms or new tools for the architect to

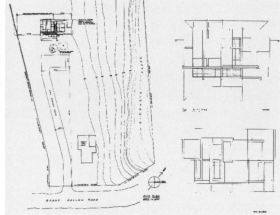

**21-25** House VI, Cornwall, Connecticut, 1975

work with. The programmatic mission set at the start of his career—to elaborate a syntax that would enable him to manipulate basic figures—had been achieved. Surrounded by devoted collaborators, he discussed measurements and distances with them, proportions less so. He studied and determined the right place for shiftings, as well as how the houses should come in contact with the horizontal plane of the ground. The vocabulary and syntax he developed were well assimilated and handled with familiarity by his collaborators. His repertoire of graphic/formal mechanisms—which reached a peak in projects like House VI—was consolidated as the essence of his architecture, impregnating his future works. Anyone embarking on a study of the graphic/formal conventions established by Eisenman will be impressed by his consistency, which is truly admirable.

Actual use of the house gave rise to transformations of the spaces, carried out by its proprietors with great care but not always to the architect's liking. It was Massimo Vignelli who set about to "decorate" House VI with furniture and flowers for publication in *House & Garden*. Despite his good relations with Vignelli, Eisenman took offense. As far as he was concerned, the house had been defiled. Indeed, House VI lost some of its value and interest as soon as it took on the dynamics of everyday life. It wasn't given to a flower vase or breakfast appearing on the table. What mattered to Eisenman was the whole process that gave rise to an object, and to the extent that the object resisted use, it acquired a near-surreal air when subjected to it. The clear message was that these houses were, first and foremost, objects.

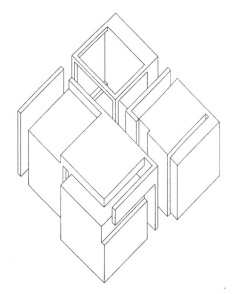

26 House VIII (project), 1975

26 House VIII of 1975 was never built either. The nuclear orientation we saw in House VI here becomes a four-part centered division that can be considered a precedent of the systems of voids we will now see in House X.

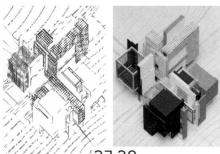

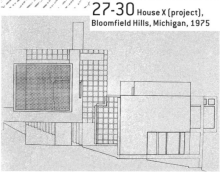

**27-30** House X (project),
Bloomfield Hills, Michigan, 1975

**27-30** House X for Bloomfield Hills, Michigan, dated 1975, was a first opportunity for Eisenman to work for a client with the ambition and resources to build a house worthy of becoming a part of architectural history. Eisenman worked on this project for three or four years. Though it was never carried out, it gave him some formal experiences that would be important in subsequent stages of his career.

The cube, previously a self-contained figure, here is the result of gathering four quadrants that gravitate in L-shapes over the axes that divide the cube. Each of these volumetric quadrants would define another cube if the void shaped by the L were filled. As the dimensions of the voids are altered, the volume of the quadrant is transformed, and eventually the full dimension of the cube is attained. Such versatility of figures, which can be considered identical structurally, makes it possible to associate the quadrants with diverse functions and to address the different conditions of the four cardinal points by virtue of the dimension of the void and the building materials used. The staircases and a chain of ancillary services are placed in the gaps between quadrants.

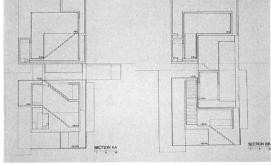

SECTION AA

SECTION BB

**31-34** House XIa (project), Palo Alto, California, 1978

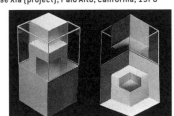

**31-34** The unbuilt House X can be considered to be at the origin of House XIa of 1978, a small house for Palo Alto, California, that in a way synthesizes the body of Eisenman's work of the seventies. It was designed for the architectural critic and historian Kurt Forster. Here Eisenman discovered the architectural potential of the ground. Also, working with two familiar figures, previously explored in the House X project, allowed Eisenman to work out the encounter of concave and convex, a relation that henceforth would be one of the most characteristic formal mechanisms of his work, and which would later stretch to schemes based on the Möbius strip. On the other hand, the fact that the staircases are situated on the outer edge gives rise to an attractive loss of center. This makes House XIa quite different from House X, despite similar figures. The concave/convex relation in turn makes apparent the sky/land and interior/exterior dialectics. And thanks to it, Eisenman manages to give the architecture a certain symbolic content, without iconographic contaminations.

By 1978, many things had happened. Times had changed. The abstract was beginning to give way to the figurative, and this must have been disturbing to Eisenman. The high tide of the Five Architects (early seventies) had given way to a low tide of a clearly postmodernist flavor (late seventies). Michael Graves, as one of the Five, had started out with the same theoretical interests as Eisenman. With all his baggage in tow he now switched to the postmodernist camp, and his Portland Public Services Building was the banner of the new tendency. In those years, only the appearance of Gehry, the noble savage, could steal the limelight from the proposals of Graves and his followers. Aware that pure formal investigation had grown out of fashion, Eisenman sought to move on to something else. In a way resuming the strategy of earlier years, when he had preached that the modern spirit had fallen short of coming to full term, he now proclaimed that humanity was at the threshold of a new stage of history, a new way of understanding the world. After what had happened in World War II, people were going beyond the horizon that had been discerned at the start of the century, and architecture was obliged to take part in the expression of a new vision of the universe. Eisenman recycled himself, leaving aside his pure abstract neutrality and redirecting his discourse to a new, transcendental, teleological vision, one tantamount to a reflection on the course of history. He reminded us that in the Middle Ages humanity lived in a world lorded over by God, alpha and omega of the universe. Later, in the Renaissance, humanity became lord and master of its own destiny, opening doors to the cultures of the Enlightenment and the nineteenth century, which further inflated the human position by making the individual the sole reference for understanding the world around us. As recent events showed, however, in the late twentieth century such a complacent elevation of the individual was exhausted, and we had become witness to humanity's capacity for destruction. We had no choice but to admit the immanence of history and the objective fact of a cosmos that we had no control over. If Eisenman had previously begun his projects by showing us the formal origin of the process involved, now his unrelenting pedagogical vocation had him presenting his work with the help of introductory texts that are clearly teleological in nature. From then on, his projects would be inspired by metaphors having to do with destruction, with the uncertain future that awaits humankind, and with the latter's incapacity to acquire full knowledge of the cosmos. He was concerned now with ensuring for architecture a place on the pages of universal history. Evidently Eisenman had not remained foreign to the influence of Marxists like Tafuri, who at least during the middle part of his career had taken such great pains to offer a global explanation of history, and therefore architecture. What a change!

Thereafter Eisenman would try to justify his projects through texts that explicated the new themes of interest, suggesting that architecture had the capacity to reflect them. In addition to linguists like Chomsky or pure visualists like Slutzky, Eisenman began to resort to thinkers like Foucault, Lacan, Deleuze, Derrida. These were his new sources of inspiration. The "architectural ideas" he had pursued in his early works—ideas which, as we saw, were often confused with the initiation of the process—gave way to ideological proposals with real capacity to give content to his work. His projects ceased to be objective, abstract ideas, simple geometric stimuli over a neutral and universal scheme that got a process of formal development going. They were now interpretations of historic evolution that could be materialized in a form, if one grants that there is room for metaphor in architecture. Architecture was once again spurred by reality, history. The fantasy of autonomous architecture was replaced by an architecture contaminated by the outside world—a world to take into account, like it or not. Architecture should reflect the instability of history, and there was no way out of this. But how to make architecture true to the specific historic moment we are living in? How to offer alternatives to the classical world, which even the avant-gardes were still echoing? Eisenman tried to offer alternatives through the projects we will be looking at shortly. Because of the experience he had acquired in the syntactic manipulation of languages, his new projects maintained the plastic complexity of his previous works, but Eisenman was really interested in what the works had to say, what they narrated, their capacity for expressing, through accurate formal metaphors, architecture's ideological content.

As we shall see, however, the ideological argument often worked in such a way that the specific circumstances surrounding a project took on more importance than the syntactic proposal. Thus we become witnesses to a peculiar way of tackling place that often led to an affected interpretation of it, or, in extreme cases, to an entire invention of the site. The outside world became Peter Eisenman's accomplice in establishing metaphors.

Before I go on, let me offer direct testimony, through texts written by himself, of Eisenman's way of thinking. At the start of the eighties he wrote articles of great interest, among them "The Futility of Objects," [6] which must be taken as a whole program in itself. The fall of theocentrism and anthropocentrism had brought about a new situation that Eisenman described in this manner:

A new sensibility exists. It was born in the rupture of 1945. This sensibility was neither predicated in the tenets of modernism nor brought about by their failure to achieve the utopia of the present. Rather, it emerged from something unforeseen to modernism, in the fact that not since the advent of modern science, technology, and medicine has a generation faced, as it does today, the potential extinction of the entire civilization. [7]

Eisenman, who in the seventies had disdained architecture contaminated by the outside world, felt that the new situation of humanity, holding as it did the possibility of self-destruction, called for profound and real change in all human activities, including architecture. He went on:

This suggestion of an end *in* the present shattered the classical and triadic condition of past, present, and future time and, thus, its progression and continuity. Previously, the present was seen as a moment between the past and the future. Now the present contains two unrelated poles: a *memory* of this previous and progressive time and an *immanence*, the presence of end—the end of the future—a new kind of time. [8]

Eisenman offered a whole global and transcendental view of human evolution in order to introduce the concept of "decomposition," which, in his opinion, befitted the architecture of the end of the twentieth century. Naturally it was to be understood as, if not radically opposed to, then at least subtantially different from the concept of "composition," which was always based, according to Eisenman, on principles and criteria deduced from theocentrism and anthropocentrism, theories that were now irrelevant. Surely, reading the above-mentioned

6 Peter Eisenman, "The Futility of Objects: Decomposition and the Processes of Difference," *Harvard Architecture Review* 3 (Winter 1984), p. 65.

7 Ibid., p. 65.

8 Ibid., pp. 65–66.

French theorists of deconstruction had a bearing on this new attitude, but I think it's good to distinguish between a first encounter with the deconstructionists that led to the idea of "decomposition," on the one hand, and the subsequent moment when the success of deconstructionist literary criticism in the United States made him consider coining a new "ism" and agglutinating an entire architectural movement around himself. Bear in mind that the term "deconstructivism" was associated with architecture some time later, when Eisenman became the patron of a new tendency by bringing together architects as disparate as Gehry, Koolhaas, Zaha Hadid, Tschumi, and himself in a 1988 exhibition in New York's Museum of Modern Art. [9]

But let's go a little back in time and look, for a start, at "decomposition." To explain its meaning, Eisenman tells us what he understands to be "precompositional" architecture, "composed" architecture, and "extracompositional" architecture. Analysis of Venetian palaces enables him to show that "precompositional" architecture was architecture in which not the result of composition but the raw structure of order predominated. "Composed" architecture was what resulted from representing the process of the work by endowing it with an order, more than it was the order itself. Finally, Eisenman said that there was still an "extracompositional" architecture that lay on the margins of the classic idea of composition, [10] that offered a latent and alternative, "other" sensibility, and that suggested a potential rupture. Eisenman used the Minelli, Surian, Foscarini, and Strozzi *palazzi*, as well as the Fabbrica Fino in Bergamo, to illustrate his explanation of these concepts. "Extracompositional" architecture was for Eisenman a precedent of an architecture involving "decomposition."

Which architects worked in this extracompositional order that was so attractive to Eisenman? His thinking had always been characterized by a desire to go for the most subtle and most complex. Thus he preferred Scamozzi's architecture to Palladio's, and Terragni's to Le Corbusier's. In Scamozzi and Terragni we can find anticipations of the "decomposition" Eisenman so diligently pursued.

**9** Museum of Modern Art, N. Y. 1988

**10** Ibid., p. 69.

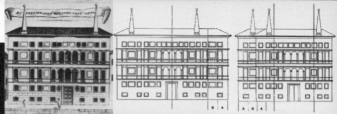

**35** Palazzo Minelli, near Bologna, drawing by V. Coronelli and compositional schemes of the facade, ca. 1709

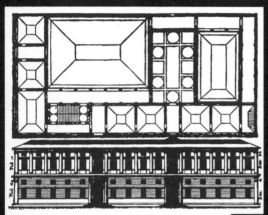

**36** Fabbrica Fino, Bergamo, by Vincenzo Scamozzi, 1611

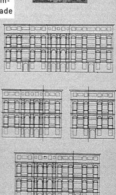

**38** Palazzo Surian, Venice, drawing by A. Vicentini and compositional schemes of the facade

**37** Palazzo Della Torre, Verona, by Andrea Palladio

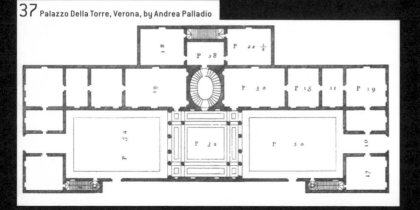

**35-38** A comparison of the floor plan of a Palladio palace with the floor plan of a Scamozzi palace reveals that the latter's work is more complex, less direct. There is a clarity in the work of Palladio that is a result of congruence, whereas Scamozzi indulges in a subtle architecture that doesn't reveal the formal criteria governing it. Neither axes, nor center, nor strict correspondence between interior and exterior gives a clue to the architecture's hidden order. How nice that architecture can be itself without immediately revealing the architect's intentions! And not because it lacks a structure, but because its formal content resists and escapes classification, categorization, standardization, or normalization. When we study this architecture, we have to recognize its uniqueness, its unrepeatability. Then we can affirm that indescribable architecture ignores norms, forgets precedent. Wherever these are dominant reigns memory, history.

But how exactly does Eisenman understand the term "decomposition"? I hope that the following Eisenmanian texts, along with the architectural examples cited, will at least make it clear that the term serves to characterize certain architectures.

**Decomposition goes further in that it proposes a radically altered process of making from either modernism or classicism. Decomposition presumes that origins, ends, and the process itself are elusive and complex rather than stable, simple or pure, that is, classical or natural. However, decomposition is not merely the manifestation of the arbitrary, the intuitive, or the irrational or the making of something simple from something complex** *[as Venturi would say]*. **By proposing a process which at root is the negative or inverse of classical composition** *[once again Eisenman's Frankfurtian interpretations]*, **the process uncovers (or deconstructs) relationships inherent in a specific object and its structure which were previously hidden by a classical sensibility. Rather than working from an original type toward a predictable end, decomposition starts with a heuristic approximation of end, an end which is immanent within the new object/process.** [11]

Eisenman still upheld the idea of architecture as a process. But he had to speak in terms of an "object/process," because Scamozzi wouldn't have started composing a building by manipulating two autonomous, familiar pieces,

**11** Ibid., p. 79.
Asides in italics are
Rafael Moneo's.

to later wrap them in crowns of peripheral rooms. Had he done so, we could take architecture as a process. But it wasn't process that counted. In Scamozzi there could be procedure or manner, but not process. Eisenman was aware that the process he had been using to show us his houses was worthless for describing the inapprehensible, indescribable mechanism of form generation that appeared in Scamozzian architecture. Eisenman on object/process:

**The result is another kind of object** *[an object that is not the Palladian object]*, **one which contains a nonexistent future as opposed to an irretrievable past.** [12] *(In one sense it is making by analysis, but not the traditional classical formal analysis.)* **The removal of the identity and significance from objects signals a uselessness** *(a futility in terms of its former conditions of being.)* **The futile object and the process of decomposition are no longer arbitrary objects and anomalous processes, nor a mutation of classicism. In this new time they may have become, albeit accidentally, the destiny of architecture today.** [13]

Despite Eisenman's rather esoteric tone, the examples he puts forward help us intuit what he understands by "decomposition": an ambitious, brilliant, attractive program. Nevertheless, it helps to distinguish between the concept of "decomposition" and that of "deconstruction," an approach that comes immediately afterward in his development. In projects like Cannaregio or Checkpoint Charlie, which we will also be looking at shortly, we seem to find an answer to Eisenman's obsessive desire to make use of "decomposition," whereas a project like Romeo and Juliet is, in my view, consciously and freely "deconstructivist." The Wexner Center, the project that wrapped up the series of what Eisenman called "artificially excavated cities," belongs to a more pragmatic realm, and has to be seen as the perfect opportunity to explore both his formal experiments of the seventies and the projects we have just been looking at. In the Wexner Center he would confront a crude reality, and the specific, with familiar instruments that he would be capable of making the most of.

At the time, Eisenman shared a studio with Jacquelin Robertson. They worked together on some of the projects being presented here. But Eisenman soon realized that there was no room in conventional professional practice for the investigations he was interested in, and the collaboration with Robertson, for which he had had high hopes, came to an end.

**12** Ibid., p. 79.

**13** Ibid., p. 80.

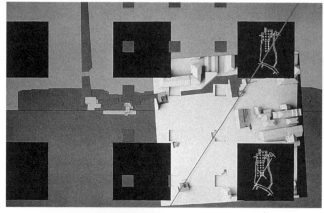
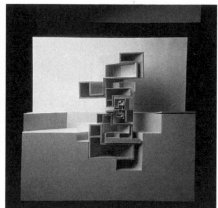

39-42 Project for
Cannaregio, Venice, 1978

39-42 The Venice project of 1978 entailed drawing up a proposal for the area around Cannaregio, the area for which Le Corbusier had proposed a hospital. Eisenman, who up to then seemed to have forgotten about place and land, now discovered the potential of these categories. So we see how he reconstructed the place, giving it new attributes by carrying out an arbitrary and virtual reading of it. On Cannaregio's land, present and past overlap, suspending the notion of dimension. Eisenman, who up to then had always refrained from seeking help from the immediate environment, here discovered that help coming from the outside world could be very useful. There was much talk at the time about the value of environmental givens. Eisenman, who had always endeavored to ignore context, now found himself forced to invent it.

When reactivated and inscribed within the universal scheme that Le Corbusier had drawn up but which was unfortunately interrupted, the category of land took on a new importance. The Corbusian grid became a reference and a material for Eisenmanian architecture. But how to make the Corbusian scheme vibrate anew? Knowing that architecture was the offshoot of the arbitrary, Eisenman connected the two bridges that serve the area with a slanting line, introducing a formal element that had nothing to do with the mechanism of occupying land that characterized the Venice project. Now turn the Corbusian grid. The overlap of the referential grid and the turned grid is manifested in the intersection of the nodes. In them appear dimensionally different versions of House XIa. Sometimes it's as if we were looking at a model. At other times the architecture acquires the dimension of a dwelling. The architecture asserts its autonomy and finds its place in a context that keeps it suspended between a future that wasn't and a present that is destroyed in its very act of becoming. The result is a project that shows us how Eisenman's arbitrary architecture might live in the midst of another arbitrary architecture, that of the city of Venice; and Le Corbusier is made the witness of an impossible future. Without succumbing to the use of context as reference, the Cannaregio project prefigured the next phase of Eisenman's career, in which it seemed to have become necessary to invent working conditions: context, hence, not as something inherited and received but as a reality that the architect is continuously forced to invent. Surely Cannaregio was a major discovery destined to illuminate Eisenman's work in the course of one of the most fertile periods of his career.

**43-48** The project we're going to look at now—Checkpoint Charlie (1981–1985), a social housing development for Berlin's Internationale Bauausstellung (IBA)—was a good opportunity for Eisenman to explain and extrapolate some of the issues he had put forward in Cannaregio. The proposals that drove his work were made explicit in his article "The City of Artificial Excavation." [14] It was clear to Eisenman that in this job which he was being offered within the framework of the IBA, it was in his power to offer an alternative to what we might consider generalized attitudes of those years. At the time, to build in the old city was to accept an architecture of nostalgia, and it was deemed necessary to comply with the

**14** Peter Eisenman, "The City of Artificial Excavation," *Architectural Design* 53 (January 1983), pp. 24–27. The text also appears on pp. 72–80 of *Cities of Artificial Excavation: The Work of Peter Eisenman, 1978–1988* (New York: Rizzoli, 1994), a book published on the occasion of an exhibition held at the Canadian Centre for Architecture in Montreal from March 2 to May 29, 1994.

architecture of nostalgia if the old city was to be preserved. The postmodern aesthetic advocated nostalgia, and this often meant simply completing the pre-existing scene, ultimately establishing a continuity between past and present that on many occasions found a natural support in the urban scheme. In retrospect, Berlin's IBA was a typical operation of darning and mending city blocks, or infilling. To accept given perimeters and complete blocks: this seemed to be the main guideline for participating architects. Hence the importance of Eisenman's proposal.

As a reaction to this failure of modern architecture to understand, enhance, or even conserve the historic centers, a "postmodern" attitude came into being: the centers were transformed into fetish objects. In general they were treated in two ways. Either discrete fragments of the old urban structure were preserved like bones or relics in a natural history museum, or the bones were reassembled, the skin and flesh restored or hypothetically recreated, and the new assemblage appeared as a kind of stuffed animal, a vignette in a "natural" setting.[15]

Eisenman didn't renounce the place factor altogether; but neither did

**15** *Cities of Artificial Excavation*, p. 73.

43-48 Checkpoint Charlie social housing for the IBA, Berlin, 1981–1985

he submit to it. He acknowledged that the place had a past, but he didn't want to be tied to it. Instead, he tried to show what could have been. As in the Cannaregio project, Peter Eisenman proceeded to invent the place, the idea being to be able to tell us how he saw and understood Berlin. His words again:

**Our strategy for developing the site was twofold. The first intention was to expose the particular history of the site; that is, to render visible its specific memories, to acknowledge that it once was special, was someplace. The second was to acknowledge that Berlin today belongs to the world in the largest sense.**[16]

**16** Ibid., p. 74.

He therefore rejected the continuity that "infilling" aspired to, and set himself the task of exploring the lot. The grid on which the remnants of the old building stood and the still-in-force order of alignments were not the only geometry of the place. The Berlin of the eighteenth century had established a different scheme, which the architect knew of but could not use. Thus, with his imagination for a tool, he took on the role of an archaeologist digging up the city that could have been. The abstract grids he had worked with in the seventies gave way to a grid that took on meaning through history. Eisenman materialized this grid with thick brick walls that speak to us of a framework that could give support to the city.

In a way it coincided with the grid used, so that the remains of the buildings still standing appear to be aligned and subject to an order. The two schemes would coexist in Eisenman's project.

But the project for Berlin also wanted to refer to a larger, universal order, and Eisenman found it in the grid of Mercator. The world we know has, ever since the sixteenth century, been defined with the help of schemes. Schemes have made it possible to represent it. The scheme of Mercator links Berlin to the universe. The schemes of the nineteenth-century enlargements of cities cannot altogether ignore the presence of other, larger, more general schemes. All these schemes were alive in Eisenman's proposal for Checkpoint Charlie, thanks to a process of excavation no longer only in a metaphorical sense, but in a literal, building-method sense. The schemes became passageways and corridors that would allow the architect to make use of a dense subsoil governed by the grid. It's important to remember the influence on his work of years of experimenting with forms, in accordance with cubist painters' principles of superposing planes. The Berlin project was the result of a formal process that can only be explained in this manner.

**49-54** The Wexner Center in Columbus (1983–1989) can be considered an offshoot of the Berlin and Cannaregio projects. It is, to date, the most important work in Eisenman's career. The images show how a huge oval in a 1920 campus gave rise to the construction of a battery of university buildings. The competition put forward the possibility of achieving a better connection between the oval and the city. With the Wexner Center, Eisenman discovered that the results of his long apprenticeship with forms, carried out in the seventies, could be applied to the schemes and grids of a city like Columbus. The site in question was afflicted with a problematic meeting of alignments stemming from different planes. The schemes were a register of history, and the architect was obliged to interpret them in an operation prior to the actual project. There were also accidents to take into account when making arbitrary formal decisions that would give rise to the project. Eisenman took the axis of the oval as reference, an axis that also served as the basis for outlining a baseball field. The axis helped him identify a scheme on which a passage is drawn. In turn the scheme embraced the two preexisting buildings, which, stretched and enveloped, took on a new significance. The latent scheme's invasion of the space transformed it radically. Everything was reoriented when referred to the new axes of coordinates. The buildings, otherwise so conventional, took on new life when turned into peculiar but actually contingent episodes. They were no longer alone. They had become key components of a new, diffuse, and extensive urban fabric that constituted a new gate for the campus.

To emphasize the "reconstruction" of context we were talking about earlier, Eisenman literally rebuilt the towers of the old barracks that had been demolished when the campus was built. An awareness of the ongoing invention of working conditions, and that life is being breathed into a new context that can come to include a past that remains only in memory, is what prodded him to build the towers, although he transferred them to a more advantageous position and later subjected them to cuts and fissures that serve to stress his artificial manipulation of them. I would say that he felt a need to exaggerate the iconography of the towers, as a way of highlighting the abstract character of his architecture. Eisenman is an architect who rejects the figurative, but he had no qualms about borrowing from memory for the image of a set of towers that helped give his project an ideological reference.

49-54 Wexner Center, Ohio State University, Columbus, 1983–1989

On the other hand, the interior of the Wexner Center clearly shows how natural and at ease he is in the formal manipulation of abstract elements (grids, planes, prisms, etc.), which cease to be abstract elements when materialized in his architecture. Yet the architecture maintains its abstract condition, and Eisenman goes to extremes to display it. For example, some suspended prisms never reach the ground. A superficial reading of the construction might well have taken them as columns.

**55-58** The Romeo and Juliet project for Verona, dated 1985, is of utmost interest, for in it Eisenman tried to apply the concept of deconstruction, in the sense in which the term is used in literary criticism, to architecture. Following the teachings of those literary critics who hold that the creative act takes place in the reading and interpretation of texts, Eisenman introduced the concept of "architectural text": architecture as the intellectual invention of a text, without this meaning that the writing of the text imposes on the reality of what is built; and therefore the architect as someone who offers an architectural text that will come alive when read. It is then up to the reader to interpret the architectural text. The reality of architecture is therefore at the mercy of the reader. The reader takes on a leading role, and the work, or text, becomes secondary. Hence, there are as many realities as there are readers. For example, Eisenman asks what it is to talk about the story of Romeo and Juliet. When we do, what are we really talking about? About the events that gave rise to the legend? About the version of it that Shakespeare immortalized? Or the operatic interpretation of the librettist Del Monte? The bells it rings in us? It is difficult, if not impos-

**55-58** Romeo and Juliet project, Verona, 1985

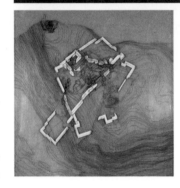

sible, to identify where the reality of the story lies, and thus the deconstructionists' insistence on the autonomy of the reader.

Eisenman tried to transfer these reflections to the field of "architectural construction." He made three design proposals of different scales coincide, literally, in models and drawings. The three projects overlap and superpose themselves on one another without

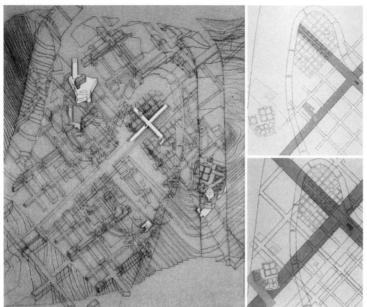

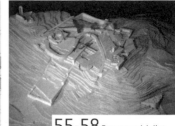

**55-58** Romeo and Juliet project, Verona, 1985

losing their respective identities completely, and without the complex, resulting object necessarily having to take on a meaning of its own. The architecture, literally materialized in the model, with its superposition of forms and images, is there for any observer to start deciphering. Topography, cities, and buildings are confused when brought together in the model, as if they existed at one same moment. To make the coexistence of disparate design categories possible, Eisenman introduced the term "scaling." The concept expresses an ambiguous desire for univocality. In coining the term Eisenman may have had in mind certain episodes in the history of architecture, such as mannerism, in which the use of elements of different scales in a single building was quite frequent. But this model is no longer about representing a future object. In interweaving projects represented at different scales, the model is a pretext for the mental exercise that the architectural experience has become.

**59-60** Biocentrum
(project), J. W. Goethe-Universität, Frankfurt, 1986–1987

**59-60** The search—outside architecture—for the trigger that produces the formal episode of any new project, and the wish that the territory of that search belong to the world of the modern, is such that in the Biocentrum for the J. W. Goethe-Universität in Frankfurt (1986–1987), the symbols used by biologists to express continuous chains of cells literally become an architectural form. Conventional blocks are activated by the ruptures that the materialization of the symbols cause. Eisenman's approach to these laboratory facilities was not unlike that of the architects who built the first airports and sought to make them resemble airplanes. Transferring biological nomenclature to architecture addresses similar principles. In projects of this kind, I am less impressed by the sources of inspiration—incongruent, unnecessary borrowings from other fields—than by whatever remains of the skillful manipulation of formal procedures. To accept the arbitrariness of a form in architecture is also to desire that it not be manifested, that it not be immediate, and that it not be perturbing.

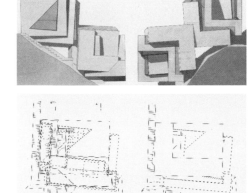

61-63 Guardiola House
(project), Cádiz, 1988

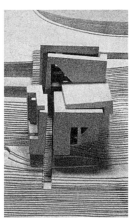

61-63 The Guardiola House in Cádiz (1988), in the south of Spain, was where Eisenman first used the slanting planes that would later abound in his work. His rejection of the idea of the house as protection, and his desire that the space in which one lives should not let one forget about the seriousness of existence, justified this "painful," slanting architecture. It's not necessary to explain why this project couldn't be named House XII or House XIII. The Guardiola House carries the name of the client, asserting its specificity. Eisenman was now at a very different stage of his career, and the Guardiola House prefigured spatial experiences way beyond the planar investigations he had until then paid so much attention to. The three-dimensionality of the Guardiola House didn't rise from the floor plan.

64-67 The Aronoff Center for Design and Art in the University of Cincinnati (1988–1996) was perhaps a less ambitious project than the Wexner Center, but it adopted the same strategy of embracing, grouping, clothing, and ultimately transforming the existing buildings. A tower and an architecture school building lacking in architectural value underwent a complete transformation when surrounded by a band of constructions characterized by a flexible geometry. Again, the idea of architecture as a process. More than anything else, the new building tells us how it was built, eloquently narrating the process. In all these constructions is a graphic mastery that counts on a building industry that, if its methods and procedures are accepted, has no trouble adapting to any formal design. Today's construction does not exhibit how one builds. Building procedures do not immediately turn into form. Form remains in the hands of architects, so long as they accept the system.

This may have been the first Eisenman project to be drawn up by computer. Eisenman was quick to realize that the computer would be a useful companion in an architectural journey where process played a leading role. It is with the Aronoff Center that we first see computer-aided images of a project's successive stages. The superposition of the flexible bands that embrace the existing buildings is computer-generated. It's important to point out the radical difference between Gehry's and Eisenman's use of the computer. In Gehry the computer is a tool with which to describe and represent forms, and then construct them with the freedom of a sculptor. For Eisenman the computer is an instrument that helps in the "construction" of a project. With the help of the computer, the complex graphics of his projects can be rendered more easily. From this project on, the manipulation and transformation of schemes and grids would no longer be the fruit of a labored, manual elaboration, but the quasi-automatic output of a computer.

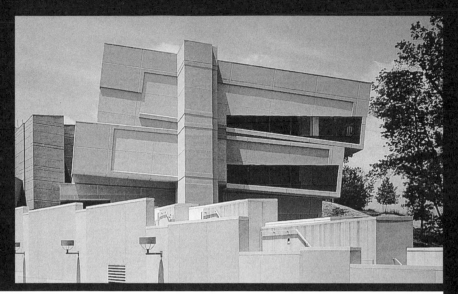

**64-67** Aronoff Center for Design and Art, University of Cincinnati, 1988–1996

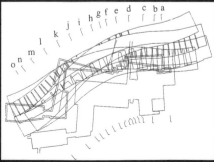

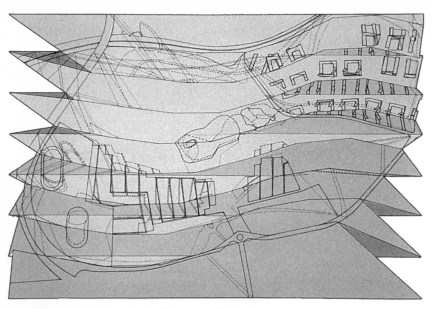

**68-69** Rebstockpark Master Plan, project
for a residential quarter, Frankfurt, 1990–1994

**68-69** In this project for a residential quarter in Frankfurt, the Rebstockpark Master Plan (1990–1994), Eisenman demonstrated his knowledge of postwar architecture. An area that would have resembled the *Siedlungen* of the thirties was transformed—and I would say also decorated—through folding techniques. Eisenman was using the metaphor that the French philosopher Deleuze put forward when he said that reality is "folded" and protected by folds, and that to understand reality we have to make an effort to unfold it. Eisenman manipulated the architectural form by subjecting the conventional masses and volumes of the residential blocks to a folding mechanism. The transition from the metaphorical fold of a philosopher to the built reality of an architect—the building—is somewhat hard to assimilate. For this reason, as I said when we were looking at the Cincinnati project, I am more interested in the architect's dexterity with forms, surely a result of his experience in the seventies. I also prefer the Eisenman who encourages us to study Scamozzi to the Eisenman who sets a trap for the German developer, telling him that execution of the unfolding operation recommended by the French philosopher will expose reality and that the industrial and urban proletariat will be pleased to be closer to reality. Maybe I should refrain from admitting that simplistic proposals of this kind are the most valuable part of deconstructivist thought.

Which doesn't prevent me from acknowledging that the formal problems addressed by the project are brilliantly resolved. Eisenman's gymnastics, put to the test in all the houses and projects so far examined, yields the kind of architecture that is never naive. Putting aside the previously mentioned evidences of arbitrariness, the project shows his mastery in the manipulation of form that is surely a fruit of the discipline and efforts of previous years. For me it's in this mastery that Eisenman's architectural talent lies, not so much in the extradisciplinary discourse with which he tries to justify his architecture.

**70** Project for Derendorf, Düsseldorf, 1992

**71-72** Greater Columbus Convention Center, 1989–1993

**70** A similar commentary would apply to this project for Derendorf, Düsseldorf (1992).

**71-72** A more conventional project was the Greater Columbus Convention Center (1989–1993). Using the outline of the railway facility that once stood on the site, Eisenman freely organized the neutral sheds of a trade fair premise. Here it's the element that gives the sheds transverse continuity that establishes movement. It also defines a dialectical relation between the naves and the transverse element, or between historic remains and new elements, which amounts to the same thing. This is the substance of the architecture. The project testifies to Eisenman's ability to tackle a large-scale commission. Note how skillfully the sheds become facades and thereby engage in a lively dialogue with the existing street.

Here again, Eisenman borrowed from the outside world. The shape of the building doesn't result from a mental operation that is translated into a pure formal gesture, but is determined by remains of the past, of memory. Again we see the importance in architecture of the concept of arbitrariness, but the geometry of the railway yard doesn't yield an evident figure as had happened in the German projects, and Eisenman's mechanisms of formal production are applied and used with greater naturalness. The same Eisenman who advocated architectural form at its purest now seems determined to show us that contamination is what he is after. Or, if you will, that the mechanisms used in the quest for pure form can live in symbiosis with other mechanisms of the most diverse origins.

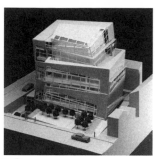

73 Nunotani headquarters, Tokyo, 1990–1992

74 Haus Immendorff (project), Düsseldorf, 1993

73 In a city like Tokyo, the agitation that dominates the form of the Nunotani Headquarters Building (1990–1992) seems completely unnecessary. Or, at the least, it falls short of the desired degree of provocation. On the other hand, the message may be that any kind of construction is acceptable on such high-cost land, or that Eisenman's capricious architectural proposal is acceptable if it addresses the high cost of the land. The sense of inevitability that seems always inherent in good architecture is completely lost here. A certain feeling that it's the building's exterior skin that matters makes one think that projects like the Guardiola House are better, more intense representations of the spirit of Peter Eisenman.

74 In the 1993 project for Haus Immendorff in Düsseldorf, a relatively conventional structure is catalyzed by a curve from contemporary physics that is called a solitron. It's what produces the superficial vibration of the facade. So once again Eisenman looked outside architecture to begin the process of arbitrary form construction.

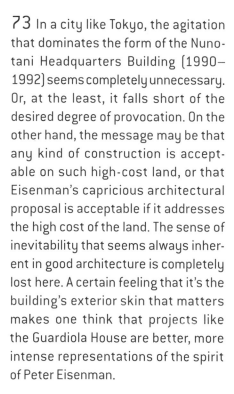

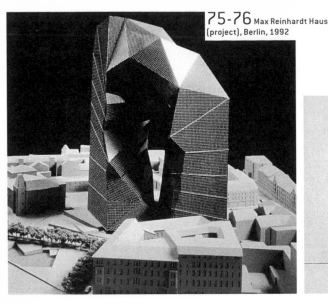

**75-76** Max Reinhardt Haus
(project), Berlin, 1992

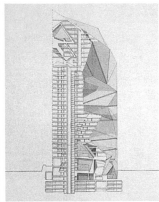

**75-76** The Max Reinhardt Haus in Berlin, of 1992, is an ambitious and exaggerated project in which the aleatory—bringing to mind Gehry—is supported by a dense and complex volume that bears allusions to the Möbius strip. Present in this project are the explorations of the concave/convex relation that Eisenman had initiated in the late seventies. This is curious, considering that the Max Reinhardt Haus is more about volume than about space, or, if you will, that it is a project where the spatial experience is generated in the volume. In the final analysis, the constructive problem here was centered on executing differential elements that would make construction of the volume possible. The Max Reinhardt project heralded what seems to be a characteristic of the nineties: a kind of aversion to Cartesian volumes and spaces.

# Postscript

The foregoing interpretation of the evolution of Eisenman's architecture has recently been endorsed by the publication of his book *Diagram Diaries*. It, too, puts emphasis on a change of attitude that took place at the start of the eighties, when he realized that the discourse of abstract architecture had exhausted itself. The search for an alternative to what his contemporaries were doing made him look to external factors, and so it is that his architecture opened itself to inputs of place, metaphor, history, and sentiment. As previously stated, Cannaregio can be considered a turning point. Recent past and remote past come together here, and so it is that in a place as specific as this Venetian quarter, the inevitable and the arbitrary join hands. Eisenman explicitly confirms this when he writes:

**The Cannaregio housing project in Venice was the first project to use what might be called an external text in that it is the first of six projects to consider site as an exteriority. . . . This corresponded with my psychological work at the time, which was attempting to move my psychological center from thinking to feeling, from the head to the body or to the ground.** [17]

In *Diagram Diaries*, Eisenman makes great efforts to inscribe his work within the broad arc of an overall and continuous career. After confirming that Cannaregio had marked the infiltration into his work of components previously ignored, he proceeds to classify his works, arranging them in a table that reveals the first stage of his career as faithful to "diagrams of interiority," using grids, cubes, L-shapes, and bars, and the second stage as dictated by "diagrams of exteriority," using notions like place, text, mathematics, and science. (It's natural that as Eisenman's work grows in every sense of the word, it should shift from interiority to exteriority.) The table shows that interiority was the rule until Cannaregio. Eisenman's earlier architecture was characterized by a penchant for finding norms and mechanisms within the discipline. It didn't try to have any particular meaning or significance, and wasn't preoccupied with making contact with an outside world that would only serve to contaminate an ideal world of forms. After Cannaregio, exteriority took over (the Virtual House is an exception). Eisenman's post-Cannaregio work must be understood

**17** Peter Eisenman, *Diagram Diaries* (New York: Universe Publishing, 1999), p. 173.

as the result of receiving external stimuli and applying them to known formal schemes. The architect feels familiar with those stimuli, or finds them in texts by the latest philosophers, or in recent scientific research. Fortunately for him, the experience of his previous stage always maintains a presence and the arbitrariness of the stimuli is concealed by the forest of forms that the architect deploys so skillfully. In other words, Eisenman's current architecture uses both his own formal resources—those he had explored in the seventies and which fall under "interiority"—and incentives from the world around us, which come under "exteriority."

To give the course of his career a certain continuity, Eisenman has coined the term "diagram." The concept of diagram is not new. It has been used not only by those who have explained architecture in pure visual and formal terms, such as Wittkower, but also by functionalists like Gropius. But Eisenman tries to stretch and broaden its meaning: **"Generically, a diagram is a graphic shorthand. Though it is an ideogram, it is not necessarily an abstraction. It is a representation of something in that it is not the thing itself."** [18] Later on in the text: **"The diagram is not only an explanation, as something that comes after, but it also acts an an intermediary in the process of generation of real space and time."** [19] The role of the diagram as a generator of architecture is what seems to currently interest him, though in the knowledge that **"[as] a generator there is not necessarily a one-to-one correspondence between the diagram and the resultant form."** [20] Although Eisenman enlarged the concept of diagram to the point of identifying it with the neutral structure of the "nine square grid," I believe that the early part of his career would be hard to explain in terms of "diagram." Previously he had put a lot of emphasis on the process that followed an arbitrary first movement, a movement that shook the neutral, generic mass of grids—these understood as formal structures. The first movement was called "formal strategy," and, in my opinion, this way of referring to the beginning of a process is more suitable for explaining Eisenman's early career than a discourse on diagrams. He was interested in making a testimony of the process, a register of the formal evolution of architecture in the making, and one has only to look at his past projects to grasp that his architecture was attentive to the concept of process and relied on formal strategies more than on diagrams. That none of his

**18** Ibid., p. 27

**19** Ibid., p. 28.

**20** Ibid., p. 28.

projects can be said to spring from a generative diagram is confirmed by this: "**In House II, the built object becomes a diagram of the process. The object and the diagram are both one and the other; the real house operating simultaneously as a diagram.**"[21] The object—the result of the process—is the diagram, which is tantamount to affirming that the notion of diagram was not at its origin.

**21** Ibid., p. 67.

Neither is the diagram concept relevant, I believe, to the projects Eisenman groups under "places of artificial excavation." The metaphorical return to the earth, the doubting of all principles, surely present in such significant projects, can hardly be subsumed by the concept of diagram. I am more inclined to understand these projects as unfolding with the intention of introducing the notion of "decomposed" architecture. Romeo and Juliet—in my opinion one of Eisenman's most interesting projects—is particularly difficult to relate to the notion of diagram. It escapes it, becoming a brilliant academic exercise in applying to architecture the concepts and criteria used by the deconstructionist literary critics. When exactly does Eisenman feel a pressing need to incorporate the notion of diagram into his architecture? I think that as external pressures like program and scale grow stronger, it becomes more necessary to use such a concept. I would say that the concept is indispensable in a project like the Biocentrum. The arbitrary selection of form—in this case the symbols biochemists use to describe the DNA chain—makes the concept of diagram highly relevant. Of course diagram doesn't mean, for Eisenman, the direct application of graphic abbreviation to architecture—although the graphic component of the diagram is in fact quite present in the Biocentrum case.

Eisenman takes pains to tell us that the diagram is the origin, the generative matrix of all architecture. There has always been a certain sanctification of method in his work. Nowadays, any methodology incorporates the computer. Eisenman understands the computer's incredible potential in the transformation and manipulation of form. But this potential needs a starting point, a graphic abbreviation, a diagram. For Eisenman, the diagram is to computer-generated architecture what the *parti* was to the architecture governed by academic compositional criteria. With the computer as a tool, Eisenman decided it was possible to present the beginnings of his career through the notion he so enthusiastically puts forward in this latest publication.

*Diagram Diaries* is also a commendable effort to reconcile present and past. In an interesting chapter titled "Diagrams of Anteriority," Eisenman offers a synthesis of the history of Western architecture in just a few pages. In true reconciliatory mode, he writes: **"In the interiority of architecture there is also an a priori history, the accumulated knowledge of all previous architectures."** [22] It is this accumulated knowledge that Eisenman means when he says "ante-riority." Inclined once again to consider his work the latest turn in the road of Western architecture, he starts out by reminding us of the role played by Vitruvius, whose treaty established what "architecture had been and should be." The architect with full responsibility over architecture then disappeared—**"The cathedrals began in one style, in one century, and were finished sometimes three centuries later in an entirely different style"** [23]—but after a long impasse the architect as subject reappeared in the person of Alberti. Eisenman makes it clear that **"Alberti suggests that Vitruvius did not mean that buildings should be structural, but that they should look like they are structural. . . . With Alberti, architecture for the first time concerns not only its being—the facture itself—but also its representation both inside and outside of its being."** [24] In other words, architects want to make the interiority of architecture present, visible. For Eisenman, "normalization"—submission to the norms inherent in history—is a risk that is implicit in the notion of anteriority. And to oppose it he coins the term "presentness." To define it: **"Presentness is that condition which allows the object to remain unabsorbed into the normalized interiority of architecture. It allows the object to remain outside of its original time as a critical instrument."** [25] The diagram would give architecture a formal structure, making presence possible. Finally: **"It is this level of criticality in presentness which inhabits the diagram as a second degree of representation."** [26]

22 Ibid., p. 37.

23 Ibid., p. 38.

24 Ibid., p. 38.

25 Ibid., p. 42.

26 Ibid., p. 42.

The book ends with passages I believe are key to an understanding of architecture's current situation. In the closing chapter he says: **"The diagram as a form of writing, because it introduces a non-presence as an absence in presence, allows the possibility of overcoming the idea of a motivated sign."** [27] The diagram, hence, as a hidden generative matrix giving rise to internal shiftings. Eisenman's recent work has made him write these disturbing lines: **"It seems ironic that only now, in the last few years, when the diagram seems to have had a theoretical rebirth, . . . our work of thirty years on the same subject has become relevant. In one sense, this book stands as a critique of that rebirth, and in another sense, it is an acknowledgment that the larger the projects become, the less control that any architect has, no matter what the process."** [28] The diagram as a hidden spirit that architecture instills in buildings, an affectionate, sentimental sigh of one who doesn't want to lose his critical powers, the "present-ness" that Eisenman associated with the diagram: **"In this context, the diagram begins to separate form from function, form from meaning, and architect from the process of design. The diagram works to blur the relationship between the desiring subject—the designer, the user—and the desired object in order to move both subject and object towards an unmotivated condition. But at the same time, as Massimo Cacciari points out, it is problematic to act as a negative agent in architecture."** [29] Eisenman ends by telling us that this way of interpreting things brings about a "desire for fulfillment." The consolation would be the diagram: the hidden figure that only the architect's eye can see, and where all his fantasies come true.

**27** Ibid., p. 214.

**28** Ibid., pp. 207–208.

**29** Ibid., p. 214.

# ALVARO SIZA

Álvaro Siza Vieira is a complete personality; a many-sided figure, without a doubt an architect very different from those that we have seen in the previous lectures. For some he is the most genuine representative of an architecture that is a continuation of the tenets and principles of the modern architects. Indeed, Siza's work can be considered the quintessence of the modern movement. Alvar Aalto is present in his architecture. So are the likes of Wright and Le Corbusier, especially in his early works. Another master whom Siza knows well, and whose influence pervades his work, is Adolf Loos. We will have the opportunity to verify this in the illustrations reproduced here. Unquestionably, the architecture and the architects of the modern movement are very much a part of the work of Álvaro Siza. Yet in the opinion of others, Siza is the leading representative of a certain architecture that engages with the popular, with traditional building. As we know, it is Kenneth Frampton who has most drawn attention to professionals of relatively peripheral countries who have managed to develop local architecture of high cultural quality. From their marginal cultures, they have turned resistance (to international styles) into a virtue. Such resistance begins with accepting immediate realities, knowing their ins and outs, and trying to transform them from within. It amounts to criticism, meaning self-criticism, which in good hands can prove a very useful and far-reaching tool.

The acceptance of reality begins with knowledge of the place. In discussing Rossi we came across prototypes and a Platonic view of the world. In Eisenman we perceived an obsession with method. Now we have before us an architect who addresses the contingent, or the unexpected, without forgetting the importance of finding the origin of the architecture. With Siza's work, we discover what is most essential, what most forcefully characterizes the architectural phenomenon. Architecture at its purest: this is always at the heart of his work. We have seen Rossi insist on serving primary ideas. We have seen Eisenman's interest in solving linguistic problems by exploring the meaning of syntax. In contrast, Siza seems to want to tell us that he simply wants his work to "reek" of architecture. And it is this "aroma of architecture"—or, if you wish, of what we understand as architecture, what we were taught to understand as architecture—that we breathe in his works. In his hands, architecture becomes something close to poetry. Especially in his early works, we get that feeling of having stumbled upon a transcendental reality, a feeling similar to the one that comes over us when we read a poem. As a matter of fact, Siza has often been compared to the famous Portuguese writer Fernando Pessoa. Like Pessoa, Siza tries to convince us that he doesn't *act*, that he simply reveals what he presently surprises us with. Siza doesn't like to be the star of a scene. As we will later see, however, he does like to have command of a situation, or control over the script. So it is that his recent architecture lends itself to analogies with a theater work, with its plot and its cast of characters. Siza may tell us or have us believe that everything he does is inevitable, but in the final analysis his work is peopled by characters governed by him, characters who have a part in the play—the drama of architecture—and whom he, the author, directs and uses. The poem has given way to a comedy or, if you will, a tragedy.

Although Siza doesn't relate himself to Fernando Pessoa, I will quote paragraphs of the Portuguese writer that I believe can help shed light on Siza. I understand that it is somewhat of a cliché to draw a parallel between the two, but I think that devices of this kind are valid when useful in depicting a person's intellectual profile. Pessoa says:

**I enjoy speaking. Or rather, I enjoy wording. Words for me are tangible bodies, visible sirens, incarnate sensualities. Perhaps because real sensuality doesn't interest me in the least, not even intellectually or in my dreams, desire in me metamorphosed into my aptitude for creating verbal rhythms and for noting them in the speech of others.** [1]

We can look at Siza's work in terms of "wording," as a compound of many autonomous words connected by the scheme he has plotted around them. Once we acknowledge that such a scheme exists, we are able to recognize in Siza's work the words that Pessoa celebrates. I would even say that they jump and move about in the built realm with the same integrity as in a pictogram. Poets relish the euphony that certain words have when played with, and when Siza deploys the elements he has chosen to build his architecture, we understand what Pessoa meant by "tangible bodies." With Siza we are overcome by the knowledge of being privy to the phenomenological experience of architecture, and the impression of tangibility that his architecture produces—which we don't

[1] Fernando Pessoa, *The Book of Disquiet*, trans. Richard Zenith (Harmondsworth: Penguin Books, 2002), p. 224. Original title: *Livro do desassossego*.

find in Rossi or Eisenman—encourages us to put to practice our tactile capacities, stimulated as we are by Siza's handling and use of materials. And so it is that expressions used by Pessoa, such as "visible sirens" or "incarnate sensualities," can be applied to the built realm.

The second sentence of the quote is harder to understand, and therefore harder to use for interpreting Siza's work. But aren't the words of architecture—those that Siza holds captive in his work—arranged according to rhythms and references of the kind described in the quote?

Says Pessoa:

**Certain pages from Fialho and from Chateaubriand make my whole being tingle in all of its pores, make me rave in a still shiver with impossible pleasure. Even certain pages of Vieira, in the cold perfection of their syntactical engineering, make me quiver like a branch in the wind, with the passive delirium of something shaken.** [2]

I can't help thinking of Siza when I read these lines. In the manner of Pessoa, who speaks of the "delirium of something shaken," Siza in his architecture tries to seize the moment. Pessoa again:

**Like all who are impassioned, I take blissful delight in losing myself, in fully experiencing the thrill of surrender. And so I often write with no desire to think, in an externalized reverie, letting the words cuddle me like a baby in their arms.** [3]

With Siza, too, we have the impression that everything he knows and touches, everything he has been able to give life to, possessed him first, as it possesses us now, like a "baby in [its] arms." Pessoa:

**They form sentences with no meaning, flowing softly like water I can feel, a forgetful stream whose ripples mingle and undefine, becoming other, still other ripples, and still again other. Thus ideas and images, throbbing with expressiveness, pass through me in resounding processions of pale silks on which imagination shimmers like moonlight, dappled and indefinite.** [4]

Obviously feeling is important to Pessoa, proof that the "flowing reality" so well represented by the waves had a definite form, even when destined to vanish, with time, into the whole.

This last passage offers a way to read Siza's architecture: as the capturing

2 Ibid., p. 38

3 Ibid., p. 38

4 Ibid., pp. 38–39.

of something in motion, as the presence of something contingent, as a continuous allusion to the constant change that gives rise to temporal succession and makes it possible for us to enjoy moments, specific objects that architecture gave rise to by freezing them at a certain instant, in a specific work. In Rossi, time was stopped at a particular point of the clock. In Siza, time is trapped by an architecture that makes itself felt sensorially. We are affected by it both tangibly and materially. To describe Siza's architecture, there is nothing better and more indispensable than this final Pessoa quote. It needs no commentary.

**Blessed be instants and millimeters and the shadows of tiny things, which are even more humble than the things themselves! Instants.... Millimeters—how astonished I am by their audacity to exist side by side and so close together on a tape measure. Sometimes these things make me suffer or rejoice, and then I feel a kind of gut pride.** [5]

We now have to ask: so how exactly does Siza work? As he himself has often said, he works by acknowledging reality. He is attentive to the landscape, to materials, to building systems, to uses, to the people who will inhabit his buildings. Architecture helps define the reality from which one must start out. Therefore, it is necessary to know the reality. Siza has stressed this concept on numerous occasions. In "Essenzialmente," final chapter of *Immaginare l'evidenza*, he says: "To begin [a design] and be obsessed with being original is to be uncultured and shallow." [6] As we know, Pessoa published his work under four or five names: it is *others* who write and act for us. And this is exactly what Siza tries to do. The Évora development, for example, almost makes one think it was carried out without an architect. Siza would have his figure as an architect disappear, and indeed in Évora he does disappear, both literally and virtually. The fragile houses are transformed, destroyed, rebuilt. The only thing that remains is the structure, which Siza borrowed from the city itself. The architect's personality doesn't impose on the project obtrusively. What prevails is the structure, and we perceive the accidents that are trapped in it. Siza says: "Each of my designs seeks to capture, with the utmost rigour, a single concrete moment of a fleeting image, in all its nuances. To the extent to which one manages to capture that fleeting quality of reality, the design will emerge more or less clearly, and the more precise it is the more vulnerable it will be." [7] The same shadows Pes-

**5** Ibid., p. 436.

**6** Álvaro Siza, *Immaginare l'evidenza* (Rome: Laterza, 1998), p. 133. The English version used here is a translation from Rafael Moneo's translation of the original Italian.

**7** Álvaro Siza, "On My Work," in *Álvaro Siza: Complete Works* (London: Phaidon, 2000), p. 71.

soa talked about: "the shadows of tiny things, which are even more humble than the things themselves!" The shadows speak of the sun, the light, the moment, the instant. Of the "doing" of things, not of "how things are done," which is what preoccupies Gehry, who is obsessed with showing how architecture is made. Siza has other concerns. He likes to be witness to how a structure captures fugitive time, and likes to demonstrate its continuity to us. Time gives reality the contingency that architecture indulges in. So it is that Siza's architecture recognizes the value of the momentary, and relishes the being of things that might have turned out another way. Nothing in his architecture claims to have been inevitable. Siza opens our eyes to a precise and specific instant that, to our surprise, is materialized in his architecture.

Aristotle made a distinction between actuality and potentiality. In Rossi's architecture we contemplated the fullness of the act. The idea one started with was exhausted, its image consumed in the process of materialization that construction necessitates. In Siza we relish the potential condition of works, which demand to be finished by those who contemplate them. Works become works only when enjoyed. Though we often contemplate Siza's works in a state of total physical decrepitude, close to ruins, they never actually become ruins, in that they are always capable of offering us new discoveries. If we are ready to understand that Siza's work cannot be seen as something abstracted from the person who contemplates it, we will understand the fluidity of an architecture that recalls the attitudes of thinkers like Heraclitus or Bergson: the works of Siza always offer us unexpected and diverse architectonic experiences.

But again, how does Siza go about his work? Let's use his own words to answer the question. Siza has written relatively little, but we have at our disposal fifty pages or so—dense and all very useful—in which he describes how he works and offers as many as eight considerations about what we could call his method. I believe it worth putting them down here as a preamble to our run-through of his work:

[1] I start a design when I visit a site (the program and the conditions are almost always generic). Other times I start earlier, from the idea I have of a site (a description, a photograph, something I have read, something I have

overheard). This does not mean that much is kept from a preliminary sketch. But everything has its beginning. A site is valid for what it is, and for what it could or wants to be—perhaps these are opposing things, but they are never unrelated. Much of what I have designed before (much of what others have designed) flows within the first sketch. In a disordered way. So much that little appears of the site which is invoking it all. Nowhere is a desert. I can always be one of the inhabitants. Order is the bringing together of opposites.[8] Often Siza's architecture is born of the dialectic generated by the encounter of opposites. Program and site, for example. A case in point is the swimming pool of Leça da Palmeira. Turn difficulty into virtue: such a motto could well serve to explain a good part of Siza's oeuvre.

[2] I hear it said that I design in cafés. . . . It is one of the few places—here in Porto—where you can remain anonymous and concentrate. . . . [The idea] is to overcome—and that is the word—the bases for working.[9]

Siza goes to work in cafés because it's there that he physically feels himself merge and blend in with others who look to public space for the privacy they are entitled to as individuals. This, without altogether annulling one's awareness of the "other." To Siza, Porto's cafés are not so much places of leisure as opportunities to grasp the meaning of the social body. So it is that he considers the café the perfect place for conceiving a work of architecture. To Siza, to concentrate is to feel the weight of his obligations to society.

[3] Some of my latest projects have involved long discussions with organized groups of residents or future residents.[10]

With this statement Siza reaffirms the functional importance of architecture. The users-to-be of the architecture should always be kept in mind. After all, the work that the architect pins all his hopes on ends up in the users' hands.

[4] They tell me that my work, both recent and earlier, is based on the traditional architecture of the region. . . . Tradition is a challenge to innovation. It is made of successive grafts. I am a conservative and a traditionalist, that is to say, I move between conflicts, compromises, hybridization, transformation.[11]

**8** Álvaro Siza, *Writings on Architecture*, ed. Antonio Angelillo (Milan: Skira, 1997), pp. 204–205; translation by Dekryptos, Brussels.

**9** Ibid., p. 205.

**10** Ibid.; translation slightly altered.

**11** Ibid., pp. 205–206.

Siza refers to the role of conflict, and with it, "compromises, hybridization, transformation." He is wary of purity and willing to accept architecture's hybrid character as a starting point. As far as he is concerned, architecture does not come about from a tabula rasa. To Siza, making architecture is transforming what is already known and, through compromise, coming up with a hybrid.

[5] They tell me (some friends do) that I do not have a supporting theory or method. That nothing I do points the way. That it is not educational. A sort of boat at the mercy of the waves. . . . I do not expose the boards of our boats too much, at least on the high seas. They have been split too many times. I study the currents, eddies. . . . I can be seen alone, walking the deck. But all the crew and all the equipment are there. . . . I dare not put my hand on the helm, when I can only just see the pole star. And I do not point out a clear way. The ways are not clear. [12]

**12** Ibid., p. 206.

**13** Ibid.

For an understanding of Siza's working method, this paragraph is particularly beautiful and revealing. He doesn't like to see the pole star, he doesn't want to know too well where he's going. He prefers to come across a solution unexpectedly and enjoy the surprise. He knows that the contingent implies multiplicity and ambivalence. He likes to be aware of the conflicts, because it is through them that contingency is manifested. Only by recognizing the contingent can one address the specific problems that architecture presents.

[6] I would not like to make what I design with my own hands. Nor design all on my own. [13]

With this statement Siza stresses how important it is for architects to set a distance between themselves and the work. It's not a question of solidarity and giving others a chance. When he says he doesn't like working alone, what he's saying is that he doesn't want the architecture to be the result of what he does with his hands. A far cry from what we will later see in Gehry, in whose opinion architecture must come about with no discontinuity whatsoever and with absolute immediacy, resulting in works that carry no trace of the construction process and that therefore bear the direct stamp of the architect, who asserts his presence as energetically as a sculptor in the clay—later bronze—that he works with.

[7] My unfinished, interrupted, altered works have nothing to do with the aesthetics of the unfinished, nor with a belief in open work. They have to do with the enervating impossibility of completion, with the obstacles I cannot manage to overcome. [14]

**14** Ibid.; translation slightly altered.

**15** Ibid., p. 207.

Siza here tries to annul any possible interpretation of his buildings as open, unfinished works, in the tradition of the purest modernism, and in the process he confesses that if any of his buildings fall short of reaching the degree of fullness required, it's attributable not to aesthetics but to mere circumstances.

[8] . . . to rediscover the magical strangeness, the peculiarity of obvious things. [15]

After reminding us of how he addresses the observations artisans make of him, Siza acknowledges the importance of the presence of things, something which, aware of its uniqueness, he encounters in a way of feeling that he doesn't hesitate to call "magical strangeness."

Reduction is always risky, but Siza's observations could be simplified in this manner:

**place**: origin of all architecture.

**distance**: provided by the fact that it's others who build.

**discussion**: pay attention to those who will be using the building.

**contingency**: the solutions to the specific problems of each job are to be found in the conflicts that accompany the reality of the context of the work.

**uncertainty**: thanks to the vagueness of the goal being pursued at the start of the job. The reaction is not resignation. On the contrary, that all well-done jobs end in surprise is a source of satisfaction.

**mediation**: architecture as something that calls for group work, accepting one's limitations (constructive, functional, legal, etc.), sacrificing direct personal expression.

**nonsatisfaction**: every architectural work is, in the eyes of its architect, unfinished; the architect necessarily feels that his solution failed to resolve all the conflicts inherent in the surrounding reality.

**evidence**: architecture as the opportunity to test the uniqueness of things, the uniqueness that in their evidence allows us to discern their very essence. This idea of Siza is somewhat related to the Augustinian definition of beauty as the splendor of truth. On a more Franciscan note, Siza recalls the beauty of "the singularity of evident things," suggesting that among them is a place for architecture.

We will now see how Siza's work has developed over time, with good illustrations for the principles put forward above. When we talk about Siza, we have to think of an architect who is extraordinarily endowed for the practice of the profession. If we accept that architecture has to do with the visual arts and a certain capacity for the formal manipulation of reality, and if we should have to speak of Siza along with Stirling, Rossi, and Eisenman in terms of capacity and talent for practicing the profession, there would be no doubts about naming Stirling and Siza as the most capacious and gifted. Rossi and Eisenman have made great efforts to come up with a formal expression of their own, and we could say that their work has acquired more coherence and complexity over the years, their early works having been richer in good intentions than in actual achievements. But Stirling and Siza demonstrated mastery from the very start, so it could be said that their early works are not too different, quality-wise, from their later works. To be sure, both Stirling's career and Siza's show rising paths that reach a peak with works like the engineering faculty of Leicester or the bank in Oliveira de Azemeis, but we have to acknowledge that both were astonishingly precocious.

1-6 Boa Nova restaurant,
Leça da Palmeira, 1958–1963

1-6 Siza was only 25 when he started to draw the plans for this small restaurant, the Boa Nova, in Leça da Palmeira (1958–1963), but already he demonstrated the mastery that justifies talk of precociousness. A fundamental element in the landscape is the small hermitage that, resting on a platform that introduces the horizontal line at the center, and despite its modesty, acquires the character of an artificial and autonomous object. Siza understood that the hermitage would be an inevitable reference for the restaurant. Inclined to mark differences, he fragmented both its overall volume and the walls rooting it to the ground, making fracture and discontinuity the essence of the building's form. The ground was a key element, confirming from the very beginning of his career the importance of place in Siza's work. The rocks are literal manifestations of the importance

1-6 Boa Nova restaurant, Leça da Palmeira, 1958–1963

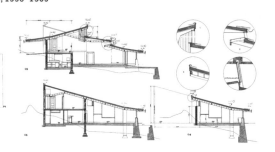

of the foundation, the primary operation in any construction. The building is therefore an encounter between construction and ground, which on this occasion is also the foundation and, as such, speaks of nature expecting to be constructed on, establishing a dialectic that indulges in contrast.

It isn't difficult to note Wrightian echoes in this project. The idea of an opening disappears; there are no windows. On one hand we find platforms at different levels on which the tables are arranged, enjoying splendid views. On the other hand there is the roof, connected to a system of walls which it relates to in a way very different from, if not altogether opposed to, what we saw in the hermitage. For a very early work of an architect, it is extraordinarily elaborate. Siza had been practicing as an architect only four or five years, and this restaurant can be considered a kind of takeoff point. Perhaps what's most relevant is how the system of walls dissolves to the point that we forget it's there. Other than this, which addressed the more structural aspects of the project, it's important to pay attention to the painstakingly rendered articulation of the access and the connection to the kitchens. Hence the importance of the sections, which show us a skillful use of the gaps produced between the roofs. On the other hand Siza explores the value of materials and makes extensive use of wood, entrusting it with the job of creating a certain atmosphere one might call domestic or private.

This is an architecture that is attentive to the slightest inflection, the smallest of slants. Álvaro Siza has always given importance to alignments. He knows that spaces change, both inside and out, when they defy orthogonality, and surely the slight obliqueness of this project has a definitive effect on the building's form. On the other hand the obliqueness establishes a certain continuity with the roofs that, though constructed according to traditional models, are handled with as much freedom as care. In this way it manages to draw a broken and picturesque profile that allows the building to harmonize with the landscape. Needless to say, I don't mean picturesque in an English way, with the volume taking shape through an additive manipulation of elements. I am referring to an attitude born of a picturesque perception of the landscape.

Lastly, in this early work Siza showed how drawn he was to the construction process. And though he would make use many times of traditional systems, at other times he would make efforts to put traditionally opposed materials in direct contact with one another, giving rise to unexpected, interesting juxtapositions. In Siza's hands, materials want to be themselves. They endeavor to preserve their integrity, precisely, by not subjecting themselves to the mediation that comes with an acceptance of their traditional uses, and it's easy to see this in some elements of this project, such as the windows.

**7-11** Swimming pool,
Leça da Palmeira, 1961–1966

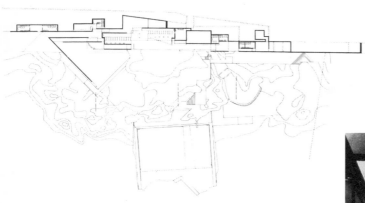

**7-11** The swimming pool of Leça da Palmeira (1961–1966) is a project of great maturity. It demonstrates a capacity to make the most of the meeting of opposites—on one hand the natural environment and wild ocean beyond, on the other the artifice of the construction, the calm enclosures of the pools. The ocean is represented in the rocks, which are like fossilized waves, and the pools are sustained by a system of vertical walls that give rise to an artificial sea, a captive Atlantic where one can bathe because a portion of the ocean has been isolated and pacified. In this case the landscape/seascape is not transformed by conventional elements like porticoes and pergolas. Instead, Siza has built a system of platforms that modifies our perception of the rocks, endowed as they are with a relief they didn't have before. The platforms give the landscape a horizontal order that engages in dialogue with the horizontal plane of the premises defining the pools. It is in this new horizontal territory that the meeting of opposites happens, giving rise here to the creation of social life.

With its austere forms, important transformations in the environment, this Siza work anticipates minimalist architecture of the eighties. Simply by building a concrete wall that protects and separates us from the road, Siza managed to isolate the premises and facilitate its encounter with nature, the prime interest of this project. The wall makes us forget the panorama of a polluted coast that lies across the road, and at the same time it leads us to a lower, darker plane where we discover the dressing rooms, showers, toilets, etc. Everything constructed in this plane is a filter that leads us to the sea, distancing us from the everyday world and giving us the peaceful solitude that comes with an encounter with nature. Wrightian nuances are very present in Siza's early works. All those horizontals, all those set-back walls, all that repetition of wooden beams—wood, not concrete—indicate how much Siza had studied Wright. There will always be those who prefer to paint the picture of an instinctive Siza, a noble savage, as against that of the cultivated architect who has made knowledge the support of his profession. Needless to say, I think otherwise. From his earliest works, Siza's career is the career of an extraordinarily educated and cultured architect who acknowledges the influence of the masters he admires. Of course Siza also has powerful instincts that enable him to go beyond learned architectures. One of the most necessary and most difficult tasks of an architect is to liberate his own instinct. For an architect to do this, it may help to examine the work of someone as liberated as Siza.

12-17 As with the previous project, here we can talk about a Siza who accepts reality, the limits within which he must work, and yet adopts an attitude we could well call "possibilist," because he simultaneously proceeds to transform reality, in such a way that the conditions that seemed to limit the possibilities of the job actually become the origin of the work. To assess the Magalhães House (1967–1970), it is important to consider the modest residential Porto district that is its context. Siza surprises us when he shows the potential of the lot's perimeter. We will come to this when we look at the floor plan. First I wish to draw attention to the importance, in Siza's view, of thinking out the architecture of this house in terms of its frontal character. This Siza project coincided in time with subtle critical readings of Le Corbusier. And like a bullfighter inclined to face up to the beast with his left hand over and over again, Siza went about resolving the different episodes we now encounter as we go through the volume of the house. In doing this, he insisted on its frontal nature, and developed the architecture in terms of it. From the street, we confront the facade. Later we find the door and a new frontal plane appears. Everything is made frontal, even when put together in a complex scheme of lines and planes, walls and volumes. So it is that a series of abstract formal episodes is transformed into something as real and everyday as a house.

Let us now look at the floor plan. Siza leads us to the rear of the lot, where the garage is. With this he manages to colonize and make intensive use of the lot, incorporating all of it into the house. The paving establishes a distinction between the garden and the construction, using a subtle geometry of slants that, through a slight twist, creates a dialectic between the void of the garden and the mass of the house. The subtle twist is responsible for the slanted access, doubly slanted if we consider that one can also enter from the garage. The structure of the house comes out perfectly defined with the living room looking inward toward the garden/patio, which the kitchen also faces. Notice how carefully Siza has handled the small area that prolongs the kitchen, separating

## 22

**12-17** Manuel Magalhães House, Porto, 1967–1970

**12-17** Manuel Magalhães House, Porto, 1967–1970

it a bit from the garden area toward which the living room gravitates. On the other hand, there is an intimate relation between the living room and the bedrooms, which are grouped together with exceptional skill. With the Magalhães House, especially in relation to the neighboring houses, it makes sense to speak of a destruction of the cubic figure, which has a certain neoplasticist flavor. We can identify mechanisms that recall Wright, such as the lateral accesses to the house and to the rooms. But the truly surprising thing is the passage from the void generated by the path leading to the garage, a void that is still public, into that formed by the low walls containing the volume of the house, the void of the garden, a private void that becomes the heart of the architecture of the house. By looking at things this way we are better able to understand the pertinence of the house's frontal development.

We are at the close of the sixties. Siza's talent would soon be widely recognized. People of my generation remember the issue of the magazine *Hogar y Arquitectura* in which Nuno Portas introduced Spaniards to a new generation of Portuguese architects, with an extensive analysis of the work of Siza. [16] Shortly afterward Siza would be discovered by the ever-alert Vittorio Gregotti, and he has since been among the architects that students and professionals alike most take an interest in. This is not surprising. The Magalhães House was in itself a work of astonishing maturity, and more so considering that the architect was only 34 when he drew up the project. So early on, Siza was already a master. Earlier I referred to the dialectic he introduced with the subtle manipulation of alignments and geometry. There is also a dialectic in the access to the house, where he puts together two materials like concrete and metal. The bright white of the metal sheet contrasts sharply with the concrete of the wall, establishing some linguistic terms that, by continuous extension, ultimately define the figurative world of the house. Awareness of the value of dialectics intensifies at the thought that the figurative world of frontality—metallic white and concrete—has the drabness of the neighboring houses for a background. The skill of Siza—who uses the same materials as those houses, so that no one takes offense—lies in knowing how to set his house apart from them just through formal devices. As we see in the images, he manages to do just that.

Siza's early maturity is also manifest in the interior. There is a lot of sophistication in the entrance to the house, the design of the doors, the way the window is made to handle the encounter of two different planes, etc. The construction displays itself, yet maintains its abstract condition, literally. Notice the way the walls meet the floor. As always happens in Siza's architecture, even in a modest dwelling like this, the interior space is an entity of its own. Observe how light enters from above. It looks like a tribute to Le Corbusier. With this we find ourselves before evidence of the possible, the contingent. How many other ways could the entrance of light have been handled? Nothing is inevitably linked to the structure of the house. Very much to the contrary. Faced with a whole series of singular episodes, we have the feeling that each is simply the result of a momentary desire, at a precise instant, on the part of the architect. Hence the arbitrariness, the aforementioned sense of the contingent. Siza may insist that he does not want to be a protagonist, but here is a fluctuating world in which we invariably and continuously perceive the architect's presence.

**16** *Hogar y Arquitectura* 68 (January-February 1967), pp. 34–84.

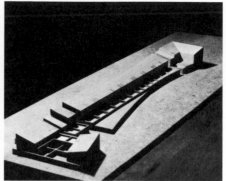

**18-20** Housing in Caxinas, Vila do Conde, 1970–1972

**18-20** At the start of the Portuguese revolution, Siza felt obliged to accept more modest commissions. He decidedly put himself on the side of the progressives, helping in the development of their housing policy. For a better understanding of the programs, he set out to communicate with the people, and he came to accept the fact that his houses should allow for transformations of the kind not always in line with his idea of architecture. The dwellings in the Caxinas district of Vila do Conde (1970–1972) clearly illustrate this attitude. Knowing that the houses would eventually be altered, he manipulated their profiles and volumes in such a way that at least the interventions of their neighbors would not interfere. Hence the added value of the proportions of the windows, of the chinks separating the blocks, or of the finishes, which are resolved in an Aaltoesque manner. On the other hand there is an insistence on rhythm—and here we can't help remembering Pessoa anew—that makes our reading of the work waver between the individual and the unitary. Siza may even have entrusted the architectural expression of the project to this rhythm.

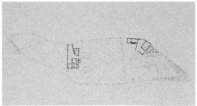

**21-25** Alcino Cardoso House, Moledo do Minho, 1971–1973

**21-25** The project for the Alcino Cardoso House in Moledo do Minho (1971–1973) is a particularly clear example of Siza's attitude of complacency toward conflict. This was a small house amid walls and paths, looking over a small vineyard, to which the proprietor wanted to add a few rooms and a swimming pool. Accepting the job, Siza decided to revitalize and transform the conventional bay by means of new openings and the introduction of a kitchen, in a way that deviated from the orthogonal order of the stone walls. A project of this kind, where the system established by the geometry of the walls seems to allow for new uses, calls for a transformation of the inert spaces. To achieve this Siza capitalized on the interstitial spaces, emphasizing their importance through the addition of conventional bedrooms in alignment with the terraces of the vineyard. The conflict is resolved in the manner of an encounter, without the character of the unfinished and fragmentary being allowed to dominate. The new construction—which is light and not costly—insists on the geometry defined by the terraces, positioning

**21-25** Alcino Cardoso House, Moledo do Minho, 1971–1973

itself independently of the preexisting building. The roof, light and metallic, accentuates the differences between new and old. Its various inclines help the two parts of the house maintain the distance that separates them in time, at least in the eyes of one looking from outside. Inside is another matter. The interior space lets it be used as if it were a single building.

It could be said that once an architect dares to produce such encounters, reality rewards him with unexpected spaces, surprising architectures. In the Moledo do Minho house there is the unexpected meeting of glass and stone, oblique space and orthogonal space, tiled roof and metal roof, etc. In the surprises that such encounters create for us, this architecture freezes the moment at which it came about, keeping it alive. The coexistence of two very different architectural pieces speaks to us of that moment, and architecture makes this capturing of the instant a pretext or justification of its permanence.

**26-27** Siza is admirable for taking on social housing projects, for not minding the modesty of that line of work. In the project for Bouça, Porto (1973–1977), the "accident" or "first support" was a low wall that incorporated a small sample of old architecture. As in the Caxinas dwellings, Siza here resorted to mechanisms of typological repetition, with the section ultimately defining the masses. Through skillful manipulation of the section, the substantial volume acquired a vividness that would allow it to survive in the complex world of constructions surrounding it. We also have to laud his courage in accepting fragility as a norm in itself. Paradoxically, the strength of the project lies in its fragility. An architecture built with modest means seems not to demand elaborate treatment, seems not to call for any sort of restoration. It accepts its use, the loss of that pristine condition it had at the start. Unlike other modern architectures, where maintenance of original conditions is obligatory, Siza's architecture is comfortable with the passing of time, even when it entails a loss of integrity. Siza simply recognizes and accepts the mission of the construction, which is, above all, to address the needs of its users.

**26-27** Social housing, Saal da Bouça, Porto, 1973–1977

28-33 The Beires House (1973–1976) is a contemporary of the works we have just been looking at, and yet another sample of Siza's capacity to transform programs. The mission here was to build a residence outside Póvoa de Varzim for a retired army officer who had returned to the country after years of being stationed in the colonies. The modesty of the surroundings did not prevent Siza from undertaking the work with amazing ambition.

Here he created an autonomous universe on a small lot, making the house gravitate over a garden, an element that must be seen as something intimately linked to his architecture. The garden, which can be thought of like any other space of the house, is shaped by an angled glass wall with recognizable echoes of Stirling. Through a small house, Siza may well be explaining to Stirling how Queen's College could have been resolved. The house presents itself as a gigantic window capriciously turned over the broken fragment of the garden. But then doubt comes over us. Maybe Siza wasn't so much trying to show the value of the erosion of a volume. Maybe he was more keen to stress the potential of the line—in this case the broken line—that marks the limit between interior and exterior, a limit that architecture has gotten us so accustomed to. And I will venture even further: the broken line prefigures the hypothesis that there is no distinction between inside and outside.

Again the importance of the entrance. As on other occasions, Siza indulges in a lateral, slanted access. Such an entrance is necessary in this case, given the house's narrow front. There are actually two accesses, one through the kitchen and the other into the living room. On the kitchen side, with its window protected by a circular canopy, Siza creates what is more or less a service space, including a bathroom, a bedroom, and a storage room. Completing the service program of the ground level is a back bedroom. But the protagonist of the ground floor is the living room, bordered by the broken wall of glass on one end and the lot's actual rear perimeter on the other. It is in the living room that one gets a sense of the autonomy of the house. This room seems to want to tell us that there are no distances to be established between the natural world that is still present in the garden and the manipulated, artificial world of the construction. They are brought together by the architecture, and made one. This is the conclusion to be reached when one contemplates the indissoluble internal/external space that

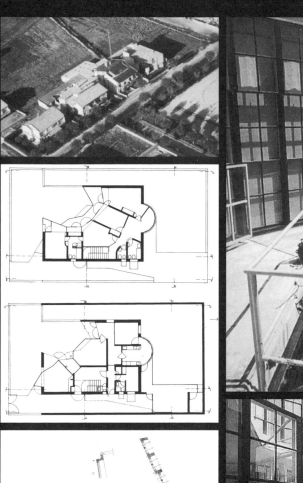

28-33 Beires House, Póvoa de Varzim, 1973–1976

the glass wall defines. The upper floor, in turn, is characterized by its flexibility and the efficiency of its interstitial spaces.

The Beires House is the result of a small/large exercise in geometry, and the strategy established in the project prevails. The unrepeatability of Siza's architecture comes to the fore. It would be hard to find other circumstances where such a basic mechanism as a bite could open the facade as much and still allow most of the rooms to look over it, just as the brief demanded.

As for language, this is a generically modern house whose most prominent feature is perhaps the tightness of the measurements. This brings about what we might call a miniaturization process. I remember being surprised when I visited it: it's such a tiny house. Because it's so small, many elements become objects of contemplation in themselves, and the visitor feels pressured to address the issues that are implicit in them. In other words, it's a house that constantly makes us perceive the presence of architecture. Its geometry gives rise to an infinite number of unique solutions that lure us and provoke admiration of the architect's sensibility.

**34-39** We are now in the year 1974. Siza is by now a mature architect. The Banco Pinto & Sotto Mayor building in Oliveira de Azemeis is a work of astonishing mastery. It is difficult to find an architect more in control of his own work. Siza speaks of uncertainty and of himself as a captain who, pacing on deck, can't discern the pole star and therefore doesn't know what direction the ship is moving, but projects like this bank are more likely to make us think of him as one of the few who are able to guide a ship to port in the thick of night.

Once again we have a minimal program, and once again we have a side access. The side access is so recurrent in Siza's work that he seems to be consciously averse to the idea of fronts generating the architecture of buildings. The entrance to the bank, which is to exploit the curve that resolves the corner, is created by means of an energetic cut that turns this curve into a fragment—a gesture prefiguring certain mechanisms of fragmentation that would become commonplace in the eighties. The break in the continuity of the curve results in a sophisticatedly resolved access, as anyone who observes the break in the step that materializes it will admit. From the main

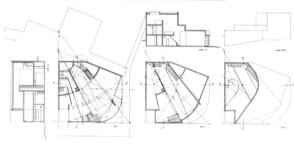

34-39 Banco Pinto & Sotto Mayor,
Oliveira de Azemeis, 1971–1974

door one sees the space revealed in its entirety, acquiring huge dimensions in the wake of a process opposed to the aforementioned miniaturization, disconcerting us with its immense complexity. This magnifying of space is achieved by means of the multiplication of levels, which are reached by stairs that section them, and through the accompanying proliferation of ceilings. The result is a chain of interesting formal situations.

The stairs are a key element. They explain how the space takes shape. They actually structure it, and

proof of this is their tangential position. But contrary to what happens when a space is conceived as a *promenade architecturale*, the stairs of the Banco Pinto & Sotto Mayor are not places from which to contemplate architecture. In other words, the space of this architecture is not obligatorily perceived in the light of motion. And a final word about the stairs: note that Siza uses them to establish a subtle distinction between public and private spaces.

At first sight, the Banco Pinto & Sotto Mayor could be interpreted as an attempt at linguistic exploration, as

**34-39** Banco Pinto & Sotto Mayor,
Oliveira de Azemeis, 1971–1974

an assertion of the continued validity of the rationalist language. To defend such an interpretation it suffices to examine the signage, the emphasis on curved surfaces, the smooth plastered planes, the absence of elements applied to these—not a single lamp, not one heater that might alter the surfaces. But I believe there is more to it: an attempt to show architecture at its purest, devoid of phenomena or events. The complexity of the space obliges us to go beyond exclusively linguistic considerations. Here is a building that speaks of architecture and tries to offer the architectural experience in terms of what is thought to be its very essence: space in all its purity, space without the limitations that use confines it to in buildings. It can then be affirmed that Siza, whenever possible, dispenses with all typological references. In this architecture of his, geometries so disparate as to seem irreconcilable come together in harmony. It is the spectator, immersed in the space, who gives them that unitary condition that makes it possible to speak of the presence of architecture. In a way, all this makes us understand architecture as something perceptible, as a tangible sensation consolidated in the specific and exact instant that defines the space. We could also speak of a cultural instant. It is as if the architectural references we perceive in the work were frozen at that precise instant, that exact moment at which the building was constructed.

The interior spaces are enthralling in their complexity. Imagine going up the stairs, and make an effort to grasp the importance of light in the definition of the spaces. The light literally dazzles us as the spaces appear before our eyes. Before us is a continuous unfolding of architectures. Can we speak of a concrete, specific space? Though we are lured by the variety of architectural episodes being offered us, the work does not lose its oneness. In the next lecture we will see how for Gehry the quest for unity was something to incorporate into his career only later on; before that, the thrust of his work involved manipulating fragments. In contrast, a sense of unity was present in Siza's work from the very start of his career. And yet he never altogether dispenses with the discontinuous. It's wonderful to see how discontinuity has been incorporated into a more global reality. The images of the Banco Pinto & Sotto Mayor speak of his architecture with more conviction and eloquence than I could ever do. A work like this is certainly Siza at his best.

Not to mention that everastounding mastery of scale that allows him to touch base, seamlessly, with the most disparate architectures. In my opinion, this feeling for the scale of a context acts as a protective cloak when he deals with architectures we might consider opposites. It is interesting to see how interior and exterior relate to one another in Siza's architecture. At first it seems that the exterior is dictated only by the interior. Not so. Awareness of the surroundings counts just as much. Siza has an extraordinary ability to deal two cards at the same time, in such a way that all gestures that are important outside are important inside as well, and vice versa. Of course the resultant continuity reinforces the work's unitary character.

**40-45** We could say that the career of the young Siza culminated with the Banco Pinto & Sotto Mayor, although the house he built in 1978 for his brother, Antonio Carlos Siza, was already a work of extraordinary maturity. But we should also speak of sadness, of deep *saudade*. And so profound is the sadness that we also ought to talk about daring. A house like this can only be offered to a brother. On the other hand this is a premonitory work. It anticipates many of the formal proposals he would elaborate on later. This is a curious, strange architecture, which explains why it has gotten so little critical attention.

Siza has said that place lies at the origin of his architecture, that external circumstances have a bearing on a project from the very start. The place that is the setting of this house seems to lack any qualifying attributes. We might call it a "no-place," its one characteristic feature being an altered perimeter. Still Siza finds in it the elements with which to begin the project. A line we might consider the most arbitrary of gestures, and which divides the area inscribed within the perimeter, becomes the motive and foundation of the architecture. I would even say that with this line, Siza works on the lot as forcefully as Lucio Fontana made a cut activate the rectangular surface of a canvas. Arbitrary alignment is the tool Siza uses to begin structuring the house. At the same time, it allows him to colonize the rear of the lot. Here again we have an architecture that pays full attention to the access, the gate. In this case Siza makes cars and persons coincide. Through the dimensions we recognize the different functions of the spaces, and it becomes clear that the access to the house has the character of an initiation rite. This explains the broken movement Siza forces us to perform in order to reach the raised platform on which the house sits. The whole game unfolds on the way from the gate to the platform. One crosses the threshold and the house reveals itself in its entirety, with no transitions between spaces. From the threshold we take in the living room and dining room areas, the kitchen, and finally the courtyard, which leads to the bedrooms. A private room directly connected to the kitchen speaks of a last redoubt of privacy.

If you take a look at the floor plan you will not be surprised at the mention of concepts like fragmentation and rupture. Only the bay window, which asserts its presence in both the courtyard of the facade and the more private service one, gives the architecture a certain unitary character. But what the architect

## 22

**40-45** Antonio Carlos Siza House, Santo Tirso, 1976–1978

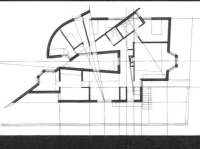

really seems to indulge in here is the endeavor to bring together disparate elements: the living room, whose apparent regularity and symmetry is destroyed by a subtle intervention in the ceiling; the complex dining room space, livened up by the choreography of two columns; the children's bedrooms, skillfully grouped with a tinge of ironic reference to a modern architecture that otherwise seems to be deliberately ignored; and lastly, since we have to cut short any enumeration of spaces and elements, the bathrooms, the simple schemes of which, to minimize costs, could well be the direct job of a plumber. Maybe you've noticed that I've left out the courtyard, a key element around which all the above-mentioned spaces gravitate, and which makes it possible for the house to unfold in accordance with the comprehensive brief. The strategy that involves organizing architecture around a courtyard is something Siza would frequently resort to in future. At some point it is hard to tell if the courtyard gave rise to the spaces or if it is simply a residual space, a mere result of accommodating the program so freely. One thing is sure: the courtyard is lord and master of the house. It is as if the whole spirit of the house resided in the void. The rooms around are other "houses" whose character and meaning will depend on the uses assigned them. Each of them has easily discernible features of Siza's architecture that we are already familiar with. There are traces of the Banco Pinto & Sotto Mayor in the children's bedrooms. The relation between dining room and kitchen bears experiences of some of Siza's early houses. The living room upholds the tradition of a domestic architecture that Siza learned from Wright. But the disparity of elements and architectures fades away when seen from the house's most private area. From here the mother of the family has a sweeping view of her children's rooms, like a guard keeping watch over the inhabitants of a panoptic jail. The view unifies, and, materialized in a drawing, it becomes a tangible possession of the house, a sensation at once virtual and real. Only the aforementioned maid's room beyond the kitchen is exempted from the tyranny of the courtyard and the schemes it generates. The result is that the house has a new territory, private and virgin, that produced by the arbitrary line that gave rise to the architecture.

The house borders on the irrational. Nevertheless it consciously explores all the geometric mechanisms and formal operations that have their origins in Gestalt theory. The house can be understood as the result of activating a conventional and symmetrical U scheme through inclusions, cuts, or projections. The unique and specific spaces of each room maintain their autonomy, but, with the help of the visual projections we were talking about or that of the shift over the line of origin, they are incorporated into the undeniable unity of the house. On the other hand, if we look at the private garden area as a whole, as a ground, figures appear—as much the solid defined by the children's bedrooms as the bay window of the room next to the kitchen. This house is highly important as an introduction to Siza's subsequent architecture. The courtyard experience, for example, would be relived in a definitive work like Porto's School of Architecture, and repeated in the School of Education in Setúbal, the Carlos Ramos Pavilion in Porto, the office of the rector of the University of Alicante, and so on. The Antonio Carlos Siza House is an entire program, a whole repertoire of the has-been and the yet-to-be of Siza's architecture. In it, certainly, he retested the potential of interstitial spaces. But allow me one more comment. The Antonio Carlos Siza House is a lesson on independence. The private and intimate breathes life and spirit into the architecture. In addition, the house is a sample of what in my opinion is one of the most valuable aspects of Siza's work: his belief in architecture as a medium that can accommodate our sentiments. The interiors of the Antonio Carlos Siza House are spaces that exude intimacy, a density of feelings that find expression in a diverse chain of architectural episodes through which the discipline becomes a witness of history, a trace of life. That is why the word "daring" appeared at the start of this commentary.

**46-51** The Quinta da Malagueira project of 1977 was one of the commissions Siza undertook in the context of the social housing policy of Portugal's progressive regime. In Siza's eyes, the architecture of these projects mirrored a particular social group. They were a paradigm of a specific class. Needless to say, he identified with the group he was working for. The site here was on the outskirts of Évora, a very beautiful old city where, as in so many others, today's problem of typological continuity comes to the fore in new projects. Siza was commissioned to build in an area where spontaneous construction had yielded a street and a series of alleys perpendicular to it. He was asked to enlarge the quarter. In doing so, he looked kindly upon the logic of the spontaneous urbanization preceding him, and proceeded to work around it with the experience he had acquired in works like the Beires House. Hence the courtyard houses aligned and organized by streets. Again, Siza planned for the houses' potential to undergo transformation. The courtyards would help preserve the energy of a social group that certainly would eventually want its houses to grow. Admirably systematic, Siza put forward his own version of the different phases of a house's growth. At a time when attached one-family dwellings with closed, definitive forms are proliferating and repeating trivial models *ad nauseam*, such capacity to plant the seeds of a house's evolution is very welcome.

Let's now turn our attention to Siza's urbanistic strategy: the total occupation of the buildable area. Such a strategy creates continuity between his project and the spontaneous construction previously at work in the area. In both developments, public space is reduced to streets. This leads us to appreciate Siza's mastery in establishing the measurements or dimensions of things. In a project of this kind, defining the width of the street is crucial. The width is exactly enough to allow parking and circulation, no more and no less. Some may chide me for praising this decision and clamor for a solution that provides for greater parking space, but in my opinion Siza here once again demonstrates an extraordinary sense of reality. Parking is an important aspect of everyday life. By giving the street a width that is just right, without recourse to restrictive regulations, he is able to guarantee organized parking.

I would also like to draw attention to the fact that a certain picturesqueness saves the project from the monotony and massification that otherwise

**46-51** Social housing,
Quinta da Malagueira, Évora, 1977

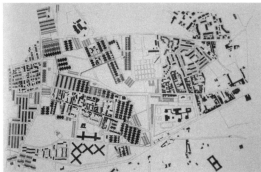

**46-51** Social housing,
Quinta da Malagueira, Évora, 1977

characterizes social housing. Siza's strategy here is simple: adjust to the topography. In this way, his constructions come across as an architectural cloak that wraps or completes the territory. The peculiarity of the territory lies in the undulation of the topography, and this is reflected in an architecture that is intrinsically diverse and varied, an architecture that has the same picturesqueness we have so often admired in vernacular constructions.

I have only one "but" about the Malagueira project. Apparently at some point Siza entertained doubts about his own work, specifically about its simplicity, and his response was to give the complex an architectural episode of greater impact. Transferring Kahn's criteria of servant and served spaces to the urban sphere, he injected Malagueira's modest fabric with a flamboyant, monumental duct. It's easy enough to guess the historic examples it is modeled after. In my view the Malagueira complex could have done without such an evident, rhetorical element. This infrastructural spine may for a moment serve to justify the geometry of the quarter, but it can hardly compete with the wealth of forms born out of respect for topography, nor with the constructive elements, whether doors, windows, or chimneys, that together mark distances and rhythms.

**52-57** We are now in another small Portuguese city, Vila do Conde, in a modest urban environment where Siza's Banco Borges & Irmão (1978–1986) rises autonomously and inoffensively. It is autonomous in the force of its curved surfaces, a novelty in that area, specifically in the curious asymmetry created by the building's two main facades. The floor plan and the section are complex. The architect painstakingly exploits the multiplicity of levels. Access to the different levels is along the curved glass surface, which from the start professes faith in an architecture that, through transparencies, endeavors to show how interior and exterior can come to be one same thing. From the very beginning we can observe the role that the staircases play in defining the structure of the spaces. The staircases unfold in opposite directions, producing something not far removed from the movement we perceive in the Möbius strip. This creates access from two levels. It also produces a longitudinal shift that isolates the building from the party walls, reinforcing its autonomy. By asserting the unique character of the building, Siza manages to distance it from the surrounding constructions. The very structure of the building separates it

**52-57** Banco Borges & Irmão, Vila do Conde, 1978–1986

from its neighbors and allows it to be different, without ever lacking respect for its surroundings.

This architecture must be seen as a constant celebration of the extraordinary and exceptional, as a continuous opportunity to appreciate accidents. There is nothing in this building that can be considered generic. Its space is a whole that brings together individual episodes designed to highlight its structural aspects. There is constant movement, as much in the external surfaces as in the geometry of the ceilings. With Malagueira it made sense to recognize Siza's debt to known types, but in this case he deliberately stays clear of typological references. What prevails is the global character of the whole.

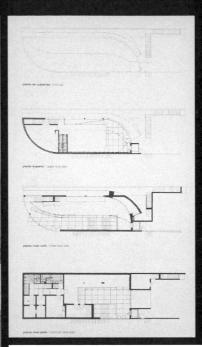

**52-57** Banco Borges & Irmão, Vila do Conde, 1978–1986

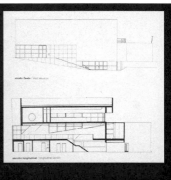

Maybe we should recall some of the formal mechanisms we observed in the Banco Pinto & Sotto Mayor, and again acknowledge the importance of interstitial spaces, the "cuts" and "erosions" of horizontal planes, slanted lines, and so on. Everything contributes to the congruence of and continuity between interior and exterior. The dichotomy between inside and outside that so often takes place in architecture vanishes. A good illustration of the desire for integration and continuity is the way the curved window stretches onto the marble surface of the interior and blends into the curved plaster surface outside. Complementing the masterful manipulation of spaces and volumes is this no less impressive capacity to revitalize surfaces. Marble, with its echoes of Loos, is used for both floors and walls. By not materially differentiating these, Siza comes up with spaces that are more abstract in character. As he has done elsewhere, he does away here with furniture elements. Everything in this architecture is fixed. Furniture is superfluous, and when in fact furnishing elements are put in, they seem strange, removed from the architecture. In his determination not to add elements, Siza dispenses with lighting fixtures, and light just shines from the gaps and interstitial spaces, all the more reinforcing the importance of these. Every now and then a conventional item will make an appearance, such as the porthole in the staircase, but these are rare. As we were saying, the whole architecture can be taken as a celebration of the unique and specific, as an answer to accidental questions. Someone once defined Catalan art nouveau as an architecture of uniformly consistent, unrelenting quality. So it is with Siza's architecture, which has no hierarchies. Everything in it has the same high quality. Understanding architecture as something tangible, something we perceive, a phenomenon, he tries to give all his ingredients the same importance. Hence the global and unitary character of his architecture. There is no doubt that the desire to make architecture a perceivable spatial experience is present in this work. So we needn't speak of architecture in partial, linguistic terms.

**58-59** Mario Bahia House (project), Gondomar, 1983

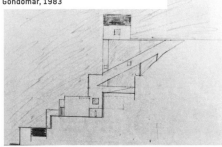

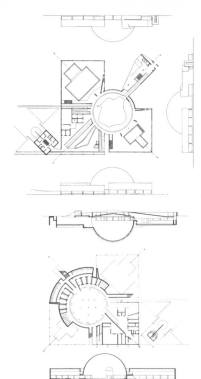

**60-61** Görlitzer Schwimmbad (project), Kreuzberg, Berlin, 1979

**58-59** The exploitation of the exceptional sometimes takes on near-caricaturesque tones, as in the Bahia House project of 1983. This exaggerated house, bordering on the grotesque, emphasizes the slope of the hill by ignoring it and letting vertical structures reach the horizontal. Siza indulges in the artificiality of the elevator, applying mechanisms of the public architecture of both Porto and Lisbon to private space. His mastery of architecture gives him license to undertake experiments of the capricious or outrageous kind.

**60-61** Excess also characterizes his 1979 project for a swimming pool facility in the Kreuzberg district of Berlin, the Görlitzer Schwimmbad. Siza is much more schematic abroad than in his own land.

**62-64** Avelino Duarte House, Ovar, 1980–1984

**62-64** In the Avelino Duarte House (1980–1984), Siza seems to allow a certain narcissism to lead him back to known experiences. Once more he pays special attention to the access, which, again, is lateral, ignoring frontal symmetry. Siza builds on the asymmetry both inside and out. The iconographical references that played such a key role in the house he built for his brother are nowhere to be found. The protagonist here is space, which is made an entity in its own right from the viewpoint of a center dominated by a dramatic staircase. Interest in space explains this project's continuous Loosian references. It is a refined and subtle work, but perhaps lacks the categoricalness of other Sizas.

65 Schlesisches
Tor, Kreuzberg, Berlin,
1980–1984

65 International acclaim of Siza's work led to numerous commissions abroad. A project for the rehabilitation of a Berlin block, namely the Schlesisches Tor (1980–1984) in the Kreuzberg district, confronted him with a familiar problem: social housing. So it was that with brilliant mastery he resolved in the plan the corner of a very consolidated block of the Turkish quarter. Everything seems to be entrusted to the facades, which come across as pliable both inside and out, thereby eliminating intersections and the encounters dictated by geometry. But the promising plan falls short in terms of architecture. The facades become strange when subjected to strict German codes and overuse of standard elements. Siza seems to be aware of this, and decides to turn the bulk of his attention to the building's rather academic crown. Paradoxically, the residents adorned it with the words "Bonjour Tristesse," as if to get across that such architectural license failed to overcome the cruel reality of that facade. Siza took the irony in good spirit, telling us that under such living conditions there is no room for disciplinary alternatives.

What went wrong in this project? Why is it that a subtle floor plan came to nothing in the actual construction? I think it's because there was no room for accident, no chance of a unique intervention, in the particular environment of Kreuzberg. Siza did try—in the undulating facades, in the unnecessary pointed canopy that strikes too sharp a contrast with the rounded corner, in the building's unusual encounter with the adjacent buildings, and so on. But the image of norm prevails in the end, and Siza knows it. We have seen him tackle similar commissions very gracefully in his country, but there he counted on accidents and turned necessity into virtue and conflicts into allies. Nothing of that takes place here. When accidents are invented fictions and become artificial mechanisms of architecture, reality comes marching into the scene, as in this Berlin building, where all we perceive is crude reality, devoid of architectural pretensions.

66 Rehabilitation of the area of the Campo di
Marte in the Giudecca (project), Venice, 1985

67-68 Social housing,
Schilderswijk, The Hague, 1984–1988

66 This project for the Giudecca in
Venice, dated 1985, is a minor work,
but it shows that Siza had learned
his lesson in Berlin. There is no architectural artifice here, or if there is, it's
only on a very small scale. Obviously
the architect pragmatically accepted
the reality imposed by the surroundings, and stayed clear of flourishes.

67-68 The social housing development in Schilderswijk, The Hague,
dated 1984–1988, is not a bad project,
but it's not exceptional either. We could
make a list of clichés, a whole chain of
forced discontinuities. If discontinuity
were the point, then I'd sooner choose
the discontinuity of the house Siza
built for his brother, which is much
less forced. But that house is not the
only reference here. The main entrance
recalls the Avelino Duarte House. Neither the Duarte House nor this apartment building has the freshness we
saw in previous housing projects, such
as at Quinta da Malagueira.

**69-70** Two dwellings in Van der Venne Park, The Hague, 1985–1988

**69-70** Still in The Hague, these two dwellings in Van der Venne Park (1985–1988) are very interesting. We could consider them "caprices," and this would give us license to speak of an approach that would subsequently

abound in Siza's work. His architecture becomes pure narration, with identifiable figures or characters engaging in dialogue with one another. Invention from here on would rest not so much in exploiting accident as in inventing that dialogue: the architectural work as a colloquy between different characters, each with a voice of its own.

**71-74** If I had to choose one project out of the many that Siza has carried out in recent years, I would tend toward this small Carlos Ramos Pavilion in Porto's School of Architecture (1985–1986). Here again he was faced with limitations imposed by the surroundings, and responded with an approach he had tested before: reduce the virtual dimensions of a long bay by folding it to a U shape around a courtyard. Where lies the origin of the architecture? In the void of the courtyard? In the subtle manipulation of a distorted perspective created by an inversion of terms? To be sure, asymmetry prevails in this space: the corners are diverse; the projections protecting the windows defy any reading based on regularity; the openings shift along the facade, disregarding any set geometry, etc. Nevertheless some symmetries exist, introduced with deliberation and subtlety, such as those produced in the corners by the entrance staircases and the lavatories.

If you take a good look at the work, you'll see that I'm not exaggerating. It's small and simple, but the architecture is intense, full of events incessantly drawing our attention. Siza makes efficient use of ambivalence. The figures are simple, elemental, yet one perceives an instability that makes them captivatingly unique. An example of this is seen in the photograph of the inverse perspective created by the courtyard and roof plane with the trees of the garden beyond. The elements of the construction, strict and resistant, are key components of the composition. This is illustrated by the use of pillars or the encounter of the ground level's floor slab with the terrain.

A visit to this pavilion in Porto is recommendable. I am convinced that it always proves rewarding, even if the classic Siza—he of the Beires House, the Banco Borges & Irmão, or the Banco Pinto & Sotto Mayor—seems to have disappeared into thin air. One wonders what happened to those brilliant mechanisms we saw in his early works. Siza here has dispensed with

243

**71-74** Carlos Ramos Pavilion, School of Architecture, Porto, 1985–1986

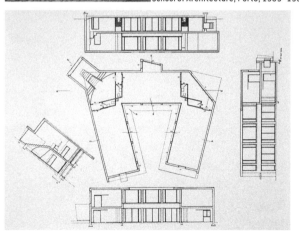

cuts, interstitial spaces, encounters, dislocations, and the like, to focus on the most elemental of architectural strokes, the outline of the floor plan. Everything that we can consider anecdotal or accidental has vanished and given way to the strictly essential. And yet with only an admirable control of the floor plan Siza is able to create spatial situations that are full of emotion and interest. Moreover, this pavilion reveals a perverse indulgence in the encounter with the conventional. Weren't we already accustomed to the defenseless abstract walls that defined his volumes? In this pavilion, Siza protects the surfaces by making an assertive slab jut out provocatively. Would there be a more conventional way of using a roof slab? But this is no reason not to describe the architecture as subtle and complex. It may in fact be reason to.

Let's now make a stop along the way. By the mid-eighties Siza was getting a great amount of work, and his projects began to be less singular and more schematic. One might say it was simply his drawings that were getting schematic. In my opinion, however, if the drawings are schematic, so are the projects. Architecture then becomes "characters in search of an author," elements/characters he knows well that later take shape in the interior spaces, whether through skylights, structural elements, or exaggerated architectural figures that are not hard to identify from his previous works. So it is that looking at Siza's more recent works is like watching a drama or a comedy. What counts is the invention of the plot that brings to life the characters acting out the scene, the architecture around us. This architecture is born occasionally without that sense of reality that was responsible for the freshness of his early works. In my opinion, Siza's architecture gains in autonomy, but loses that spontaneous contact with reality that characterized it before. Each of the architectural characters he presents, meaning the spaces and images of his architecture, remains important, and we are able to understand their lively dialogue. But it

**75** Centro Cultural de la Defensa (project), Madrid, 1988–1989

is all inevitably spoiled the moment the architectural stage is put in a place and subjected to reality. The artificiality of the project then comes to the fore, and this is when we feel a certain longing for an earlier Siza.

**75** What I've just been saying can be applied to the sophisticated project for the Centro Cultural de la Defensa in Madrid (1988–1989). We won't dwell on it now. Let this be an opportunity for private reflection.

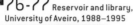
**76-77** Reservoir and library, University of Aveiro, 1988–1995

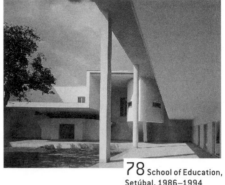
**78** School of Education, Setúbal, 1986–1994

## 24

**76-77** The library for the University of Aveiro (1988–1995) is a very interesting project, both in plan and in section. We quickly note, however, that it offers no surprises, that Siza here uses familiar tools. By now he is an author who knows how his audience will react. Whereas his early works needed an audience, or were to be understood as unsuspected experiences that were set in motion by the presence of an audience, now things work the other way around, with spaces whose impact we could predict. The windows are attractive, they could be considered new versions of the *fenêtre en longueur*, masterful replicas of Le Corbusier. But what are these brilliant accents for, if the architect fails to maintain the character of public space throughout the project? As we were saying before, reality, the presence of the ordinary, the instrumental condition of the building prevails, counteracting the most valuable aspects of this architecture.

**78** In the School of Education in Setúbal (1986–1994) we find the same formal mechanism that appeared in the courtyard of the pavilion for Porto's school of architecture. Once in a while there are sophisticated episodes, but the project also suffers from a schematism that is patent in the drawings.

**79-84** Galician Center of Contemporary Art, Santiago de Compostela, 1988–1993

**79-84** With the Galician Center of Contemporary Art (1988–1993) Siza again showed his mastery in blending a building into its environment. He established a relation between the masses of the new construction and the facades of the Convent of Santo Domingo de Bonaval by creating an intense urban ambit in which a distinctive material, granite, becomes the protagonist. The sharp contrast between the roofs of the convent and the flat roof of the center clearly reflects distance in time, while the masses, similar in proportion, speak of the stability of spaces. Finally, the impenetrability of the convent's volume, a solid without fissures, contrasts with the epithelial character of the granite of the center, a building one perceives from the start as a play of voids. Convent and center jointly enjoy the green slopes of an abandoned cemetery. The masterful lines of Siza's walls define a subtle geometry that dissolves in the preexisting network of paths and grids. Siza skillfully turned the broad ambit composed of the convent, the center, and the new park into a single whole.

In my opinion, Siza's real feat in Santiago is this capacity to embrace different architectures in one whole. The museum is full of that "aroma of architecture" we mentioned before, that presence of architecture as a perceptible phenomenon which we have so often seen in his work. Now, however, above all, we can sense his mastery over the material he works with. Gone is that sense of risk of his earlier works, where bona fide accidents gave rise to the architecture. The accidents are now simply architectural inventions, rhetorical games, that no longer make us think of the inevitability of the design, or of architecture's capacity to address and reconcile opposites. How else do we interpret the artificial slot that produces the metallic beam that supports the wall shaping the portico? What other meaning can we give the slanting lintel accompanying the ramp? The center is full of interventions of this kind. They continuously attract our attention, even if we consider some unnecessary.

The interior spaces are very beautiful, though much of what's already been said can be applied to them. The efficiency of obliqueness as a space-generating mechanism comes to the fore in the dramatic and always well-resolved meetings of stark surfaces. The museum as an architectural experience first. Or architecture at its purest as a frame for works of art. So it is that many things considered important in museum architecture, such as lighting, ceiling height, and routes, are not that important in the Galician Center of Contemporary Art. The ceilings of some of the rooms are dubious, if these rooms are to be places in which to hang paintings and display artworks. The measures are not always adequate, the itineraries not always clear. In my view, the center is more a collector's unique and private house than a public space. Perhaps the house that Siza envisioned as his fantastic "imaginary museum"? Despite all these reservations, I cannot forget the emotion of discerning the city of Santiago through the building's sophisticated openings.

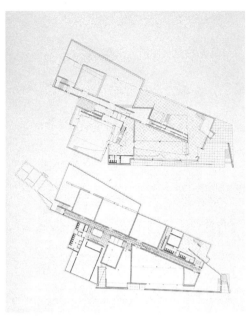

**79-84** Galician Center of Contemporary Art, Santiago de Compostela, 1988–1993

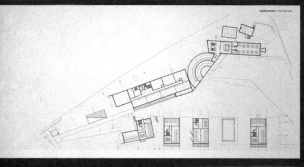

**85-90** School of Architecture, Porto, 1985–1996

**85-90** This larger project for Porto's School of Architecture, finished in 1996, is perhaps the work that most clearly represents the latest phase of Siza's career. An architecture of architectures: this is perhaps the way to define a school that endeavors to teach the discipline. There are no more conflicts. Whereas it was still possible to think in terms of conflict when he built his earlier pavilion for the school, which was about reducing the scope of intervention and thereby improving the open spaces, here the buildings' relationship to their environs is less important. What matters is the drama, or hitting upon the personality of the characters that appear. Because of the pace at which he must work, Siza has to be schematic, and the result is an eminently narrative architecture. He manipulates characters that are almost anthropomorphic, equipped with eyes, noses, and mouths, figures alluding to the history of modern architecture. Without a doubt such manipulation warns us that modernity has given way to the ambiguous situation of turn-of-the-century postmodernism. By leaning so much on the diverse character that the architectures (or characters) acquire, a certain literary tone appears that heretofore was absent in Siza's work. And it is this cutting edge that makes the architecture something of interest. This is no longer pure architectural experience, but an intellectual game. Architecture of architectures. Architecture of references. One is attracted to the provocative simplicity of the characters and the feigned awkwardness of the design of the elements. If we consider the sudden appearance of a near-Venturian canopy, the exaggerated breaks in the corridors, the oblique windows, the conventional frames, and if we remember what Siza's career has been before this, his virtuous design abilities, we know these are play times and that Siza indulges in drawing architecture with his left hand. We all know that he could do it with his right hand, but maybe some wouldn't forgive him for it.

In Porto, the architecture Siza has so accustomed us to lives side by side with this new, turn-of-the-century sensibility. Maybe this camouflage is necessary for a smooth transition from the architecture of the second half of the twentieth century to the one that people of the twenty-first will soon be initiating.

# FRANK O. GEHRY

Of all the architects whose works we are examining in these lectures, perhaps Frank Gehry made the clearest and most decisive breakthrough in the seventies. I believe it can be stated, to wide consensus, that his work has been the most influential in the eighties. Let me begin this lecture with a long quote from an article I wrote on Gehry for the magazine *A&V Monografías*. Reading it over again, I thought the ideas presented remain valid, and would serve well as an introduction to a review of Gehry's work.

**You can't talk about Frank Gehry without immediately mentioning his city, Los Angeles.** *[Actually he was born in Toronto in 1929. He lived in several cities, studied on the East Coast, then settled in the city that can now be considered his own.]* **. . . Los Angeles is, first and foremost, the epitome of mobility, a celebration of individual rights and liberties. The automobile encourages such mobility and becomes something like a last physical redoubt for the individual, assuming, so to speak, the role of a protective shield that allows him to exercise his rights and liberties.** *[The car, as it were, as something that ultimately protects and defends us, our last shell of privacy, our most personal possession. As guarantor of our ultimate and most personal rights, the car becomes something more than a mere instrument. The car becomes a symbol of a way of understanding society and individuals' relation to it.]* **The city reflects this omnipresence of the automobile, and the result is an image in which freeways stand out and dominate a topography hidden under an infinite cloak of one-family homes that flaunt the diversity of their occupants.**

**If in traditional cities continuity rests in what is built, in Los Angeles continuity lies in movement. The built domain expresses the pluralism of those divided into diverse social groups and immersed in the unceasing flow of automobiles. A pluralism that without a doubt reflects the ethnic diversity of American society, but which clearly also reminds us of the unyielding determination of Americans in defending individual rights. High on this list is personal expression through one's dwelling, which implies the right to an architecture understood as the unmistakable manifestation of every citizen's own aesthetics, a refusal to accept formal obstacles leading to unity of style, a last wish of an ecumenical culture.**

**But along with such pluralism one must stress the importance of the**

ephemeral in a city like this, the awareness everyone there has of the perishability and volatility of things, a certain sense of obsolescence linked more to consumerism than to any finality or teleological view of the universe. One could say that mortality and mobility are complementary terms, or, as it were, that one follows the other. Needless to say, such ephemerality includes architecture. Everything in Los Angeles, even that which is built, is in constant motion. Constant change creates a climate of absolute freedom from norms, and to such an extent that L.A. can be said to be the paradigm of the "non-norm," proof that the highest of conventions is the lack of them, the "non-convention." Los Angeles is in perpetual transformation, an ever-changing, diverse city where fixed terms of reference do not exist. The architect finds himself without the support ordinarily provided by context, which amounts to saying that his work cannot be taken to be any type of "consolidation." There is nothing to consolidate in Los Angeles. What is more, to "consolidate" would be to negate some of L.A.'s most characteristic attributes and bestow value on permanence, in open contradiction to the changeable, unstable, mobile nature of the city.

So Gehry's architecture starts out by accepting L.A. for what it is. It is based on a desire to respect and maintain the city's structure. This requires a thorough knowledge of the city and the mechanisms it is built with. Gehry's way of integrating himself into the city has nothing to do with camouflage or contextualist procedures. To be contextual in Los Angeles is to ignore context. Gehry's integration is more profound and more radical because it involves building *like* Los Angeles and not simply *in* Los Angeles. His architecture can be interpreted as a reflection on how to build in the city.

And thus the architecture of Frank Gehry, like the architecture of Los Angeles, escapes the monumental, ignores typological criteria, and bears the mark, the stigma, of the temporary, the ephemeral. The architect is not boxed in by circumstances. To him, environmental preexistences do not count: he will respect a way of doing things, a procedure, but never a given environment or context. He goes about his work free of prejudgments, knowing for sure that when he lays a first stone it is the seed of an organism, an organism meant to grow in a future that no one will have any power over. Thus the absence of interest in composition. Form is not something closed and perfect. Few architects are farther from the Platonic ideal than Gehry. With Gehry there is no preliminary idea, there is no vision of what the construction will be. A building is the evolution through time of what originated as a dialogue between primary, elemental shapes. [1]

It might at this point be good to remember the temporal coordinates that surrounded Gehry's beginnings as an architect. Gehry became known as an architect at the end of the seventies. The weaknesses of the postmodern proposals were then starting to come to the fore. To be sure, Michael Graves's building in Portland, Oregon, was received with a lot of enthusiasm in 1982, as were buildings like Philip Johnson's AT&T in 1984, but the postmodernist tendency had definitely lost steam by the mid-eighties, as illustrated by the general disapproval of Graves's project for the Whitney Museum extension. (Let me add that if interest in Graves's architecture waned, even more so the interest in the architecture of his followers at that time.)

In the United States there was a feeling that postmodernism was something too European, too dependent on historic styles. Actually one could detect a certain hidden disdain for history in postmodernism, hence the caricaturist character of postmodernist architecture, but for many American architects, postmodernism meant servitude to classical languages that were unnecessary and obsolete in a society like America's—as had the academicism of McKim, Mead and White at the start of the twentieth century. Curiously, the architects who opposed the postmodernist excesses could themselves be considered Europeanist. Naturally, I am thinking of the Five. To the wide American public, the architects comprising that group were sophisticated intellectuals who, busy as they were in the search for an abstract architecture, and with no other concern than finding meaning for the expression of a language of their own, forgot all about the link to reality that had characterized American architecture since Jefferson's days, and which had made common sense, or pragmatism, its banner.

So when the architecture of Frank Gehry burst onto the American scene, breaking away as much from the historicist endeavors of the postmoderns as from the linguistic pursuits of the Five, the American public took it as a breath of fresh air. It was like the straightforward view that is only seen by those who

1 Rafael Moneo, "Permanencia de lo efímero. La construcción como arte trascendente," in *A&V Monografías de Arquitectura y Vivienda* 25, "Frank Gehry 1985–1990" (Madrid: Arquitectura Viva, 1990), pp. 9–12. See pp. 83–84 for English version: "Permanence of the Ephemeral: Building as Transcendental Art," trans. Gina Cariño. The asides in italics are Rafael Moneo's.

look at things with total freedom, unencumbered by the prejudgments that convention imposes. Gehry's image was that of the pioneer, the free spirit who takes it upon himself to invent a new architecture. American culture is recognized for its pragmatism and immediacy. Gehry's architecture is, in a nutshell, an expression of the individualism of Los Angeles, an individualism that in the final analysis is the greatest stamp of the glory of American society. In this way, his position is diametrically opposed to Rossi's. The Italian architect anxiously pursued a collective architectural expression, the anonymous architecture of a society that gives no protagonism to the individual. In contrast, Gehry's architecture reflects and celebrates American individualism. It shouldn't be forgotten that the eighties were to be the years of a profound affirmation of Americanism.

Interpreting Gehry's work in Americanist terms helps us view his work as that of an architect primarily interested in showing "how things are done." In the previous lecture we came to the conclusion that Siza's endeavor is to give poetry a presence in the built realm, but without showing the cards he uses to make that happen. Gehry, in contrast, is concerned with the materiality of "doing," and with showing us "how." The act of "doing" prevails. Never mind if the circumstances surrounding the "doing" are not given much importance. To build in Los Angeles is to start from zero, like working on a tabula rasa. Again contrary to Siza, who always refers to the reality he started from, finding in it all the elements needed to sustain an architecture that is, by extension, poetic. The other side of the coin: Gehry does not look to the city for support or justification of what he will be building in it. He does not take surrounding circumstances into account, nor does he work with types, images, or preconceived ideas of how a building should be. In his own words, **"What I like doing best is breaking down the project into as many separate parts as possible. . . . So instead of a house being one thing, it's ten things. It allows the client more involvement."** [2] For Gehry, this rupture of the oneness of a work is not a merely aesthetic matter. It has other important implications. Above all, it allows a freer analysis of the program. Gehry likes to come across as a practical architect who respects programs and budgets and is useful to the client. Contrary to what some think, his houses are not objects for purely aesthetic satisfaction. Whatever they may look like, they address the

**2** Frank Gehry, from an interview with Barbaralee Diamonstein in her *American Architecture Now* (New York: Rizzoli, 1980).

wishes and requirements of their owners. They comply with a program. Whereas for Siza place is important, for Gehry the fundamental thing is the program. When presented with a program, he proceeds to dismember it, a process that his language reflects with utmost clarity, and that gives rise to a concept transcending fragmentation and rupture. The elements Gehry works with do not result from rupture of the unitary. More than fragmentation and rupture, we ought to talk about the moment at which independent elements, members of diverse organisms, are put together.

So Gehry starts out by dismembering a program. A house is dismantled, and uses are identified with forms. Living room, kitchens, bedrooms, workshops, etc., are associated with cubes, cylinders, pyramids, hemispheres, etc., the elements that make up the construction. The architect knows these elements well, and how to build each of them. They are abstract geometrical shapes. Unlike Rossi's architecture, which is essentially representational, Gehry's is abstract. Since it doesn't always have figurative references, in a way it could be interpreted as architecture that respects modern tradition. We will elaborate on this point later on.

When the program has been broken apart and the elemental geometrical figures that will form the construction have been identified, the architect subjects them to the forces of the environment in which they will have to live. It's in this way that the architecture is consolidated. In a way, the real job of the architect is to "detect" how the elements will position themselves under the effects of a field of forces. But how exactly does Gehry, as a professional, confront a project? How does he "detect" the place to be occupied by each figure? How does he locate the right position of each of the primary elements he is building with? Eager to have a presence in the construction, Gehry tries to eliminate any kind of mediation. He wants his work to manifest itself fully in the construction. The question of the architect's presence, both direct and indirect, is resolved in the process of constructing the model. Once he has defined the pieces that will accommodate the different parts of the program, Gehry is ready to enter the battlefield of architecture in earnest. He anticipates the future through the model. The model becomes the vehicle of the work. The architect touches the pieces, feels them, and in this direct contact with the pieces the form of the construction is forged. It is in manipulating the predefined shapes that Gehry detects the place to be occupied by each in the whole, and discerns the potential of each shape to break, erode, etc. Such proximity to the gestation of the architecture suits the architect. The idea is to eliminate outside mediation or interference. For Gehry, hence, models are not mere reductions—or versions at another scale—of future reality. They are architectures in themselves. The challenge of the architect is to maintain the immediacy of the model in the actual building. Inevitably some is lost.

Previously we saw the ambiguity involved in Eisenman's passing from one scale to another: architecture was removed from matters of scale, so to speak. Not so with Gehry, who likes to be bound to the construction in the same way that he is bound to the model. Salvation lies in maintaining the immediacy of the object. Gehry likes to maintain the aura of the individual and unique that accompanies any work of art. Paradoxically, the weakness of his work is offset by its very nature as a singular, unique work of art. Indeed his works are fragile, especially the earliest ones. His work is weak in the most literal sense of the word, as befits anything that is part of the ephemeral and ever-changing context of Los Angeles. And a fragile object will only survive if considered a work of art. In L.A., a building deserves to be preserved only if it is considered a work of art. The durability of a building doesn't come so much from the resistance of the materials used, but from the value conferred upon it by its being considered a work of art. Paradoxically, spirit lasts longer than matter.

To simplify things, we could say Gehry works like a sculptor. We could talk about how he works. Nevertheless, it is easier to zero in on what he ignores. Gehry ignores traditional representation. In his work, the building, the architecture, is not thought out in terms of floor plans, sections, and axonometries. In discussing Eisenman, I stressed representation being so linked to his architecture that there are moments in his work when representation and architecture become one. In contrast, Gehry dispenses with all linkages between architecture and representation. Gehry prefers to go straight to the point, namely the architecture, the ultimate reality, skipping the intermediate rung of representation. Through deliberately imprecise sketches, he intuits what the masses of his building will be, and proceeds to construct the model. Drawing the floor plans, and especially the sections, is a formality to comply with, but it never occurs to him to make them the origin of the architecture. In the final analysis, to make architecture is to know how to build a model.

This approach to construction implies a prior knowledge of the techniques of constructing elemental figures. Gehry is an experienced professional who knows the procedures practiced in the building industry of the United States. He had his own wanderings in the desert during the fifteen or twenty years of professional life that preceded his being discovered. During this period he got to learn all about commercial architecture, architecture totally devoid of the sophistication that would come later. He got well acquainted with the business of the architect and the techniques of American construction—techniques we can describe, to be sure, as simple and restricted. American construction is much simpler than one would assume. The conventions to respect, always linked to the tyranny of the powers that be, are imposed with extreme rigor. So it is that innovation and change are much harder to carry out in the United States than in other countries. Gehry learned his lessons well during those dark early years of his career, so when the time came for him to manifest the meaning of his architecture, he had no trouble constructing elemental figures. Using the conventional techniques he had learned before, he went on to build his prisms, cubes, cylinders, and hemispheres. Gehry also knew the structure of the balloon frame, the kind of cladding he could use, etc. He was familiar with industrial products, metal plates, etc. Gehry is against fiction and the simulacrum. American architects of the seventies constantly flirted with the simulacrum. Poststructuralist architects such as Eisenman like to think that architecture is a world of fiction, and the postmodernists, including Venturians, indulge in another kind of fiction by turning the figurative into camouflage. Gehry is more modern in that authenticity matters to him. His architecture never falls into the trap of fiction, and it never indulges in simulacra.

This leads us to something that is key to an understanding of Gehry's architecture: his need to feel the physicality, the reality, of the construction. It is important to speak of the value he puts on materials. Gehry is a builder in the greatest sense. He enjoys manipulating the materials that the building industry puts at his disposal. Like some artists of his generation, he explores the potential that materials have when not used conventionally. Hence the continuous exploration of textures in his work. A fresh look at construction and materials creates a new architecture. Gehry has on more than one occasion said that he prefers buildings while under construction: "Buildings under construction look nicer than buildings finished. . . . Buildings that are just done by ordinary people—they look like hell when they're finished—but when they're under construction they look great."[3] There is a whole logic of construction inherent in the sight of an unfinished building that vanishes completely when we have before us the finished work, the construction that has reached a permanent state of stability. Take the case of this building we are in right now, the Círculo de Bellas Artes by Antonio Palacios. There is no more room for imagining the whole construction process lying behind those plaster columns decked with moldings. Yet there was a time, during construction, when the logic of that process was patent: when the columns were still pillars made of steel profiles and the absence of a false ceiling left a system of vaults and beams exposed. We could then have asked the architect: Don't you think the essential elements of the architecture—contiguities, proportions, etc.—are already present? Isn't it therefore unnecessary to go on? Why pursue an academic final point? Gehry might have advised the architect Palacios to hold it. He is accustomed to the fact that nothing ever reaches a goal, or definitive final point, in Los Angeles. Materially he would like his buildings to stay at their most essential. That is, unfinished. The aesthetics of the unfinished as an objective per se. Gehry is very familiar with metal *déployé*, plywood boards, new paint, stones. He likes to maintain the presence of materials in the finished work. In fact he does things in such a way that they are seen, perceived, in all their splendor. Of late, in his studio, computer-aided designs go directly to robotics workshops. In this way, the design tool has a direct bearing on the construction process. Unlike Eisenman, Gehry is not too interested in the concept of process—that is, in the sequence arising from the mental elaboration of the project. What he wants is a process that traps the architect between design and construction. In discussing Siza there was a need to introduce the concept of distance between the architect and his work. Gehry tries to ignore it, or eliminate it altogether. He would like to be able to work like his artist friends. That is, put on work clothes and execute his projects with

3 "'No, I'm an Architect': Frank Gehry and Peter Arnell, a Conversation," in *Frank Gehry, Buildings and Projects*, ed. Peter Arnell and Ted Bickford (New York: Rizzoli, 1985), p. xiii.

his own hands—without intermediaries, whether drawings or builders.

In sum, Gehry dismantles a program, identifies the figures he wants to build with, and explores the incentives that the site offers. But soon he discovers how important the notion of arbitrariness is in architecture. We have been insisting on it in these lectures. Rossi was very conscious of the idea that architecture rests arbitrarily on figures and images. His entire oeuvre is a recognition of this arbitrariness. Eisenman understands arbitrariness in another way, but arbitrary certainly are the decisions that govern the languages we find at the origin of his architecture. Siza may be less arbitrary, because his respect for the contingent prevents him from indulging in a capricious invention of forms. He doesn't feed on forms he is unfamiliar with, or doesn't grasp the meaning of. He doesn't let these become the support of his architecture. Gehry himself stayed clear of the arbitrary early on in his career, when he would materialize specific architectures out of a set catalog of elemental figures. But later, as the method consolidated and expanded and he learned that any form could be turned into architecture—thanks to his desire that his models immediately take on the character of architectures—he discovered the unavoidable presence of the arbitrary, and this discovery let him witness the tyranny of the architect. He was overcome by mixed feelings. On one hand, awareness of the arbitrary made him believe that the immediacy he desired was possible. On the other hand, the anguish of seeing a form stripped of its content, of seeing his fish turned into a discotheque, transported him to unknown territory where everything is possible.

Gehry has reacted to this unexpected discovery by trying to show us that his work does not belong to the conventional built realm. In other words, he does not want his works to be taken for buildings. He would like them to be seen as something else. As we've said before, the permanence of his buildings, their duration in time, comes from their being considered works of art. And indeed they have been taken for art by contemporaries, both institutional and private, who have followed his work en masse in recent years. Gehry's success has been spectacular. Nowadays there is probably no architect as recognized as he is, and this explains his long list of works, which are never easy to examine with conventional critical devices. But despite a consistent method, one can discern a certain evolution in his work, and this is what I want clarified by the end of this lecture. The fact is that I've noticed a curious change of approach in his recent works. Particularly since the Vitra project, I've observed an interest in a peculiar vision of the meaning of a unitary, continuous architecture. Perhaps Gehry has perceived symptoms of exhaustion in the mechanism of recomposing the fragmentary, in the procedure that follows the dismantling of a program, and is now attracted to an architecture where a breath of the unitary makes itself felt. It must be understood that such desire for unity has nothing to do with a totalitarian architecture. What I mean will be clearer when I associate the concepts of continuity and unity to that of movement. Of course there is a contradiction of terms between architecture and movement. But there is in fact a certain agitation—or movement—in Gehry's latest buildings that is of utmost interest to us. In my opinion, there is something new here. It is an idea of movement that we may have had premonitions of in the undulating facades of the baroque architects of Italy, Germany, or Austria, but some projects of Alvar Aalto may be a closer precedent. Gehry has sometimes spoken of movement in architecture as an alternative to ornament. So it is that we are witnessing an attempt to address what has been a constant in twentieth-century architecture: the inevitable, inexorable, and irreversible death of ornament. The agitation or movement that Gehry seems to be looking for in his latest works has little to do with the fractures, fissures, ruptures, and folds that characterize a good part of contemporary architecture. The abstraction underlying those experiences is giving way to a new organicism, a new image of architecture, an architecture more aligned with orientations in favor of life. Let us now take a look at what Gehry's career has been and what may still lie ahead.

1 Steeves House (project), 1959

1 This first work, the Steeves House, is from the year 1959. Gehry had studied on the East Coast; after taking his master's in urban design at Harvard, he moved west to Los Angeles, where an uncle of his was involved in the movie industry. So it was in L.A. that he got his first clients. The Steeves House speaks of its place and time. It has echoes of Wright, and it is the result of superposing two identical pieces, as if an allusion to the convenience of repetition. The cruciform structure is of unmistakable Wrightian origins, as are some Orientalist elements. This is a very strict architecture, one that manipulates form through a geometry governed by symmetry. But, though designed at a time when Kahn dominated the architectural scene, it is fundamentally a Californian house. It has the lightness of wooden constructions, and the lightness of an entire building tradition whose models are the architectures of Schindler and Neutra.

2-3 The Danziger House of 1965 is a more sophisticated work. Rising in the midst of the urban jungle of Los Angeles, indifferent to any nearby stylistic reference, it was for Gehry an opportunity to declare which architectures he was most attracted to. We could again mention Schindler, the restless Austrian architect who had moved to California and taken to Wright and Japanese architecture, and we shouldn't forget his compatriot Loos. Schindler's intense view of space is also present in this austere architecture whose most distinct feature is a firm handling of volumes and openings. The Danziger House speaks of an architect who knows what he's doing but has yet to develop a language of his own. This is still a referential architecture. Comparing it to one of Siza's early

2-3 Danziger House, Hollywood, California, 1964–1965

works, the Magalhães House, we have to admit that the work of the Portuguese architect is more refined, more elaborate, and more complete. More than detail, what's attractive about the Danziger House is the force of its form. In this way, it prefigures Gehry's later works. In other words, Siza's architecture reached maturity very early on, whereas Gehry's initial works presented a series of intentions that would become explicit over the years, gradually giving rise to a language and expression of his own.

4-6 The first project in which Gehry openly drew up a distinctive architectural program was this one for a house of the California artist Ron Davis, built in 1972. In his paintings, Davis arranges objects in broad perspectives of open, distorted spaces. Gehry tried to come up with something similar. The house can be said to have an open plan, and its large spaces foster a life of few restrictions. The house is therefore not a machine for living, but a place for life. A slanting, uninterrupted roof unifies the different spaces while enriching and energizing them through a series of cuts and fissures. Gehry worked on the roof with the freedom of an artist. From the very start of his career Gehry wanted to be close to the art world; just as painters of the period injected their works with materials and textures that were foreign to the canvas, so Gehry set about to discover and exploit materials that industry produced but construction had yet to learn to assimilate. In this house Gehry showed the extent of his interest in the potential of the most diverse materials. To him, architecture would always be linked to the materiality of construction.

4-6 Ron Davis House, Malibu, California, 1968–1972

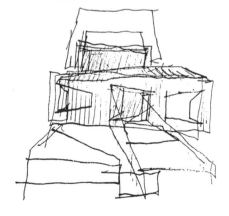

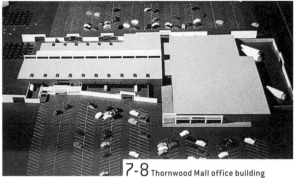

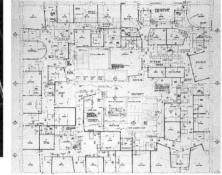

7-8 Thornwood Mall office building
(project), Park Forest South, Illinois, 1976

7-8 Gehry somewhere refers to himself as a survivor, as one of those persons who across generations of immigrants stay afloat in the waters of history. Whereas Rossi was always inclined to magnify his personal drama, Gehry renounces the heroic status, and as a survivor he accepts any kind of work. Thornwood Mall of 1976 is an ordinary office building with a parking lot. The construction is very simple, although a certain formal play learned in the Ron Davis house helps break up the spaces and soften the tyranny of the orthogonal. The floor plan is drawn up with total freedom, subject only to the specifications of the brief. It may be relevant to speak of an aggressive smugness in the intensive use of space, exaggerating architecture's servitude to the system. The Americanism we mentioned before is loud and clear. Function prevails over aesthetics.

**9-10** Santa Monica Place,
Santa Monica, California, 1972–1980

9-10 In the very celebrated Santa Monica Place (1972–1980), Gehry seemed to be saying: if Venturi talks about defying the stylistic puritanism of modern architecture by putting graphics on buildings, I'm going further and turning a whole building into a giant sign. Letters—graphics—appropriate the entire facade. The architecture is the signage, nothing else, and it dissolves in the jungle of messages that L.A. is. We saw how Peter Eisenman manipulated the volumes of the Columbus Convention Center, how he tried to blend the masses into the context through a camouflage operation. The idea of the "whole" prevailed. Ignoring content, Eisenman planted the convention center onto an existing context by "remaking" it in terms of respect for form. Here Gehry does exactly the opposite. He constructs and organizes the interior spaces according to the logic dictated by the shopping center program, then wraps the inert built mass with a veil of red metal. The building is present in the city not as an architectural form or gesture, but as a huge sign saying "Santa Monica Place."

**11-12** Cabrillo Marine Museum,
San Pedro, California, 1979

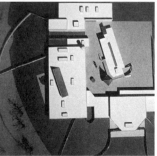

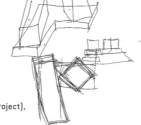

**13-14** Familian House (project), Santa Monica, California, 1979

**11-12** The Cabrillo Marine Museum in San Pedro, California, a 1979 project, is a small building with a large presence. The roof illustrates how Gehry makes his architecture transcend mere compliance with the brief. Elements that are conventional, commercial, and modest—a window, for instance—are invigorated by clever screens or diaphragms that cover and transform them. The screens and diaphragms are made of industrial materials, and the unexpected use of them here captures the attention of the spectator, turning an otherwise common building into an interesting architecture.

**13-14** But it was in a series of private houses—such as the Familian House in Santa Monica, the Gunther House, the Wagner House, and his own house, the Gehry House, all from around 1978—that the direction his investigations would take first became truly clear.

The Familian House was Gehry's first exploration of what a building can be if stripped of a skin. What lay behind the stuccos of his friends in the New York Five? We see wooden frameworks, panels of *déployé* metal, insulation elements, etc. Beneath the surface is that world of construction that Gehry is so drawn to, and which makes it possible to think of his work as an anatomical exploration. The world of "muscles and bones" underlying the image of architecture is what interests him. Slanted elements appear to prop up and brace the verticals. A marked sense of instability pervades the built reality, manifesting an approach not far removed from provocation. It comes from an attitude that takes pride in individual freedom, in this case that of the builder. A kind of freedom, to be sure, that differs much from what we saw in Siza's works. The Portuguese architect transmits all personal baggage into an object that, in the end, comes across as autonomous, whereas Gehry has always been determined to show that the architect has ultimate responsibility over the work, which must then be understood as an expression of individual freedom. Today we are shocked at the capricious constructions of deconstructivist architecture, yet Gehry's projects of the seventies prompted reactions not so much of anxiety as of surprise and admiration.

Curiously, this architecture takes off from the orthodox modern. In the Familian House, it isn't difficult to identify the original cube or discern Corbusian references in the white prismatic elements. But the Platonic phantom of orthodox modern architecture that is at the origin of Gehry's works vanishes in the field of forces he operates in. The original image distorts when it comes to capturing light or orienting the house toward specific views or points. The two volumes that give rise to the Familian House fragment and rupture, and it is in the celebration of the process of fragmentation and rupture that the building finds its raison d'être.

**15-19** With the experience acquired in the Familian House and the houses that preceded it, he set about designing his own, the Gehry House, with even more efficiency. In the previous projects there was something artificial about the way a cube was made to break apart. In this case the starting point was an existing building, a house bought by his wife Berta. Gehry presents himself as a regular American attached to his home and family. He is happy with his wife's real estate transaction and doesn't want to ruin something she has purchased so enthusiastically. He won't break up the cube. Instead he says: well, I'll fix it up. And he gets to work. Pleased to show himself as a carpenter, he doesn't come up with a replica of the Laurentian Library, but he gives the four steps leading up to the house a formal quality. Not in a static, ontologically impeccable way, as Tessenow would have. Gehry truly puts movement in the steps and delights in making the bottom one concrete. You wipe off the dirt on your shoes there before taking the other steps to a door that, incidentally, either forms part of the skin of the facade or is an extension of the step panels, one can't be sure which.

Later he would protect and enlarge the house with the same metallic fabric that he had used for the studio of Ron Davis. This is perforated when necessary,

**15-19** Gehry House, Santa Monica, California, 1977–1978

as when a window needs a view. Gehry has no problems doing this. In his opinion, it may be a Corbusian window, but beside it are all the other windows. A concrete wall with a finish doesn't bother him either, as we saw that it bothers Siza. Gehry doesn't mind a wall having the finish that custom claims for it. So he puts a finish on, with no scruples about it not suiting the corrugated sheet of the facade.

The house includes the exterior spaces that the metallic screen creates. Gehry is good at stretching relatively small spaces, at creating areas that are halfway between interior and exterior. As in Santa Monica Place and

the Familian House, here he amused himself with the surface, the skin, once again exploring and dissecting it and displaying its layers. Gehry likes to display building elements, those that always captivate him in construction sites and which have made him profess a preference for buildings before they are finished. In all this is a certain didactic mission, a desire to show us how conventional architecture ultimately betrays the construction. It is necessary to rescue the beauty of the construction, and this is done by shedding aesthetic prejudices. This is what Gehry wants in his architecture. He must have wondered: how can those people have enjoyed the view of the sky and those trees while the house was going up, only to lose it in the end? So Gehry opened the kitchen ceiling. Then he would have formulated similar questions at the sight of a wall. To liven up that plane, why buy an Ellsworth Kelly painting for hundreds of thousands of dollars when it is in my power to cut a hole in the wall and put in windows that would serve the same function? Why not demand such things from finished houses? Gehry believes it is possible. There is an optimism in him that we don't frequently find in other architects. Compared to Gehry, Siza is a stoic whose architecture has the grimness of a Seneca or Lucan.

**15-19** Gehry House, Santa Monica, California, 1977–1978

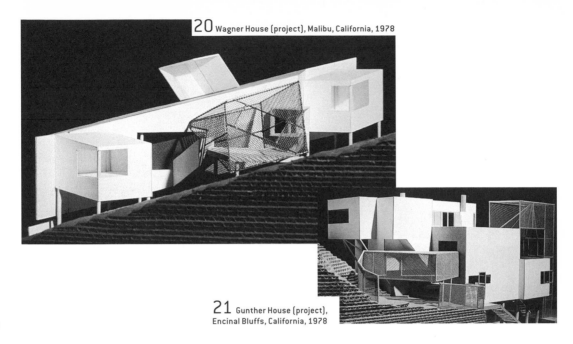

20 Wagner House (project), Malibu, California, 1978

21 Gunther House (project), Encinal Bluffs, California, 1978

**20-21** The Gunther House and the Wagner House were never built, but the projects drew on the principles used in Gehry's own house. Topography contributes to the instability of the volumes, which are antithetical to the architecture aspired to by his New York friends, preoccupied as they were with the continuity of modern architecture. These architectures of Gehry always have an organic component, a certain animistic air that exempts them from all conventional references. And yet the elements and materials are taken from the most frequented and conventional sectors of the construction industry. In any case, an artistic orientation distances these houses from the ordinary and, given modern architecture's insistence on the strictly functional, gives them a fresh, provocative, schism-creating tone that enraptures the observer. The viewer of these models is quickly captivated by the unexpected way in which the volume accommodates the openings, or by the seeming eagerness to systematize the use of columns, to the point that they become canonical in the corners.

22-23 Spiller House,
Venice, California, 1980

22-23 Gehry was beginning to be seen around Los Angeles. Aware of the arbitrariness of the city's stylistic attachments, he tackled the Spiller House—situated between a residence of the first half of the twentieth century and another of the second half—with utmost freedom. He also demonstrated a familiarity with interstitial spaces by skillfully placing the volume of the new construction right in between. The importance of intermediate spaces in climates like southern California's comes to the fore here in the form of the courtyard. On the other hand, built in 1980, the Spiller House shows a Gehry interested in flirting with "cultured" architecture. In a way it pays homage to modern architecture. But modernity's plain terse surfaces here erode into the stairs, windows, and cracks that are encrusted in them and that quickly become the protago-nists in the building, for they are what imperiously claim our attention. Color is important in this architecture. The neutral bluish gray renders it completely nondependent on the two houses flanking it. Gehry knew that independence would not be achieved through mere modesty of means. The Spiller House rose on a lot conditioned by the presence of older buildings on the adjacent parcels, but thanks to its architectural independence, the house is an interesting piece worthy of our attention.

**24-25** Gehry's works had been well received in the late seventies. With the Benson House of 1979–1984, he set out to make an entire manifesto against the postmodernism of the day. But first let's look at the drawing. Far removed from the Giacomettian character of Siza's drawings, it is a reminder of the way Gehry dismantles a program into different volumes. We identify a tower and a lower construction, both ready for the uses that have been assigned them. We can even guess from the picture what the materials will be. But there is no indication of perspective, nor any use of shadows. All the drawing tells us is that the house will be set on *pilotis*. Everything is vague. It's as if Gehry can't or doesn't want to anticipate the architecture, as if he has to or prefers to wait until the very moment of construction. So what he does in the meantime is draw our attention to singular elements by designing them with special care, giving them an imperious presence. Take the case of the undulating shingles coating an otherwise plain construction, or the strong image of the exterior staircase banister. There it's as if Gehry were saying: if the regulations demand protection on the stairs, I'll put protection, but make people forget there are regulations. Hence the exaggeration,

**24-25** Benson House, Calabasas, California, 1979–1984

to the point that the railings take on a leading role in the house. The arbitrary rearrangement of the sections and the emphasis placed on displaying the most elemental construction together result in the appearance of a safety element with a formal and figurative value of its own. Gehry knew that building the banister conventionally would have yielded something we expected, and not a new episode which in taking shape would be able to capture all our attention. Now we understand why Gehry isn't interested in conventional drawings, floor plans and sections. As far as he is concerned, anticipating reality with drawings is not the way to go about architecture. To him, the architectural phenomenon is always close to the direct and immediate. Architecture unfolds in the process of construction.

26-27 Easy Edges and Experimental Edges, 1969–1973, 1979–1982

**26-27** Gehry's interest in materials led him, in the eighties, to what he called Experimental Edges. With his penchant for exploring the potential of new materials, he designed a series of chairs using common corrugated cardboard. There are curious differences among them. Sometimes they are merely translations of old Bauhaus models. Sometimes Gehry seems to have been indulging in deterioration, for we find ourselves looking at objects—furniture pieces—whose patina is its deterioration. But all of them have a fragility not far removed from that of the works of the conceptual artists. Gehry's chairs invite respect, not use. Through subtle design operations with a material normally used for something else, objects originally of purely instrumental value take on the character of works of art.

**28-29** It seems that everything in the House for a Filmmaker project of 1981 is aimed at showing us how Gehry feeds on the production mechanisms of other fields. In this case, it's as if he wants us to see that architecture doesn't differ much from what film directors call montage. The model didactically reveals the house as the result of assembling separate episodes: a studio for the filmmaker to work in when inspired, a kitchen for his culinary passions, a sitting room for friends, a stairway to the attic—all independent scenes joined together to form a house. Architecture, hence, as a montage of diverse experiences and uses. Architecture not so much as landscape (although Le Corbusier's *promenade architecturale* is definitely present here) but as a range of possible activities that give rise to a spatial scheme based on a "script."

But the project also contains a statement on materials that deserves commentary. It's in this project that Gehry explains the shifts in the use

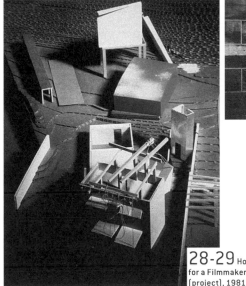

**28-29** House for a Filmmaker (project), 1981

and handling of materials that would henceforth be a characteristic feature of his work. By shifts I mean using new materials in arrangements taken from traditional construction systems. Plywood panels are installed as if they were stone walls, and strips of sealing compound act as mortar joints. The texture of the panels resembles the veining of stone, reinforcing the simulacrum. The new materials outweigh the rhetorical force of the traditional images. Gehry is fully aware of what is happening, and chooses a bright blue sealing compound to avoid confusion. The literalness of the arrangement dissolves in the subtlety of color use. Some of these gimmicks could be dismissed as bordering on postmodernism, and Gehry was therefore operating on slippery ground, but the energy with which he manages these opposites is unmistakable.

30-32 Here now is an example of shapes dictating the construction in a totally arbitrary way, which would lead to a theory of shape in architecture that is detached from any explanation outside of itself. Architects are always trying to escape from the arbitrary, but we ought to admit that arbitrary form lies at the very origin of our work.

Gehry seemed to have arrived at this conclusion when he drew up his 1980 proposal for the Chicago Tribune and renounced the opportunity to formulate a new high-rise structure. With clear intentions of disconcerting and provoking his colleagues, he decided to transform a molding or a baluster, however one looks at it, into a skyscraper. That the idea wasn't that convincing to Gehry himself becomes patent in some of the alternatives he subsequently offered. In one of them, he more imaginatively crowned the building with a newspaper. The formal digression that began with a baluster thus ended up with a newspaper sculpture, in playfully ironic recognition of the importance of the arbitrary in architecture. Here, again, Gehry pursued the path of his artist friends. His proposal for the Chicago Tribune has to be connected to the work of Claes Oldenburg.

## 27

30-32 Competition entry for the Chicago Tribune Tower (project), 1980

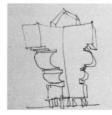
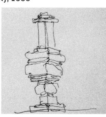

33-34 Follies (project), 1984

**33-34** Three years transpired between the Chicago Tribune project and the Follies, but they are presented together because both say much about Gehry's confidence in the architecture-originating value of shapes. Gehry has frequently talked about his attraction to the fish shape. He sees it as a paradigm of all shapes, and used it here to construct a lamp. In 1983, for an exhibition in Leo Castelli's gallery, Barbara Jakobson asked twelve architects to come up with a capricious invention, or folly.[4] Some conceived pavilions in gardens. Others designed ornamental objects, water watches, the works, but always from and for the world of huge houses where people allow themselves such extravagances. In contrast, Gehry centered on the image of the fish/lamp, anticipating his use of the fish shape—quintessence of the arbitrary form—in larger constructions like the discotheque in Japan and the building in Barcelona's Olympic Port.

**4** B.J. Archer and Anthony Vidler, *Follies: Architecture for the Late Twentieth-Century Landscape* (New York: Rizzoli, 1983).

**35-37** Norton House, Venice, California, 1982–1984

**35-37** Built between 1982 and 1984 on the California beach, the Norton House can be understood as a complete programmatic manifesto. Here it's as if Gehry were telling us that he had the formula to build all the houses he wished. The Norton House is a whole repertoire, or better, a whole synthesis of what can be said with a vocabulary and syntax that he had by then a full grasp of. The house has nothing, but it has everything, and it doesn't suffer the process of miniaturization that the architect had previously used so enthusiastically. There's a ground floor, a floor that is partly a terrace, a watchtower, and one can climb even higher through an exterior staircase. The largest possible domestic program is accommodated in a 4-by-20-meter lot. There is room enough for the theater of a life, and even for the contemplation of the lives of others. Indeed, the Norton House can also be considered a monument to the voyeur. Everything is resolved with humor and with a tinge of aggressiveness if we think of his colleagues, who take great pains to design a handrail.

I understand why many architects find Gehry disturbing. Familiar as he is with all that preoccupies professionals, there are many occasions when he solves a design problem as if saying: I know what you would do, but that's so irrelevant that I'd rather collect capricious elements, which in the end create a more intense architectural atmosphere. Though on a smaller scale, the Norton House—please don't crucify me—has the same architectural ambition as the Villa Savoye or Villa Mairea. One could also take the Norton House as a humorous commentary, a joke. But I can't take it as such when I consider how the architect indulges in the making of the house, how the elements are manipulated, how the materials are handled. Again, to understand how the architecture has come about, it helps to look at the drawing. We saw how Siza's interstitial spaces were empowered phenomenologically. Here we have a Gehry sketch telling us that interstitial spaces are exactly that: interstitial, irrelevant.

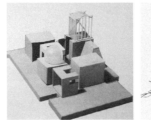 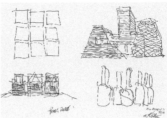

**38-39** Tract House (project), 1982

**38-39** Gehry put his colleagues to shame again in the Tract House of 1982. While they were busy with the nine-square grid, with all the seriousness that the grid and the cube impose, Gehry in his search for the origin of a house was indulging in the most genuine expression of the house, associating elemental figures with particular uses and forms. Subjected to a recomposition process that would give sense both to the parts and to the whole, each of the nine squares forming the nine-square grid acquired

a character of its own in his project—a small courtyard, a room crowned by a hemisphere, another room covered by a lantern, and so on. An exterior area helps the house fit into the urban fabric, establishing the desirable transition between private and public. Of course no one looking at the model misses the fact that one of the pieces is brazenly and deliberately turned over. We hear Gehry saying: don't correct the error, that's how I want it, that's how I like it. Maybe we can interpret such indulgence in the erroneous or ambiguous as proof that ours is not the homogeneous society it was before, and that we must therefore be ever alert for cryptic individual messages.

40-41 California Aerospace Museum and Theater, Los Angeles, 1982–1984

40-41 Because of the publicity Gehry was getting in those years, institutions began to take an interest in his services. So it was that 1984 found him busy with a major commission: the Aerospace Museum in Los Angeles. The sudden change of scale, and possibly also the awe and respect that an institution inspires, might explain the more contained nature of this Gehry work. Definitely it didn't have the intensity of his previous, smaller and more private works.

42-45 Loyola Law School, Los Angeles, 1978–1984

**42-45** The Loyola Law School (1978–1984) in Los Angeles is one of the finest works of the first stage of Gehry's career, which would end in the mid-eighties. Actually it is difficult to classify and catalog his work chronologically, but Loyola marks the apogee of a way of doing things. The assignment was to build a university complex in an area that could be considered degraded, and the challenge rested, precisely, in understanding what could be done there. It is important to acknowledge the awareness of place and the capacity to adjust that characterize Gehry's work. In my opinion, Loyola is the work not of a snob but of a responsible architect. He thinks the way he thinks, and applies the architecture that he believes best addresses the exigencies of a reality he knows well. In this case it seems he was saying: I have to defend myself from the modest circumstances in which I find myself, and what better way to do it than to draw a clear line to separate the classroom and administration building from the rest; this will allow me to give more visibility to the elements of the program that have greater architectural potential, such as the library, the conference room, the student club, etc.; these will take over the open space, which will then connect

with the classroom and administration building via a spectacular staircase. Indeed the staircase is a daring gesture that turns the cheapest windows on the market, those of the administration building, into something else. The staircase plays a key role in relating the different parts of the program to one another, but more importantly, it is the tool Gehry uses to provoke a shift—as I said, the windows are transformed—ultimately making the architecture more dynamic.

Certain postmodernist echoes here lead him to pay tribute to classical architecture, a distant phantom haunting the profession of the law. But it's a frank, explicit allusion that has nothing of the staircase's scenographic force. Climbing the stairs is a worthy experi-

ence. The viewpoints it offers are like those of a movie camera: architecture as a sequence of itself. Gehry doesn't indulge in the promenade. His architecture envelops and surrounds us as if it were alive. Curiously, his architecture can exist on its own; the staircase proves this. In a way, what occurs here is foreseen in the script. There are no surprises: we already had our surprise the first time we saw it. Whereas Siza's architecture needs people for it to acquire its full significance, Gehry's needs no spectators. It is in itself a scenography and needn't know who the actors are.

Everything about Loyola is simple and elemental. The mechanisms of rupture are commonplace, so to speak. And yet the complex, the way each and every one of the pieces helps to create unique places, manages to transform it into something one can recognize as a university campus. The Loyola Law School is much more than a set of buildings. With his architecture, Gehry has been able to create the conditions that make one feel one is in a campus, and this without resorting to the rhetoric of costly materials, and without ignoring the setting. As we have said, Gehry is not a contextual architect. Yet few architects would have handled the commission with the same instinct for what can be done in a neighborhood. Basking in the good fortune of being offered a university project and professing respect for the client institution, many of us would have drawn up an architecture of the "near-sacred" kind. Without disregarding the religious denomination of the client institution—one of the elements of the program is a small chapel—Gehry's architecture skillfully dispenses with affiliations. And so it is that what prevails is the celebration of architecture. In its modest Los Angeles neighborhood, the Loyola Law School seamlessly reproduces the entire architectural scenography of university campuses.

We should also say something about the handling of materials. Still on the confident staircase, one might wonder why the engineer didn't add a couple of inches to the profile. Then the stairs could have been spared all those devices that hold it up. The answer is that Gehry sometimes goes for what looks dificult, as this always brings some added value. And he likes to show that he is not afraid of the difficulties that the reality of the construction might bring. Finally, let's stop and look at how the tower was constructed. Again we see evidence of Gehry's constructive mechanism, but what's surprising now is the way glass is used over the wooden framework. The contrast of glass and wood accentuates the attributes of both materials. Gehry maintains the independence of each of them, and this respect translates into an attractive and ambiguous definition of the architecture. Is the glass a substitute for the surface of a stone wall? And towers generally assign load-bearing responsibilities to their perimeters, but if in this case the perimeter is just a fragile skin, is the resistance of the tower entrusted to the wooden framework? Without a doubt the dialectic between glass and wood, between the virtual and real structure of the tower, contributes to the ambiguity in which lies the lure of this architecture.

**46-47** Expansion of 360 Newbury Street, Boston, 1985–1988

## 28

**46-47** In the enlargement of 360 Newbury Street, Boston (1985–1988), a unique eave totally transforms an early twentieth-century commercial building that must, incidentally, be acknowledged for the perfection of its stonework and its meticulous terra-cotta finishes. It's as if Gehry recognized that its architecture dated back to the Renaissance, and thought that by completing the composition and turning the building into something close to an Italian palace, the eave would justify the filiation. Again I would like to harp on Gehry's constructing architecture directly in the model. There the braces and struts look woody, with no regard for the material they are to be built in, namely steel. As built, their lead-coated copper lining dematerializes them. What matters is the form, which was established when the model was built. Notice the careful design of the corner. True to the avant-garde project of his architecture, Gehry dispenses with traditional examples.

**48-51** The Winton Guest House of 1982–1987, in Minnesota, is a very good example of this way of building in which architecture is consolidated early on in the model itself. One could almost say that construction of the model annuls the need to construct the building. The construction of the model establishes how the building's shape will be manipulated. The mission here was to complete the program of a mansion with a guest pavilion. Gehry decided at the outset that every room should have a character of its own, taking a particular shape and a particular material. Three bedrooms and the cubicle containing the fireplace and chimney surround a communal space crowned irregularly with a pyramid. Gehry arranges and composes the fig-

ures in a way that doesn't differ much from the composition of Morandi still lifes. There is no intention to be organic, no intention to build a whole. We simply feel the proximity of the parts, which pile up to create an image, the image that results from accepting the formal independence of each of the elements. Modesty is something we saw in his earliest projects. The more modest the program, the more intact and fresh his methodological intuition.

The Winton Guest House is one of the best examples of an architecture that is better understood in the model than in the actual building. Contemplating the images, I would even say that the building misrepresents the proposals put forward in the model. When the figures manipulated in the

**48-51** Winton Guest House, Wayzata, Minnesota, 1982–1987

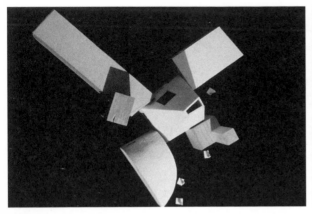

model are transformed into built reality, much of their energy is lost. Something ambiguous about scale inevitably comes to the fore when windows and doors perforate the volumes. On the other hand the composition weakens, its force dissolves, when the pieces cease to be solid and turn into volumes defined by planes containing interior spaces, these now the protagonists of the architecture. The diversity of the superficial elements comprising the actual building—stone, wooden panels, metal plates—deprives it of the force of the model's categorical solids. The Winton Guest House was built with a great deal of earnestness, so it doesn't have the freshness of the Norton House. The festive tone of the latter becomes overly emphatic in the

former, and the apparent freedom in the use of materials borders on affectation. In this particular case I really do prefer the model to the actual building, which preserves Gehry's usual intensity and freshness only at certain points, such as when the windows distort the planes and become strange frames through which to renew contact with nature.

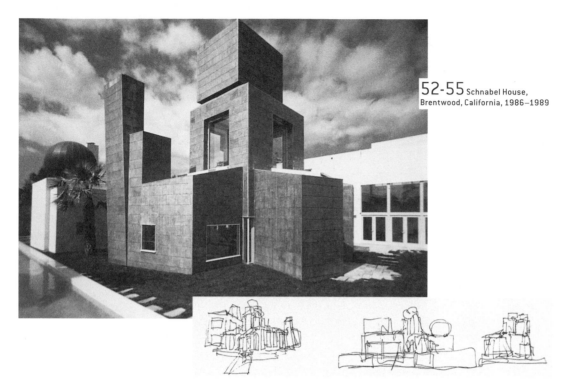

**52-55** The mechanisms explored in the Winton house were extensively applied in the following years. Gehry's architecture was now widely acclaimed, and commissions we might consider conventional came his way. A case in point is the Schnabel House, of 1989, situated in a luxurious part of Los Angeles.

In my opinion, the best thing about the house is the way it uses the lot. It takes up plenty of ground area, but not as much as its neighbors. By cleverly situating the pool along one of the borders of the lot, he virtually appropriates the free spaces of the adjacent parcels, making them gravitate around the pool, which is further enriched by the presence of an island guesthouse. The rest of the property is practically conquered by the series of pavilions that comprises the main house. Gehry is omnipresent inside and out. This, I believe,

**52-55** Schnabel House, Brentwood, California, 1986–1989

is the project's main achievement.

As in the Winton house, Gehry makes a central space give rise to a whole sequence of autonomous pieces, to each of which he assigns a use. These become the independent rooms of the different members of a single family. There is a certain desire to point out to us that opposites—prisms, cubes, spheres—can coexist, all within the framework of an artificial landscape endowed with a processional axis. The axis leads us to the tower-shaped element that is the undeniable protagonist of the house. All activities occur around it. Gehry must have been aware of this protagonism when he decided to activate it with a series of windows that attract all our attention the moment we enter the house. There is a deliberate ambiguity in the design of the windows that we are immediately taken by. For the positioning of the openings, all geometric criteria were avoided. The result is an unstable-looking tower. A relation between void and solid that is not based on questions of proportion and form is at once attractive and disturbing. So what do these curious windows offer us? The sky. The blue of the sky. Pure, undelimited by any profile.

The interiors are beautiful, and the principles of Gehry's architecture are ever present in them, even when one feels inclined to say that it loses some of its supposedly perennial virginity when domesticated by rich materials and a conventional program. Here, nothing is unfinished. No more of that, although what Gehry learned when building with fewer means now comes in handy as a stylistic resource. This brings about a certain dissociation between the chosen architectural language and the expectations dictated by the program. The contradiction doesn't escape the visitor's eye. Nevertheless, the house has a sculptural component that distorts the order of measurements and introduces us into an unreal world. Gehry's architecture indulges in an ambiguity that is hard to describe but which exploits mechanisms like the "wrong" use of proportions, sizes, measurements, materials, etc. The result is a continuous shifting and a process of decontextualization that would justify our speaking of an unreal—or unknown, unexpected—world. Gehry enjoys excess, he relishes exaggeration, and hence the appearance of unexpected elements. Even conventional furniture necessary for the life of the house's inhabitants is surprising, as is finding a grand piano instead of the electric guitars that Gehry, we have come to understand, likes to hang on the walls of the houses he builds.

56-57 Sirmai-Peterson House (1983–1988). My comments on the Schnabel House can be used here too; I will leave it to you to apply them to this other work of Gehry.

56-57 Sirmai-Peterson House, Thousand Oaks, California, 1983–1988

**58-59** Turtle Creek Development (1985–1986). Once in a while we come across an extraordinary project that is nonetheless of a purely speculative nature, in this case comprising an apartment building, an office building, and a hotel. Gehry's stamp lies in abandoning the fantasy of a single, unitary language and offering instead three different buildings. He knows that only through disparity can he address such a huge program in a single operation, and in the process dissimulate the abusiveness of the intervention. By opting for disparity, perhaps, Gehry ever so subtly criticizes the program he has been entrusted with. He might well have resorted to the trick of distribut-ing a massive project among several architects. This is sometimes done. But Gehry is able to come up with diversity by himself, and proves so here. One part speaks of New York architecture of the thirties. A second building, a volume of extraordinary vividness, shows Gehry's capacity to manipulate elements of traditional architecture in a heterodox manner. And with the third building he seems to be telling us that the models of a Philip Johnson or an I. M. Pei can be improved, that he is able to produce a glass figure that is unexpected and free, not subject to the geometrical tyranny that often governs the work of those architects.

**60-62** The Chiat/Day office of 1991 illustrates the importance that arbitrary choice of form can have in architecture. It's as if Gehry were telling us, paraphrasing Archimedes, "Name a shape, and I will turn it into architecture." Instead of form follows function, here architecture follows form.

93

**60-62** Chiat/Day office, Venice, California, 1985–1991

Chiat/Day is an artists' agency located in the Venice district of Los Angeles. When Gehry turns binoculars into an architectural form, he seems to be alluding to the work of the company, specifically what its talent scouts have to do to spot promising actors and actresses. The binoculars form the entrance to the building, manifesting the continued validity of duality when it comes to suggesting functions. But Gehry is clever and he decisively breaks the symmetry of the binoculars on the facade, both dimensionally and formally. The binoculars link up on one side with a low, slightly curving volume whose regular openings recall examples of rationalist architecture, and on the other side with a pavilion whose forest of diagonal braces echoes older architectures, halfway between medieval and popular. But the facade of disparate parts is unified in the outline of the whole, which skillfully accentuates the binoculars' central role in the composition by making them allude to classical pediments. If Gehry hasn't forgotten the lesson that is implicit in Oldenburg's statuary, then change of scale is not the only formal mechanism used here.

This reading of the facade can be applied to the floor plan, where Gehry once again demonstrates his skills. He doesn't waste time looking for a useless coherence. One can't miss the dissociation between facade and floor plan. The facade's epithelial condition manifests itself when we contemplate the conventional floor plan characterized by density and orthogonality.

**60-62** Chiat/Day office, Venice, California, 1985–1991

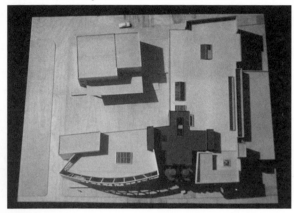

As for the interior, naturally we find mechanisms that are not too different from the usual. The boardroom, for example, is a conventional space. But it is transformed by the exaggerated lamp, the huge basket that invades and dominates the space, making our attention gravitate around it exclusively. The space is not shaped in any way. It is acted upon, and this action is what counts. The distortion involved in the lamp's change of scale is what gives rise to a new kind of space. What started out as a conventional space is now something else, because the gigantic lamp has decontextualized it. Effortlessly, and without design. Imagine a boardroom designed instead by a Scarpa, a Hollein, or a Castiglioni. Years of work, incredible effort. True to the spirit of the times, Gehry operates on terrain where such exertion is not necessary. As with the conceptual artists, the operation is mental, removed from all activity that requires a specific craft. Nevertheless the result is spectacular. The suspended lamp takes over our senses, and we can't help being captivated by it.

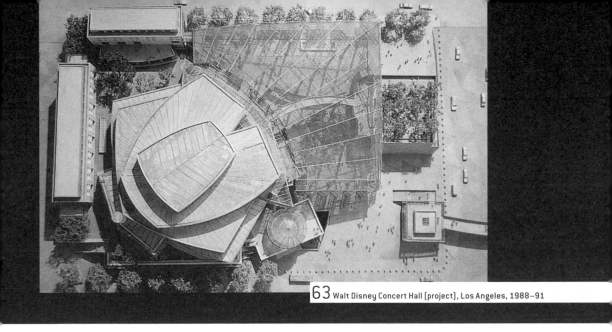

63 Walt Disney Concert Hall (project), Los Angeles, 1988–91

63 Because I've already discussed it at length on another occasion, [5] I won't now dwell on the Walt Disney Concert Hall in Los Angeles, initiated in 1987, a project Gehry worked on for years but which stumbled upon difficulties in the first phase of construction. Fortunately, the project was at last set in motion again in the late 1990s.

5 I am referring to a lecture I gave in the spring of 1990 in which I analyzed Gehry's and Venturi's concert hall projects for Los Angeles and Philadelphia, respectively. Walter Gropius Lectures, Harvard University, April 1990. Published in *El Croquis* 64 (1994).

64 Another Disney project, in this case for an amusement park near Paris (1988–1993). Professional success in the United States inevitably leads to calls from the big corporations, and Gehry's case is no exception. In recent years he has been tasked with impossible projects like this one. In this case his talent didn't suffice to dissimulate a conventional program.

65 This project for the Nationale-Nederlanden building in Prague (1992–1996) shows the limitations of Gehry's architecture. I don't see the sense in such a dance of windows in a neighborhood where respect for a certain canon has given rise to an architecture governed by restraint and order. In the Boston project we saw how accents can inject life into a structure worn out by time and use. Here, however, both the play of volumes and the anecdotal ingredients that try to liven up the building come across as groundless and unnecessary. This project incites discussion on "the necessary form" and the rejection of the arbitrary, and a certain nostalgia for a lost rationality.

64 Eurodisney, Villiers-sur-Marne, 1988–1993

65 Nationale-Nederlanden building, Prague, 1992–1996

**66-67** American Center, Paris, 1988–1994

**66-67** The consolidated Parisian context that Gehry confronted to build the American Center between 1988 and 1994 was not propitious for a display of his disheveled language. Hence the American Center comes across as a compromise between the conventional architecture that befits an administrative building and a desire to offer the kind of signature architecture that would adequately represent American culture in a city like Paris. As if it involved a method, Gehry borrowed from his previous corporate and institutional experiences, including the Chiat/Day offices, the Yale Psychiatric Institute, and the Laser Laboratory Building of the University of Iowa. But in this case the model is more attractive than the actual building. It's in the model that Gehry is lord and master of his actions. Adapted to building guidelines and legal codes, everything seems to have suffered a process of domestication. We can hardly recognize the architect. He proceeded quite freely, however, when making conventional use of the materials provided by the French construction industry, whether in the stone veneers or the woodwork. These are the only accents, accents that reveal the architect's wish to be seen one way or another. In my opinion they don't always produce the intended effects. Sometimes they fade out, blending into the mass of the construction. The skirt of the facade that was so important in the model becomes a pointless gesture in the real thing. In fact one could say that the entire project results from assimilating unnecessary norms imposed

**68-69** Weisman Museum, Minneapolis, 1990–1993

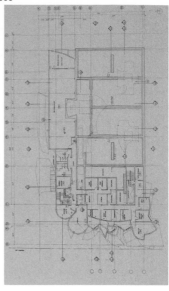

by the architect himself. The process has been inverted. An architecture seemingly born of a free manipulation of elements and materials is trapped by these norms, so the sense of freedom we have discerned in other Gehry works has vanished.

As far as I'm concerned, the best thing about the building is in the interior: some of the internal interstitial spaces. Inside the building Gehry could forget about the city of Paris and its architecture. Free of such references, he could act freely, so it is inside that his talent reappears.

**68-69** Another recent Gehry project is the Weisman Museum in Minneapolis, dated 1993. There is no need to dwell on it. It's a work elaborated according to procedures already analyzed, and using materials in a way Gehry has already familiarized us with.

**70-74** In my opinion it is more important to examine the Vitra Museum of 1987–1989, situated on German territory near Basel. As you know, Vitra is a furniture manufacturer that has commissioned an international lineup of architects—including Tadao Ando, Zaha Hadid, and Álvaro Siza—to design the different buildings on its factory grounds. Gehry was assigned the Museum of the Chair. The Vitra precinct is located in the middle of a plain that still has the attributes of farmland. But because of the invasion of industry, agriculture is in decline and the landscape has lost character, to the point that it can now be described as neutral and an architect there doesn't feel the weight of a definitive context. By this I mean that unlike in Prague and Paris, here Gehry could work with complete liberty, he was free to be himself. In examining his works so far, we have witnessed a process of dismantling and recomposing that at some point made us invoke Morandi's still lifes to explain his architecture. As we have seen in numerous projects in the course of his career, Gehry's is an architecture dominated by sculptural and visual qualities,

**70-74** Vitra Design Museum, Weil-am-Rhein, Germany, 1987–1989

even picturesque ones if you will. The Tract House, the Winton Guest House, the Schnabel House, or the Sirmai-Peterson House could serve to illustrate this. But in Vitra, Gehry suddenly discards such ways of thinking out and producing architecture. This, I believe, can no longer be called a fragmentary architecture, but a unitary, continuous, and mobile one. Contributing to the new unity is the cloak of stucco that wraps the whole building. Gone is the diversity of materials of other Gehry buildings. Here it is harder to identify, pull apart, and isolate the pieces, the elements that were so clearly discernible in his other projects. This project is much more complex. Moreover, white stucco and zinc are manipulated in such a way that it is hard to distinguish between interior and exterior and between vertical and horizontal. Since the elements that form it are not easily identifiable, the building comes across as pure spatial reality. We can draw certain parallels with avant-garde sculptures; that is, where the sculptor—Pevsner or Naum Gabo, for example, or even a certain Moore or recent Stella—tries to show us that it is possible to mold spaces. The idea of "molding space" eventually leads to a figurative or representational creation in which unity prevails and movement presents itself as an indispensable attribute. This is an important step that leaves behind the formal mechanisms derived from cubism, and in my opinion this makes Vitra a key project of Frank Gehry's career.

I will refrain from establishing references that would lead us to read this work on an expressionist note, taking the works of Scharoun and some of his colleagues in the thirties as precedents. Neither will I dwell on some less fortunate features, such as the entrance canopy, in which Gehry takes advantage of his previous experience, simply transferring to Vitra elements he has used in other projects. Nevertheless, Vitra would not have been possible without the architectural knowledge of a mature Gehry. In Vitra he deliberately ventures into new territory, abandoning what he has already explored. And yet the architecture of Vitra is the child of prior experience, even where it deliberately forgets it. Throughout his career Gehry has worked with freedom, but in Vitra this freedom is not a mere matter of negation. He is not like some of his followers who, in the name of deconstructivism, are smug in the simple and mechanical breaking of rules. Need we say that there is nothing farther from the architecture of Vitra than simplification and mechanical repetition? The freedom that Gehry has exercised in the course of his career presents itself at Vitra in all its splendor. It is manifested in the spaces contained within, so distant from all that can be understood as conventional. So distant, too, from Siza's work, which originates in the plan to be strengthened in the section. Gehry didn't start out here by drawing the interior, or the section, as Aalto surely did with the church of Imatra. In effect Aalto was explaining the dissociation of interior and exterior that has always been present in architecture. Gehry here doesn't distinguish between interior and exterior, and it's not easy for him to decide which to give preference to in the creative process—just as it's hard to determine whether a glove is the void in which a hand fits or the casing that shapes the void. In this recent Gehry we witness an attempt to dissolve the distinction between inside and out. He wants it to be impossible to make such a distinction in his architecture, and shows us that it is possible to build a reality in which the exterior, appropriating movement, and the interior, insisting on continuity and unity, are reflections of one same thing: an undefinable, fluid space.

75-79 Guggenheim Museum, Bilbao, 1991–1997

**75-79** The Guggenheim Museum in Bilbao was an opportunity for Gehry to prove that the program established at Vitra was applicable to a large-scale work. But there's more to it. The freedom that Gehry likes to wield here becomes a symbol of a city's future. Bilbao is proud of its architectures. Reason rules in the industrial constructions along the estuary, and nineteenth-century urban tradition is still felt in its fabric, but the city knows that that old world has gone and it is necessary to create a new one. Gehry's work, thus, as a representation of the new spirit that a new city desires. Again architecture plays the role of mirror of society and proves that it is capable of taking on a symbolic form and representing an ambitious program. Hence, by virtue of its presence in the city and its character as the estuary's new navel, Gehry's building embodies Bilbao's optimism and tries to be for its citizens a constant visible reminder of its new goals. This would explain the shiny surfaces of titanium that make the building an eternal flame.

But the Guggenheim of Bilbao is not just about symbols. It reveals Gehry's talent as an urbanist. His contribution in the choice of the site was determinative. From the very start, he took the bridge as an element to incorporate in the architecture. But his keen perception of urbanistic reality is most patent in the intelligent and skillful way the building literally joins

**75-79** Guggenheim Museum, Bilbao, 1991–1997

the two banks of the estuary. For this to happen, he makes access into the museum happen on a lower level, in such a way that the arriving visitor is trapped amid the active masses of the building. The experience is not unlike being in a mountain gorge. The Guggenheim necessarily reminds one of the importance in architecture of the organic analogy. That Gehry has tried to make it a nexus in a fragmented urban fabric becomes patent in the interior, which offers a crossed view of the city that makes the Guggenheim, indeed, the heart or gravitational center of a reborn Bilbao.

On the other hand, the Guggenheim allowed Gehry to refine and polish the role that the computer had begun to have in his work. The fluidity that we noticed in the last works, which had been clearly evident since Vitra, was here brought to fruition. The computer—and the application of CATIA, a software program used in industrial aeronautics—would allow him to use any form whatsoever, without fear that he would not be able to represent it. Now the most capricious of forms could be drafted, represented, and ultimately constructed. The extension of what we understand as architectural language to an infinite world of forms that do not necessarily have to be described with conventional geometries infinitely expands the range of the architect. The plane, the Platonic solids, are forgotten and the surfaces assume animate

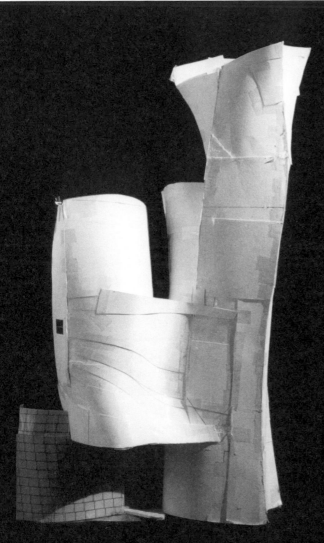

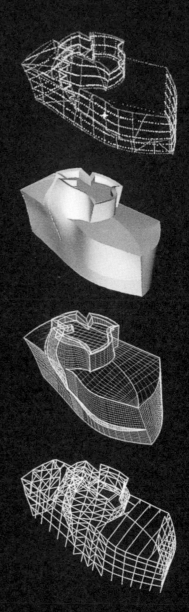

form. Architecture departs from a static reality to become a palpitating body. In this way, Gehry, liberated from the repertoire of preexisting forms, transforms himself into what he so much wanted to be, an inventor of forms. The latest Gehry, the Gehry of the Guggenheim, models his architecture with absolute freedom. He is aware that he can take all these liberties because he has a technology at his disposal that allows it. He has, little by little, acquired the capacity to build whatever form he may model, and in the Guggenheim and in later works he makes use of the arbitrary as a support for an architecture with a formal world that, you could say, is his own. If previously Gehry could transform a pair of binoculars into an entrance, insisting once more that form is independent of function, now the forms cease to be those we know and become a direct and personal expression of the architect: the computer and the CATIA program take on the role of defining, providing the builder with the necessary information. A world of unlimited forms opens before us.

But I would like to draw attention to other qualities of the museum. It seems to me that Gehry here is interested in many of the attributes we associate with earlier architecture. In the Guggenheim we are treated to a renewed sense of monumentality that, without resorting to direct allusions, transports us to experiences enjoyed in architectures of the past. Continuous changes of scale, leaps, breaks, interruptions, spans, etc. bombard our senses and transform our visit into a chain of surprises that leaves no time for reflection. The possible references are many, from the Russian constructivists to the German expressionists, from Tatlin to Mendelsohn, from the language of rationalists like Le Corbusier to that of more delicate architects like Aalto, from ambiences we might consider Gothic to others we understand as Piranesian. But as at Vitra, they are secondary to the building's sheer force as pure sensation. Gehry has accumulated experience in the course of his life, and in a work of this kind he seems to have reached his prime. Indeed, the Guggenheim of Bilbao has the unitary continuity we saw at Vitra, with no trace of self-imposed superstructural formal hierarchies. A feat in itself.

REM KOOLHAAS

This lecture is about Rem Koolhaas, and we will begin with his biography, because the key to his architecture is in his life story. Without a doubt, the events of his childhood and youth have had a great bearing on his career. Koolhaas was born in Rotterdam in 1944. He lived in Dutch colonies of Asia up to the age of ten, returning to the Netherlands as an adolescent about to embark on journalistic studies and take an interest in cinema. He wrote a few screenplays and discovered that new techniques of expression and representation were necessary to describe the universe of the second half of the twentieth century. The static framework in which architecture tended to unfold no longer made much sense, it was the architect's duty to explore new channels, and film was perhaps the medium most in tune with our times and our culture. Koolhaas's interest in cinema was therefore not mere caprice. He took film, and the mechanisms it used, as something that could be directly applied to the practice of the architectural profession.

This literary and cinematographic training that preceded his architectural vocation gave rise to his enthusiasm for the city. Maybe it was his astonishment at the city that led him to study in London's Architectural Association in the late sixties. At that time, the AA was completely under the influence of Archigram, who upheld a view of architecture in which action and technology were prevalent, with the deliberate circumvention of form. From London Koolhaas went on to the United States and taught at Cornell University, home then to two opposed personalities: Oswald Mathias Ungers and Colin Rowe. The rivalry between Ungers and Rowe made Cornell's architecture school one of the most lively and attractive centers of architectural exchange in the seventies. Rem Koolhaas was quick to become the disciple of an Ungers preoccupied with explaining urban form. The emphasis Colin Rowe always placed on history may have been instrumental in making Koolhaas lean toward Ungers. Those who were in Cornell during those years would be able to tell us how exactly the encounter took place. Ungers was linked to the modern tradition and had built some works of undeniable interest in the course of the sixties. In the wake of the student riots of '68, he emigrated to America. At Cornell he taught a theory of urban design not far removed from the principles of the architecture of the Tendenza, using the concept of type, though without renouncing the modernist education that is materialized in his earliest works.

Koolhaas benefited from his teachings, learning to make the city a compulsory reference in any architectural intervention, and to be aware of the importance of the culture of the modern movement in recent architecture. Ungers promptly perceived Koolhaas's talent, and it was he who introduced him into New York's architectural circles. So it was that in the mid-seventies, having collaborated with his mentor in some works, Koolhaas left Cornell to settle in New York and work for the Institute for Architecture and Urban Studies, founded and directed by Peter Eisenman. For years Koolhaas used the IAUS as a base from which to work on a book that, though of utmost importance for studying his work, went way beyond that, becoming key to an understanding of the architecture of the last quarter-century. I am of course talking about *Delirious New York*.

For Koolhaas, New York is the modern city par excellence. He was keen to explore it and pinpoint the true principles behind contemporary urbanism. Ever eager to proselytize, he used the watercolor skills of his wife, Madelon Vriesendorp, and the work capacity of his early collaborator, Elia Zenghelis, to disseminate his ideas. The three founded the Office for Metropolitan Architecture (OMA), and they were soon joined by restless American students, among them Laurinda Spear. Spear would later play a key role in Architectonica, one of the first groups of architects to be drawn to the principles of Koolhaas. The anagram OMA is significant. Koolhaas has always wanted to present his work as the fruit of a joint effort, as an alternative to the solitary activity of the artist-architect. In his view, the United States and New York are expressions of true modernity. As far as he is concerned, modern architecture never came to represent contemporary culture faithfully. Eisenman said that modernity never reached full term. We have also seen how Gehry tried to free modernity from the rigidity that any linguistic orthodoxy brings with it. What Koolhaas tells us in his book, what he discovered in New York, is that it is precisely in New York—the modern city par excellence, built simply under the pressure of the economy, subjected to the forces of unbridled capitalism—that the forms of true progress appear and manifest themselves in all their splendor. And Koolhaas set himself the task of showing us those forms, the forms that emerge when all respect for conventional languages and norms is done away with, when the only forces addressed are those that mold the modern world, namely technology and economics.

There is a certain anti-intellectualism in this discovery of America as cradle of modernity. Of course it's an anti-intellectualism that only one with an intellectual education, and who can afford to distance himself from the social group he belongs to, can boast. In Koolhaas's opinion, the new heroes—the protagonists of the new history of modernity—are the likes of Harrison & Abramowitz, or even Portman of Atlanta, architects dismissed by their enlightened colleagues as commercial. Mass culture, stronger in New York than anywhere else in the world, is what Koolhaas is interested in. It's this, Koolhaas says, that must be explored and investigated if we are to find the criteria and set the foundations for producing architecture. It's not a matter of indulging in the direct manipulation of models and materials, the way Gehry does, nor of coming up with a subtle architecture full of references, as Siza would have it. The thing is to explore the impact of mass culture on the city and architecture. This was done, paradoxically, in the two societies around which the history of the early twentieth century was polarized: the United States and the Soviet Union. Having closely studied the Russian avant-gardes, [1] Koolhaas knew that Russia opted for a utopia because the goals it pursued (social, and therefore aesthetic) were defined with extreme clarity. So it was that the Russians wrote manifestos and drew up and carried out spectacular projects that reactionary Stalinism would later bury in the monumentalism of the Palace of the Soviets and the Moscow Metro in the mid-thirties. The Americans also accepted mass culture, but, aware of the problems it could bring, turned weakness into a virtue by learning to build in Manhattan. Through his study of Manhattan in *Delirious New York*, [2] Koolhaas wrapped up his training as an architect. There he learned to live without succumbing to the temptation of utopia, and years later he would say:

My work is deliberately not utopian: it is consciously trying to operate within the prevalent conditions without the suffering, disagreeing, or whatever other kind of narcissism we have, all of which may be merely a complex series of alibis to justify certain interior failings. So it is certainly critical of that kind of utopian modernism. But it still remains aligned with the force of modernization and the inevitable transformations that are engendered by this project which has been operating for 300 years. In other words, for me the important thing is to align and find an articulation for those forces, again without the kind of

1 Rem Koolhaas and Gerrit Oorthuys, "Ivan Leonidov's Dom Narkomtjazjprom, Moscow," *Oppositions* 2 (January 1974).

2 Rem Koolhaas, *Delirious New York: A Retroactive Manifesto for Manhattan* (New York: Oxford University Press, 1978).

purity of a utopian project. In that sense my work is positive vis-à-vis modernization but critical vis-à-vis modernism as an artistic movement. [3]

His words reveal an intellectual who finds himself part of an elite that has lost contact with the masses. It shows us the paradoxical situation of the scholar who discovers that intellectuality is not the only engine of true progress. What counts is action, which is present in the forceful way that new techniques manifest themselves. In the final analysis, the masses are more sensitive and act more freely when faced with new historic situations than architects or intellectuals. The new course of history becomes patent in the expression of their desires, not in the manifestos of thinkers. Koolhaas has this in mind when he talks about the construction of a new city, Marne-la-Vallée:

**The role of the architect in this phenomenon is almost negligible. The only thing that architects do, from time to time, is to create within those given circumstances more or less masterful buildings. There is an unbelievable overestimation of the power of architecture in terms of the good it can do, but even more, in terms of the bad it has done or can do. Architects have been instrumental in this assessment through their accusation of modern architecture. In the vicious complaints and criticisms they developed in the 1960s and 1970s, and in howling with the wolves against the imagined misdeeds of modernism, I think architects have, in a very important way, weakened their own profession. [4]**

It won't escape one's notice that this populism of Koolhaas, this desire to link up with mass culture, is worlds away from that preached by Venturi. Venturi's populism is more indulgent toward iconography, taking pleasure in it and celebrating the entire rich paraphernalia of the American strip. In my view, this is an intellectual stance that implies condescension. Koolhaas's populism is of a very different nature. In his opinion, mass culture has the capacity to produce a city that is logical and endowed with an inner raison d'être of its own, however featureless it may look, through interventions governed by the quest for profit, never form. New York discourses on the modern city better than any urbanistic treatise. Try to make value judgments or set a priori criteria and principles on how to interpret urban science; the city of New York will negate them all. It will therefore be good to remember some paragraphs of *Delirious New York*. While

**3** Rem Koolhaas, *Conversations with Students*, ed. Sanford Kwinter (Houston: Rice University School of Architecture; New York: Princeton Architectural Press, 1996), p. 65.

**4** Ibid., p. 43.

11

traditional urbanistic treatises speak of a balanced city, where densities are distributed harmoniously, for Koolhaas,

**Manhattan represents the apotheosis of the ideal of density per se, both of population and of infrastructure; its architecture promotes a state of congestion on all possible levels, and exploits this congestion to inspire and support particular forms of social intercourse that together form an unique** *culture of congestion.* [5]

Koolhaas is amazed at this culture of congestion, which he finds as much in the amusement park of Coney Island as on the streets and avenues and in institutional buildings, department stores, theaters, the subway, etc. He upholds congestion and density as values in themselves upon which architects can and must work: **"All the latent potential of the skyscraper as a type is exploited in a masterpiece of the Culture of Congestion, a Constructivist Social Condenser materialised in Manhattan."** [6] The Russian constructivists spoke a lot about "social condensers," buildings with a capacity to provoke intense and positive reactions in people, but it was in New York that what they were clamoring for emerged, unconsciously and unintentionally. The true "social condensers" are not the drawings of the avant-garde Russian architects, but New York's skyscrapers.

**It is one of the rare 20th century buildings that is truly revolutionary: it offers a full inventory of the fundamental modifications—technical and psychological—that are caused by life in the Metropolis, and that separate this century from all previous ones.** [7]

And he adds that **"the indeterminacy of the Skyscraper suggests that—in the Metropolis—no single specific function can be matched with a single place."** [8]

Koolhaas would give a lot of importance to separating function and place, believing such separation to be fundamental in architecture, although it must also be said that he has not always stuck to this principle in his built work. It's a principle that considers that buildings have an inherent openness that renounces the specific, a certain indifference that makes them be used more freely than one would expect. How many times we architects are willing to limit or restrict the form of the building for the sake of function! Yet an examination of the city, of a city like New York, brings us to the conclusion that a building's form

**5** Rem Koolhaas, "Life in the Metropolis, or, The Culture of Congestion," *Architectural Design* 5 (1977), p. 320.

**6** Ibid., p. 322.

**7** Ibid., p. 322.

**8** Ibid., p. 324.

is removed from functional exigencies. Or, to put it differently, the city makes us see that functions adapt to the forms of buildings more easily than we think. In Koolhaas's words:

> Exteriors and interiors of such structures belong to two different kinds of architectures. The first—external—is only concerned with the appearance of the building as a more or less serene sculptural object, while the interior is in a constant state of flux—of themes, programs, iconographies—with which the volatile metropolitan citizens, with their overstimulated nervous systems, combat the perpetual threat of ennui. [9]

9 Ibid., p. 324.

The texts are long-winded, but ever present in them is the metropolitan citizen at whom Koolhaas directs his architecture. Hence his use of models. Curiously, Siza's work emerges full of references for modern architecture, but without models. Rossi's concepts of type and model pertain to the Platonic ambit of a dream world. Eisenman's models give form to a phantom where the basic syntactic structure prevails. Stirling was more preoccupied with style—ultimately with history—than with models. Gehry tries to do away with them altogether. So surely Koolhaas is the only one of the architects discussed in this book who knows what his architecture is supposed to look like when materialized. That is, he knows his models and, like a realist painter, tries to make his buildings get as close to them as possible. He abides by the reality that he has taken as a model, and this is why I have at some point described his architecture as "realist." Koolhaas's model is the spontaneous city, the city that emerges as a result of uncontrolled development, a prototype that has never come up as strongly and energetically as in American cities.

For Koolhaas, architecture has much to do with the accompanying action, the program. But he takes program literally, very differently from the way his colleagues do. The role of program in his architecture deviates much from the role it plays in Gehry's work, for example. To be sure, we must establish a link between the two, for among the eight taken up in this book, only Koolhaas and Gehry consider that program lies at the origins of architecture. But Gehry looks at program in extraordinarily concrete, precise terms—as if saying, the client tells me what he wants, and I take care of finding the shapes with which to produce the architectural organism he requires—whereas for Koolhaas program is much more diffuse and much less directly related to the architecture that is to be built. Program is an entire category that fosters the construction of imprecise, open buildings. What Koolhaas tries to avoid is an overdependence on program. He sums up the contradiction between program and architecture by calling for **"a maximum of program and a minimum of architecture,"** [10] and with statements like **"Where there is nothing, everything is possible. Where there is architecture, nothing (else) is possible."** [11] What he seems to be saying is that the architect of today should erect buildings that do not restrict freedom of action, the freedom of movement that characterizes contemporary culture. Needless to say, Koolhaas's concept of movement is something less literal than Gehry's. Koolhaas takes it that architecture finishes freedom, exhausting it. So his proposal for building is nonarchitecture, if, as he says, everything is possible where there is nothing; and that is exactly how he wants his buildings to be. And a prerequisite for this is a structure that can absorb an interminable series of meanings. He describes such a structure when talking about the Karlsruhe building: **"To generate density, exploit proximity, provoke tension, maximize friction, organize in-betweens, promote filtering, sponsor identity and stimulate blurring, the entire program is incorporated in a single container, 43 x 43 x 58 meters."** [12]

All of this is key to understanding Koolhaas's work. The truth is, however, that his architecture resists any attempt to reduce it through the classification process that all critical examinations inevitably are. It could be described as elusive. I will take the liberty of defining it as "cocktail architecture," architecture that brings together the many flavors of a cocktail. And I might add that the novelty of a flavor may be attractive and interesting but cannot compete, in my view, with the integrity of a good red wine. This is architecture whose different ingredients dissolve in the concoction. Which is not to say that they can't be identified. We could talk about "cross-breeding," but I find the term "cocktail architecture" more accurate. Cross-breeding implies the concept of transformation, but no definitive transformation takes place in the architecture of Koolhaas. The references are present, sometimes with hair-raising literalness. On one hand are images of New York, the spontaneous city par excellence. On the other hand are frequent traces of his modernist education, manifested through

**10** Rem Koolhaas and Bruce Mau, *S, M, L, XL*, ed. Jennifer Sigler (New York: Monacelli Press, 1995), p. 199.

**11** Ibid., p. 199.

**12** Ibid., p. 692.

a certain longing for the failed utopia. His works contain allusions to the Russian avant-garde architects, as well as direct references to American architects of the interwar period. Koolhaas has been quite explicit in revealing his preferences. He may be more attracted to American positivism, but his admiration of the Russian avant-gardes surfaces incessantly in his architecture. Though it is true that diverse forms come together in his work, the construction procedures he uses come exclusively from commercial, vulgar, spontaneous, and conventional architecture. It's in this kind of architecture that he finds the rationality preached by the moderns, and he glories in professing so, not without a certain delight in daring and provoking. It could be said that Venturi pursued similar goals, but it's important to stress the differences. Koolhaas believes that the spontaneous city of the twentieth century has a structure, and the thing is to discover it, whereas the populist Venturi (Venturi in his second phase) is more interested in identifying the mechanisms through which this structure is hidden. To discover the latent structure of the contemporary city, and learn to use the mechanisms used in building it, seems to have become the purpose of Koolhaas's work.

On the other hand, his architecture always reveals a desire to present his work as a product, and he likes to emphasize this, as if it were an irrefutable proof of contemporaneity. In his view, the work of the architect is not too unlike that of industrialists. Architecture is a good produced by industry, and the architect's studio a factory. This is the sort of thing the likes of Andy Warhol had already pursued in the art field. Architecture can then once again enjoy the anonymity it had in the past. So it is that Koolhaas's studio is more a workshop than a school. Its architectural output is a collective endeavor. There, the architect is not a person who designs, speculating and searching for ideal schemes as Eisenman does. For Koolhaas an architect is a catalyst who, from the design production unit that the studio is, contributes to the crystallization of forms and spaces equipped to accommodate the programs of modern life. Koolhaas has always been interested in the analysis of production. Remember that methodological studies were a fundamental part of the AA's curriculum in the late sixties. Koolhaas would go a step further, giving prime importance to the structure of his studio and combining the tasks of production and design.

Also in the name of contemporaneity, Koolhaas wants his architecture to be global, universal, unlinked to specific conditions of place. This is diametrically opposed to Siza's attention to accident, the specific. The architecture of Koolhaas wants to be useful and carry out its mission regardless of where it is, whether Japan, the Netherlands, or the United States. The place doesn't matter. A universal vision prevails over the architect's individuality. Gehry's architecture is all over the world, but doesn't aspire to be universal. Cities and institutions commission his architectural services and have a building signed by him. It's a Gehry they want, like an artwork with a personal stamp that the whole world can appreciate. But this is not to be confused with the notion of universality. In contrast, Koolhaas considers that what he produces, or what the industry known as OMA offers the market, is useful anywhere in the world. It is a trademark more than the work of an architect/artist. Industrial production addresses his desire for architecture that is indifferent to time, form, and, ultimately, person.

Koolhaas is interested in hitting upon the right scale. We will discuss this at length when we get to the illustrations of his work, but briefly for Koolhaas scale is inextricably linked to how people—individuals and masses—will use the architecture. His book *S, M, L, XL* addresses this interest in scale while serving as a framework through which to present and organize his work. At the heart of his interest in scale is the importance he gives to the use that architecture is to serve. Scale is therefore a category that leads from the private to the public. It's what makes it possible for architecture to satisfy the needs that arise in the sphere of the individual and address the spatial requirements of masses. Through skillful manipulation of scale, architecture puts itself at the service of a society defined by mass culture, thereby recuperating the usefulness it had in the past. Koolhaas considers that it's the spontaneous operators—the developers—who have best understood this new usefulness of architecture from the perspective of finding the right scale. Certainly more than his fellow architects, caught up as they are in an academic discussion about forms and icons, ignoring the fact that it's the dimensions of architecture that dictate and set the conditions of a project. Hence Koolhaas's explicit and frequently manifested determination to address reality, a reality that has nothing to do with, say, Gehry's interest in using everyday materials, or with that intangible and poetic reality that Siza finds in popular architecture. Koolhaas is interested in a more cruel reality, the reality we see in some American movies and which he found when studying New York City. It's the reality that developers build. Developers know what it is to build today. It's they who use reason in their work, much more than architects who like to call themselves rationalists. "Practical reason" has replaced all other reasons that have served Western culture after Kant. It's those who work in the construction industry who know most about the form of architecture. To be a rationalist today is to acknowledge this way of looking at things that is reflected in the contemporary city, the contemporary city that the young Koolhaas was so attracted to.

An older Koolhaas built a personal replica of the metropolis that he had so enthusiastically described in *Delirious New York*. The formal world he came across in his study of the American city is the reality that he would like to build. Koolhaas, hence, is a realist painter. But artists like Andy Warhol or David Salle can also be considered realists if we analyze their work from this perspective. Like Warhol, Rem Koolhaas tries above all to be distant. For Warhol, images are stereotypes. A portrait, to him, is a portrait of a portrait. There is nothing personal. Everything fits in the world of consumerism. Marilyn Monroe is not a person but whatever it is that she means to the public. Image is what counts. And the same can be said for elements of architecture. Koolhaas is not interested in design. He simply works with the elements given, whether by the construction industry or by popular use. He doesn't revel in invention. He prefers to preserve existing iconographies. Like Warhol, Koolhaas takes pleasure in the mere presence of known iconography. Neither of the two sees any reason to add anything else. Like Warhol, Koolhaas aggressively addresses society, insists on reflecting it in his work. David Salle's works, on the other hand, are screens equipped to receive different layers of the surrounding reality. Mechanisms of superposition are prevalent in Salle's multifaceted paintings. I don't mean the visual superposition of planes or layers, but the superposition of experiences, sensations, and sentiments; superposition not as a visual process but as a form of existence. I believe the same thing happens in the architecture of Koolhaas. He sees reality arranged in bands, like the rural landscape of Holland, and these bands constitute a basis for giving the landscape the form that people's lives require.

Andy Warhol, *Marilyn*, 1964          David Salle, *My Objectivity*, 1981

Immediately deducible from Koolhaas's reading of the contemporary city is a concept that can be understood as a corollary of it, and which I believe to be of singular value: the concept of the free section. We saw the importance of the section in Stirling's architecture, how it became the matrix of form in his work. In the early Stirling, the section determined the architecture. Knowing the section was tantamount to designing the building and establishing the program. If Le Corbusier taught us how to think of architecture in terms of the "free plan," Koolhaas has incorporated the concept of the "free section" into the architectural culture of the end of the twentieth century. Koolhaas has helped us think of architecture vertically, just as he seems to vindicate the density of the metropolis. Buildings are not structured by superposing horizontal levels. They are thought of from the section, though it is not for the section to define their forms. Buildings find their forms by addressing scale, by addressing the role they are to play in the city. Curiously, this way of looking at things leads to a renewed appreciation of the importance of iconography in architecture. In effect, the architecture Koolhaas finds in the American city is an architecture in which buildings take shape from the perspective of construction and of the scale they are to assume in the city, totally regardless of the specific forms dictated by their programs. In other words, the American city fosters the idea of the building as a container. This idea is key to an understanding of recent architecture, and surely Koolhaas's description of the city of New York has reinforced it. Sometimes we come across Koolhaas works in which a dependence on models has in fact made him replicate them too closely. But in other works the architect is in ultimate terms the inventor of the form that the building-turned-container has assumed. And so it is that he is left with the choice of an iconography that can yield an autonomous and complete building, one whose unitary and global condition reigns supreme. Aware of all this, Koolhaas can be said to have the daring to restore a global and unitary view of architecture through iconography. I have in mind projects like the transportation hub and the convention center in Lille, as well as the project for a hotel in Agadir, all extraordinarily ambitious works that in my opinion deserve respect and admiration.

If we consider Koolhaas's description of the American city, his interest in hitting upon the right scale, his contribution to a new design methodology based on the notion of free section, and his ambitious recovery of buildings' iconic character, we can understand why his architecture is so positively assessed these days, and why it is included in these lectures.

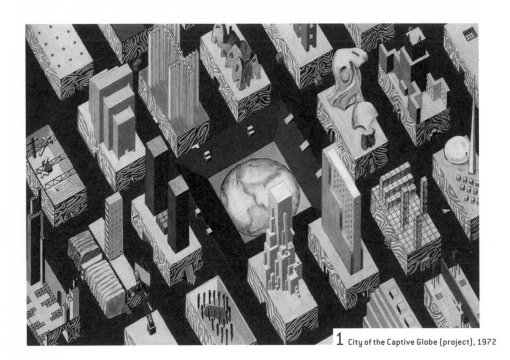

**1** City of the Captive Globe (project), 1972

**1-2** These two projects, named The City of the Captive Globe and Exodus or the Voluntary Prisoners of Architecture, both from 1972, were fruits of Koolhaas's stint in America, although the influence of Ungers is patent. In the former, the blocks of a scheme clearly patterned after Manhattan's are fertilized by a most diverse collection of skyscrapers. The force of the urban structure comes to the fore in its readiness to admit diversity. Corbusian projects are juxtaposed with towers that are unmistakably Ungerian in filiation or works inspired by German expressionism, commercial buildings are confused with institutional buildings, etc. The continuity of the scheme is not an obstacle; it does not prevent architects from going about their work.

2 Exodus or the Voluntary Prisoners of Architecture (project), 1972

The other project, Exodus or the Voluntary Prisoners of Architecture, speaks of Koolhaas's interest in the work of the Viennese conceptual artists and the investigations of the Florentine Superstudio. It tries to explore how an architectural megastructure can be simply superposed on, and live in harmonious dialectic with, the existing city.

3-4 It was in his study of the Downtown Athletic Club in New York that Koolhaas found proof that architecture can indeed be removed from the obligation to maintain a one-to-one relation between exterior and interior, that there need not be an interdependence between form and use. We talked about arbitrary architecture when looking at Gehry's work. Arbitrary architecture presents itself in a different way here, appearing when the functional variety of a building is absorbed by the arbitrary form that the skyscraper takes in the city. As we can see in the section, gyms, cafés, swimming pools, restaurants, hotels, and offices come together in the Downtown Athletic Club. The notion of the floor plan generating the building's architecture disappears altogether. In the skyscraper, what matters is the structure of the building and the position of the vertical communication shaft. Overall structure on one hand, and position of stairwell and elevator shaft on the other, define the available space, which is then open to the most diverse uses. Structure and shaft prevail. Tortuous corridors may later appear, but no matter, so long as the necessary contiguity between different spaces is maintained. The form of the building is freed from the pro-

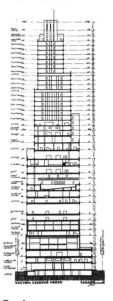

3-4 Downtown Athletic Club, New York, by Starrett & Van Vleck, 1931

322

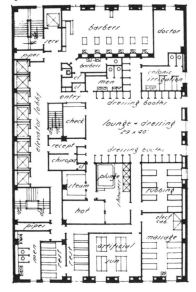

gram. The architect doesn't consider the program in defining the building's form. In this project Koolhaas discovered the principle of the "free section," which would be a source of inspiration in his future work as an architect. His analysis of the Downtown Athletic Club became his design method. In future he would undertake large-scale buildings on the basis of the section. The form of the building—including its image, its condition as icon—would be implicit in the section.

**5** The 1975 competition for New Welfare Island in Roosevelt Island, New York, was a pretext for Koolhaas to deploy an entire sequence of skyscrapers ready to serve diverse uses: apartments, offices, hotels, and so on. The "congestion" takes place under/over the bridge, and it is here that Koolhaas's personality manifests itself most freely. His proposal differs from the other competition entries in that it presents Roosevelt Island as broader and more able to make a virtue of accepting the supremacy of Manhattan. Roosevelt Island makes sense when seen from Manhattan as an incident on the East River, an incident that the city integrates by means of bridges and barges. Roosevelt Island

**5** New Welfare Island (project), Roosevelt Island, New York, 1975

is not an autonomous borough but a piece of Manhattan. The cracks Koolhaas makes on the grid of Manhattan seem to indicate so. If the cracks were one day to form other islands, these would not differ much from the one that serves as a starting point for the Welfare Island project.

Apart from the value of these proposals as design alternatives, note the sheer plastic force of the images offered by Koolhaas, thanks to Madelon Vriesendorp's skill in the rendering of perspective.

**6** Boompjes: Slab Towers and Tower Bridge (project), Rotterdam, 1980

**6** Similar comments could be made for this 1980 Rotterdam project entitled Boompjes: Slab Towers and Tower Bridge. Here Koolhaas tells us that the buildings he designs can go up anywhere, even in the unique atmosphere of places where the city fades out, as in the mouths of rivers, in ports, beside bridges, cranes, dikes, hangars, etc. Koolhaas seems to be interested in exploring the beauty behind the work of the engineers who built the infrastructure that makes our dominion of the environment possible (I say "exploring the beauty," but should perhaps speak of his awe and admiration in the face of work he doesn't aspire to claim for himself). As in the New Welfare Island project, the idea of the "whole" prevails, where "whole" eliminates all allusions to context. Koolhaas's buildings thus rise in the shadow of the cranes, like personalities removed from—but not foreign to—the urban scene, which is in the final analysis the reference and design framework that Koolhaas is so keen on. It requires a certain effort to make reflections of this kind, because the image is strong and attractive and seems to be an entity on its own. That the image is simply an illustration doesn't decrease its value as a representation of an episode of reality. There is no denying the importance of Koolhaas's contribution in the choice of such a representation.

**7-8** One of the first major manifestations of Koolhaas's talent as an architect was his entry to the polemical 1982 competition for the Parc de la Villette. For this competition—which Bernard Tschumi won with a project not unlike Koolhaas's own—our architect discarded all possible picturesque views of the park, challenging head-on the usual method adopted by landscape architects. Koolhaas didn't see why a park should offer a final and complete view of itself. He opted to see it as the scheme of a fabric in continuous evolution. This inevitably brings to mind the panorama of tilled fields that stretches beneath us when we fly over the Netherlands. Indeed, the geometry of bands that Koolhaas imposes is not very different from the geometry used by Dutch farmers. To Koolhaas, the Parc de la Villette was something that didn't have to have anything to do with axes nor with figures. Instead he envisioned activity areas defined by bands. These bands would in turn be activated by specific catalysts, and this is where the architect's job lay. There is no form. Instead we are offered a catalog of activities that are to be concretized by potential points of encounter, as in some of Peter Eisenman's schemes.

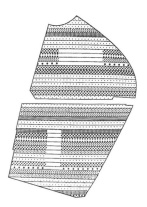

**7-8** Parc de la Villette (project), Paris, 1982

These points of encounter can serve to define a structure, which will then be given some physical entity: the network of paths and communications. The amorphous scheme is invigorated by the force of two open orthogonal axes of the kind which, to be sure, have little to do with the definitive axes of baroque gardens, and more to do with the lines of Mondrian paintings, eager as these are to define fields and areas but never to hierarchize. The idea of design as a virtual program of activities, as an opportunity to establish the availability and flexibility of space and not as a static definition of form, is much present in this La Villette project that was to go far in establishing Koolhaas's clout in Europe.

**9-15** Among Koolhaas projects, the entry to the 1986 competition for the town hall of The Hague best illustrates the degree to which he uses models as references. As an architect, Koolhaas wanted to offer the city a building as dignified as Rockefeller Center or the Waldorf Astoria. Nothing better for an administrative headquarters of a city like The Hague than one with the puritan solidness and restrained rhetoric of good New York (or American) buildings. Koolhaas went about the project by following, to the letter, the lesson he had learned in the city of skyscrapers and put down with so much passion in *Delirious New York*. True to its principles, he proceeded to construct generic architectures that could be cut vertically with the freedom and abandon he had come across in New York City architecture. Koolhaas was captivated by the visual richness of New York architecture, by the way it transcended the picturesque by accepting, without scruples, the random volumetric disposition that economic pressures regarding the use of land dictated. Koolhaas endeavored to obtain the same disposition in the generation of architectural form, even if the structural conditions here were not quite the same. Paradoxically, it would be from form—not structure—that he would come close to the models he admired. When we look at these images, therefore, the thing to celebrate is his plastic talent. Curiously Koolhaas, who in theory rejects any architecture based on visual aspects, presents himself in this project as a master of the plastic manipulation of form.

The photos of the models have an impressive plastic force. Koolhaas has the skill to photograph them with a highly efficient ambivalence that bespeaks, on the one hand, the abstract condition of the volumes, and on the other, the way an awareness of inevitable reality is manifested in the details. The volumes are structured by patterns and grids that allow them to be moved about, producing a vibration in space. This vibration relates them to New York skyscrapers, which also move about freely on the Manhattan grid. As a counterpoint, the windows help complete the image, and the randomness with which they are lit is proof of a desire not to think of buildings as something removed from their destined place in the world of everyday reality. The mastery with which Koolhaas photographed his models speaks of his devotion to film and, without prejudice to the instrumental aspect of architecture, asserts the importance of the architectural image. Indeed we discern the presence of a person who knows about filming

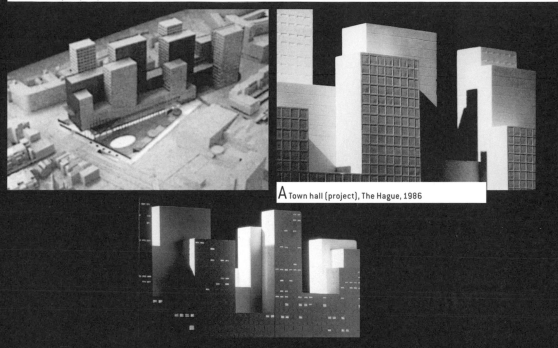

A Town hall (project), The Hague, 1986

B Waldorf Astoria, New York

C Rockefeller Center, New York

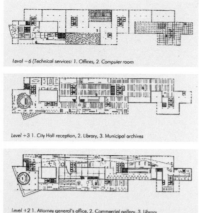

Level −6 (Technical services: 1. Offices, 2. Computer room

Level +3 1. City Hall reception, 2. Library, 3. Municipal archives

Level +2 1. Attorney general's office, 2. Commercial gallery, 3. Library

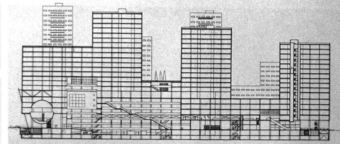

D Town hall (project), The Hague, 1986

a scene in a set. The skillful handling of double lights makes the abstract models look very real.

The town hall of The Hague is above all an administrative building, an office building. This implies an indiscriminate use of land. But it also contains a large library, as well as the bubble or sphere, in allusion to the spaces proposed by the architects of the Enlightenment, in which Koolhaas puts the town council's plenary session hall. The building is a container activated by voids that serve to structure and shape its interior spaces, whatever those interior spaces are to be. There is a certain dialectic between the construction of the solid—that is, the autonomous volume that is to play a role in the image of the city—and the manipulation of an interior that manifests the freedom Koolhaas so admired in New York, to him the paradigm of true modern architecture. Modernity is manifested in the free use of space, which we see in the sections accompanying the models.

A word, too, about the floor plans. I will not dwell on them, but note how the section reinforces the plan. By this I don't mean to say that the shift manifested in the section gives rise to an Eisenman-style floor plan, but there is in fact no question that the way Koolhaas entrusts a formal mechanism with the job of generating the entire volume of the building is not far removed from some of the experiences we came across in Eisenman's houses. On the other hand, there seems to be a certain satisfaction in eroding and molding the volume, in manipulating it in accordance with the demands of the program. This can only be explained by remembering how important it was for the orthodox moderns to free themselves of the volumetric tyranny of compositional criteria coming from outside. The volumetric freedom of Koolhaas's architecture is closer to certain neoplasticist experiments than to the Corbusian free plan, although he naturally sometimes resorts to the latter. Note how congestion, so pleasing to Koolhaas, is manifested in a studied compactness. We saw this in the Downtown Athletic Club as well.

**16-21** National Dance Theater, The Hague, 1981

**16-21** In my opinion, the National Dance Theater in The Hague, dated 1981, is not as ambitious a project as that drawn up for the town hall. Nevertheless it has interesting elements, such as the foyer. Laid out beneath the tiers of seats—an approach taken quite frequently in buildings of the kind—this is made dynamic by an assertive parabola that makes it deviate extremely from what normally results from building over a strict grid. Koolhaas desires to build in accordance with economy-dictated guidelines. Hence the upholding of the grid, and it's up to isolated episodes, or singular points, to arouse the interest of the observer entering the neutral space. The staircases and the platform over the foyer should suffice to illustrate this. It is in these singular elements that we can appreciate Koolhaas's talent as an architect. Nevertheless I believe he gets trapped—to his own dismay, I suppose—in that vulgar architecture that he claims to admire. The National Dance Theater may be an efficient building, but it is not the most specific setting for contemplating dance. There is a lack of attention to program, and this makes the theater indifferent to it. In the end the building suffers from the fact that it contains no apparent direct reference to dance. Here we have a Kool-

**16-21** National Dance Theater, The Hague, 1981

haas who is very attentive to the manipulation of surfaces, to the construction of the skins of facades that result from a conventional prismatic construction and which, in the most vulgar sense of the word, he is forced to "enliven." And this manipulation includes allusions to "cultured" architecture, such as those produced by the brusque interruption of the horizontal bands of the parapets, or the way different schemes are superposed. In a building like this, it isn't hard to perceive that the architect derives satisfaction from the mixing of diverse elements that allowed us to introduce the term "cocktail architecture." Note, for example, how the sheet metal parapets of the higher floors—undoubtedly taken from models supplied by commercial architecture—are made to coexist with the windows of the lower volume, which could well have been designed by a colleague intending to make a salute to "high culture." Koolhaas seems to have entrusted the building's image to its monumental mosaic, which brings to mind other references, such as certain Brazilian and Italian buildings of the fifties, or Matisse illustrations that were generic descriptions of dance. But none of this manages to exempt the architecture from criticism, and it remains a captive of the respect that Koolhaas considers commercial buildings deserving of. The result is unpretentious, true, and that is enough to say, but it nonetheless falls short of being a relevant architecture.

22-23 The Koolhaas who has a penchant for commercial, consumerist architecture falls into his own trap again in this 1981 project for the IJ-plein in Amsterdam. His desire to be didactic—which at some point comes across as an apology—leads him to explore how architects as diverse as Gropius, Ernst May, and Hilberseimer would have gone about it. Koolhaas's project tries to be just another option, and this is how an architecture we can call typological justifies itself. The architect insists on known types, and Koolhaas resolves this residential block by conforming with norms and using elements we have been coming across in housing projects ever since what we know as modern architecture first appeared, back in the twenties. Koolhaas is perhaps aware that this is not an exceptional project, and this may explain why the work is more often than not presented in night shots that might well serve as the opening scene of a film meant to portray the solitude of people living on the outskirts of big cities.

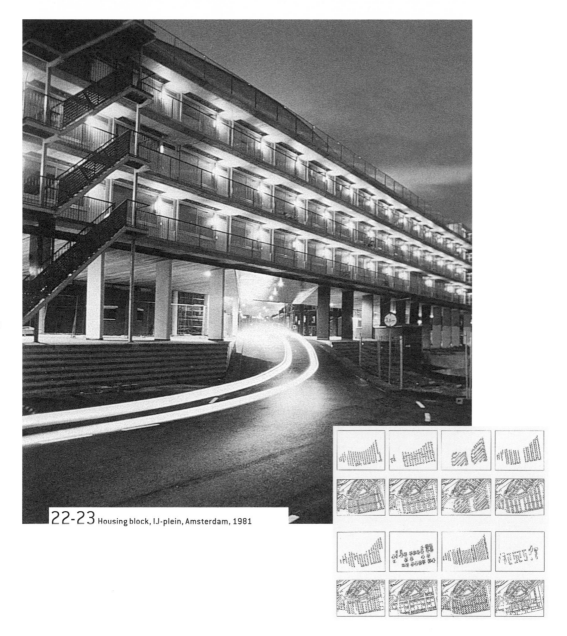

33

22-23 Housing block, IJ-plein, Amsterdam, 1981

**24-27** Two Patio Villas, Rotterdam, 1984–1988

**24-27** I believe there is a clearer definition of architectural intentions in these small houses in Rotterdam, named the Two Patio Villas (1984–1988). First let me draw attention to the maturity involved in recognizing the limits of a work. Koolhaas knows that building in a district of this kind involves limitations, and he doesn't try to surpass them. His attitude differs quite substantially from that of colleagues of his who, for the sake of coming up with sophisticated architecture, tend to proceed indiscriminately, without respect for place and program. Koolhaas knows that he has little leeway. He knows that the program, the area available, the construction systems to be applied and so on, inevitably lead to an architecture that, at least in appearance, must not deviate too much from that of the surroundings. A degree of camouflage seems in order. Nevertheless, Koolhaas manages a certain subtlety that is rare in suburban districts.

In a way, these houses give us license to pick up on the Venturian discussion of what elements adorn a construction. Koolhaas's answer to the question posed by Venturi falls within the strictest modern orthodoxy. The use of color in these houses makes us connect Koolhaas to modern Dutch architects like Rietveld. We quickly realize, however, that the slanting lines separating the different colors speak of an underlying irony that justifies the mention of Venturi. Once again, Koolhaas's architecture displays a hybrid condition that is certainly one of its attractions. But it is in the precision of the floor plan that his talent comes to the fore. We would have to look up floor plans of Mies to find a precedent of an architecture in which precision is the matrix of form. Precision as an attribute of the most exacting professionalism: the architect stays at a distance, removed from circumstances, thanks to the exactitude of the form. The ground is uneven, and the villas capitalize on this to let the car in, thereby separating themselves from the road. The stairs lead up to the level where the occupant comes in contact with another world, with nature. A courtyard constitutes an artificial component contrasting with the natural space in which the upper level unfolds, while definitively organizing the house's movement around itself. The kitchen and the dining and living areas are laid out around the courtyard/staircase core, while the bedrooms and bathrooms are situated along the party wall. It is interesting to analyze the floor plan, more so when one of the most disseminated images of the house is an exterior shot in which the reflections of the trees are confused with the frames that define the courtyard. The precision of the floor plan stands at the opposite pole from this image, which seems to want to erase all

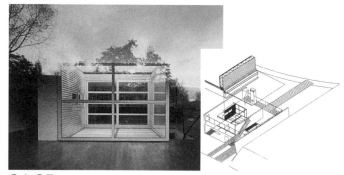

24-27 Two Patio Villas, Rotterdam, 1984–1988

references to a possible architecture. Again the paradox between the force of the architecture, understood here as the splendor of the floor plan, and what seems to be the architect's wish to show us that contemporary people live in a world dominated by reflections. Glass, hence, as a paradigm of reflection and as the material to which architecture succumbs, converted into an inapprehensible and changing image. Surely the photograph is not casual. It has that effect of strangeness that has nothing to do with the surreal, an effect we have previously come across and will continue to come across in works of Koolhaas, like a given.

**28-34** We have just seen how Koolhaas applies the criteria of a truly progressive architecture to a modest program. Glass is taken as a material that best represents contemporary building techniques, and the result is a dissolved, imprecise image whose basis and support is the glass itself and the reflections it produces. The 1989 project for the sea terminal in Zeebrugge, Belgium, is an ambitious one both in scale and in program. The approach here is very different. The iconographic proposal prevails, as all the components that give life to the building are embraced by it, whether unitarily or synthetically.

It is hard to define this building, because very disparate uses and functions converge in it. One could say it illustrates a coming century's diversity and contradiction. A building where trains and roads coincide, and which by resembling a lighthouse also alludes to maritime traffic. A building that is neither a sphere nor a cylinder—maybe we should call it a "spheroid"—and that, by the way it is anchored to the ground, challenges the vertical order of conventional constructions. Despite its perfectly unitary shape, this disturbing construction—which brings to mind, not coincidentally, the images illustrators use to anticipate an extraterrestrial world—receives the most diverse inputs: intersecting roads serving both public and private traffic, pedestrian routes connecting to the land, catwalks leading to ships, etc. The base is therefore the most unstable part, the most active area of a building that Koolhaas has quite rightly called "a working Babel." The building seems to acquire a certain calm at the point where it becomes a panoramic dome from which the horizon is recaptured and the traveler, the contemporary warrior, gets the rest he desires.

Apart from the use he makes of his principles—congestion, free section, etc.—what's attractive in this project is the architect's courage in giving importance to iconography. Although the project was not carried out, one can imagine the building's presence when seen from a ship. Lit at night, the dome undoubtedly speaks of the city of Zeebrugge's endeavor to be a crossroads for a strong and mighty Europe. The architectural project on this occasion is identified with the sociopolitical project, and the architect offers society the form that faithfully represents it. Rarely has contemporary architecture served an idea so loyally. Rarely has an architect of our times offered such a direct iconographic representation of a program. It is this aspect of the project that I believe should

**28-34** Sea terminal (project),
Zeebrugge, 1989

be emphasized, much more than those stylistic allusions that lead us to connect this way of doing architecture with Miami architects. Indeed, here is an architecture that is aware that most facades nowadays are but superficial membranes, and the architect proceeds to work on the membrane by means of a cutting operation. This gives rise to both the diversity of windows (rectangular, circular) and the slanted cut on top, without the nature of the building material making itself felt. Only in the transition from base to dome do we appreciate the triangulation that so often appears in Koolhaas's buildings and that certainly, in accordance with the teachings of modern architecture, alludes to the importance of structure in all constructions: the triangular cuts indicate that underneath the membrane stands a resistant structure with the capacity to justify the form.

Although I don't think we need to delve into a description of the spaces here, I would like to emphasize once again the importance of the section. So far we've talked about the external skin and the quasi-geographical role the building plays. But if we venture inside, we will see that the immense void is above all an available space in which the structure doesn't compro-

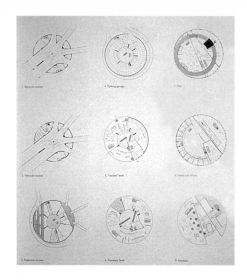

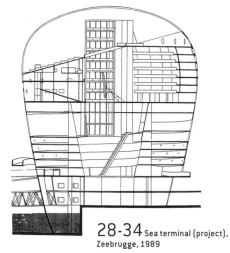

28-34 Sea terminal (project), Zeebrugge, 1989

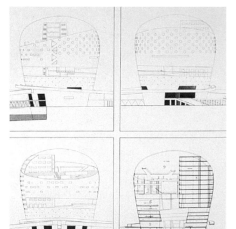

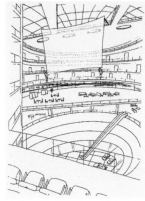

**28-34** Sea terminal (project), Zeebrugge, 1989

mise the possible section. It is true, and logical, that a helicoidal structure is used to resolve the parking lot. But the dictates of geometry are soon abandoned, and the circular schemes give way to oblique patterns that define planes equipped to accommodate the most diverse programs. The void is positioned in terms of what are considered choice views, and so both the hotel lobby and the rooms enjoy those views, while tiered seating speaks of a public use of the space whose backdrop is the ocean. The diversity that Koolhaas admired so much in New York buildings is celebrated and glorified here, supported and protected by a strong iconography. As for congestion, here we should think in terms of congestion of movements. Koolhaas's efforts to erect a building without losing sight of the traffic reference constitutes a truly interesting experience. He shows us how the contact between different modes of transportation is produced. That is how he looks at travel nowadays, as the result of the encounter of different means of transport. The energy that is implicit in any trip is manifested here as architecture.

35-38 Bibliothèque de France (project), 1989

**35-38** The series of autonomous, generalist, and global projects in which Rem Koolhaas applies his reading of New York City culminates in two projects: one, his entry to the 1989 competition for the Bibliothèque de France; the other, an actual commission in the same year for the Center for Art and Media in Karlsruhe. On different scales, they are developments of one same project. What matters is the architectural structure, and hence the confidence in buildings of a universalist nature, indifferent to program and place.

But first let's take a look at the library. The architecture, in its origins, is a cubic and translucent solid. This solid is the material that the architect works on. He has to structure it, organize it. There is a remote echo of the servant and served spaces that Kahn formulated in the fifties. The space is structured by means of a series of vertical prismatic elements in which both the resistant structure and the building services are enclosed. The vertical elements organize the space in the manner of a monumental Cartesian system of coordinates. The entire space is occupied. Remember that this is a library and that book storage and preservation alone can constitute its raison d'être. With this referential system as a backdrop, the constructed space accommodates the elements of the program: reading rooms, auditoriums, audiovisual rooms, public spaces, etc. But this doesn't prevent the volumes occupying the space from sometimes being prisms, when their functions require it. Paradoxically, since this is an architecture we could consider abstract, I would say that there is

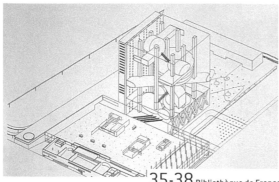

**35-38** Bibliothèque de France (project), 1989

something of a zoomorphic metaphor in the project, if we take it as a body containing organs and viscera whose positions don't seem to affect the building's final form. We could also talk in terms of a machine for storing culture in which different pieces are accommodated in a predefined chassis. There may be no contradiction in this double interpretation of the library. Remember how the inventors of machines admired living beings and nature in general. Whatever our interpretation of Koolhaas's work, the fact is that his forms do not lend themselves to being judged from an aesthetic viewpoint; true to their functionalist origins, they try to present themselves free of values unrelated to their character as servers of diverse uses.

In the Bibliothèque de France project, his representation of his architecture reaches a peak. Both the models and the drawings are extraordinarily expressive. I would like to draw attention to his ambiguous use here of solids and voids. Voids predominate in the model and one of the axonometric drawings, manifesting the essential structural elements, while solid forms appear within, suggesting functions related to them. In the floor plans and sections, however, the space fills up and is constructed by means of voids in which those functions are produced. I would also like to point out that although Koolhaas boasts that he rejects the rhetoric of traditional architecture, his work shows a plastic mastery that would be the envy of many architects who claim to use procedures of the past. Examining the cube's facades one at a time, one can't help marveling at the skill with which he introduces a note of color, or the importance that the figures he draws with uncommon dexterity acquire in the plane, whether an ellipse or a square. Koolhaas is aware of the need to liven up the plane visually, and the plastic accents he puts in it give his work a personal flavor we don't find in the works of his followers. Lastly, note how freely his architecture unfolds. The crystalline cube supports everything, including elements that here begin to be characteristic of his work, such as the rhomboidal structure acting as if it were a colonnade that we previously saw in Zeebrugge.

**39-42** The Center for Art and Media in Karlsruhe surely has much to do with the Bibliothèque de France project and illustrates how Koolhaas's proposals have the universal value we mentioned. Deliberately exaggerated and programmatic and endeavoring to be a manifesto, the library project undergoes a change of scale and here presents itself as a plausible building in which, again, theaters, dance halls, cinemas, etc. are superposed. The scale change of course implies a very different handling of the system of solids and voids. This time the resistant structure is built from the perimeter, and the system of solids this defines gives rise to the voids that make the unfolding of functions possible. Once again he explores the potential of the free section, so clearly manifested in the way he slices the model. Koolhaas, who claims to dispense altogether with aesthetics, comes across as a formidable sculptor in his elaborate models. These testify both to the energy with which the theoretical principles of his architecture are manifested, and to his fine handling of textures and surfaces. The modernity that is always behind his architecture—let's not forget his beginnings in an Archigram-dominated Architectural Association—comes to the fore in this project. The superposition of uses and activities wouldn't be possible without an extensive deployment of escalators, ramps, etc. These elements are responsible for the vitality of a space in which all the principles of Koolhaas's architecture are condensed, principles that in the final analysis amount to a single tenet: architecture is action.

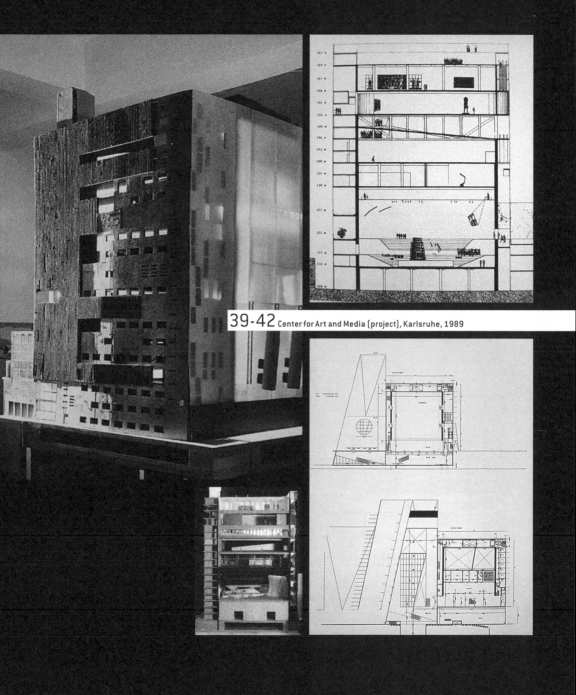

**39-42** Center for Art and Media (project), Karlsruhe, 1989

**43-50** Now we come to 1990 and what I hold to be one of the most beautiful projects of Koolhaas's career, the hotel and convention center for Agadir,
Morocco. Impossible but very beautiful. This project clearly has its origins in
Le Corbusier, but there is more to it. Koolhaas begins by reconstructing the
landscape of dunes that is to be the setting of the hotel. The project develops
an abstract idea that ends up, however, offering images that try to make us
overlook the violence of the operation. The process begins by encrusting a
square-plan prism into the rolling ground of dunes facing the sea. Now imagine
the ground fracturing and the prism splitting into two parts, both of which are
then shifted upward. As the lower one is raised, it creates a new ground level
that artificially and completely repeats the existing topography, but higher.
The other part of the prism suggests the fracture they share but unfolds more
freely, ending in its upper face with a flat surface that is eroded by means of a
sequence of courtyards, from which emerge prisms and figures whose origins
we know. The fissure—the gap between the two portions of the split prism—
helps establish the program. In general terms we can say that the convention
center activities are accommodated in the part of the prism that is underground,
whereas the hotel is assigned to the upper portion, the part we said was perforated by a series of courtyards. As an area separating public from private, the
fissure accommodates the accesses and all facilities halfway between public
and private, such as the hotel reception area, the ramps leading to the convention center, cafés, shops, and so on. As I've said, it's hard not to recall projects
of Le Corbusier, but we can also say that the integration of the car into the building had never before been put forward so radically. The whole building is now a
protective canopy for the car, but also a huge baldachin, a square-shaped cloud
from which to contemplate the Atlantic Ocean. A square, "Egyptian" city over
our heads—with courtyards, roads, and diagonals that foster movement—is
connected by escalators and elevators to the somber world of artificial dunes
that such a strange continuity establishes (despite the literal repetition of the
topography); to the entire area in which the hotel is inscribed; and ultimately to
the ocean beyond.

This is a difficult project that, I repeat, resorts to Corbusian mechanisms
with a brilliance that is rare. It is the project of an extraordinary disciple, a

**43-50** Hotel and convention center (project), Agadir, Morocco, 1990

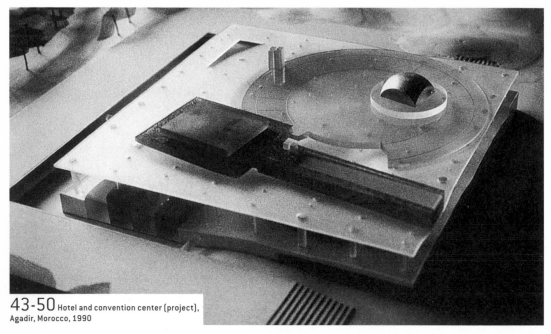

**43-50** Hotel and convention center (project),
Agadir, Morocco, 1990

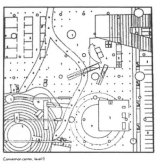

Convention center, level 0

Urban plaza, level +4-18m

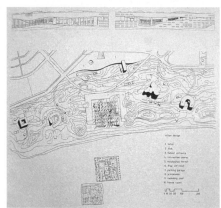

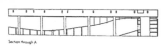

Section through A

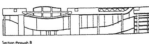

Section through B

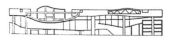

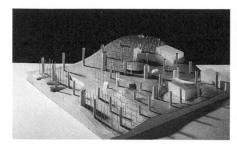

**43-50** Hotel and convention center
(project), Agadir, Morocco, 1990

project that would have deserved to be executed so as to proclaim once and for all the validity of certain principles: the *pilotis*, for example. Koolhaas handles the *pilotis*—the new *pilotis*, if you will—with an extraordinary freedom. The columns aren't identical. The diameters vary, and the complex is as alive and diverse as a forest. It helps that the columns/cylinders are encased between two undulating surfaces and not between two horizontal planes, as they might have been in Le Corbusier. In the forest we also find prisms that contain functions and reinforce the artificiality of the landscape, much more than one might think, given the insistence on a literal replica of the topography. The artificial landscape that the fissure creates is enthralling, and, considering the effects of light and shadow that the voids of the hotel would have produced, it's not difficult to imagine the spatial richness it would have had, had it been built. The combination of the elements of the program—hotel, open space, conventions—gives rise to an architectural form of singular value, one in which symbolic elements, place, functions, etc. are not ignored but, on the contrary, allowed full expression. The method is most attractive, yet didn't occur in any of the projects so far discussed. And all this right by the sea.

**51-56** Although the Nexus World residential development in Fukuoka, Japan (1991), is a small part of a complex in which a large and diverse selection of architects from all over the world participated, Koolhaas made the most of the opportunity and drew up a housing proposal that could be considered generic and universal. Against a use of land that seemed to lay stress on the specific, Koolhaas chose to build a sample of a broader fabric that could be extended further if circumstances demanded. The desire for a universal architecture prevails anew. The road taken on this occasion is that of the courtyard house. But the lot's conditions of centrality send the inhabitable patios upstairs, in contiguity with others, by establishing the required conditions involving ventilation and opening, making possible an intensive and continuous use of the land. In the paradox of making density and independence coincide lies the lure of a project of this kind. Koolhaas accepts Japanese congestion, but at the same time works toward the complete autonomy of the individual, absolute owner of the space that is generated around the courtyard.

On one hand I would like to point out how, despite the limited size of the

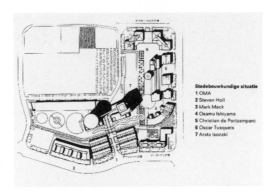

Stedebouwkundige situatie
1 OMA
2 Steven Holl
3 Mark Mack
4 Osamu Ishiyama
5 Christian de Portzamparc
6 Oscar Tusquets
7 Arata Isozaki

**51-56** Nexus World residential development, Fukuoka, Japan, 1991

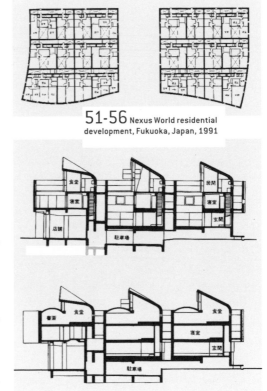

51-56 Nexus World residential
development, Fukuoka, Japan, 1991

lot, Koolhaas works out two different types of housing, thereby acknowledging border conditions. This allows him to give a special plastic value to the undulating front that features the entrance to the residential development. On the other hand, something must be said about the handling of materials. The whole project shows a desire to "build nature" that explains both *il finto rustico* and the appearance of small green mounds in the courtyards. The undulation of the roofs and walls contributes to the creation of the vague naturalist atmosphere that, as we said, is one of the project's characteristic features.

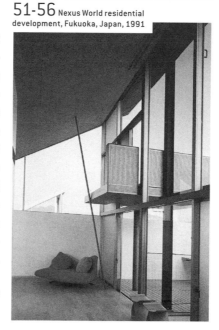

**57-64** The Villa dall'Ava (1985–1991) is a small house outside Paris. Here again Koolhaas ignored context. With no regard for the bourgeois surroundings, he went about building a manifesto of the ambitious social and aesthetic program that both he and the clients desired. The house is a whole reflection on suburban life that among other things considers how suburbanites resort to humor in order to survive. On one hand Koolhaas emphasizes the geometry of the lot by exaggerating the house longitudinally. On the other hand, in an appropriation exercise that is quite like that of painters when they use others' works as reference, Koolhaas seems to want this project to be a commentary on the excesses of Corbusian architecture. But apart from all this, the house offers an infinite sequence of spaces and sensations. The longitudinal shape of the floor plan is made to coincide with the movement of the house. One could say that the entire architecture is focused on leading us from the narrowest to the widest space, and from the most public to the most private. (The shortest side of the trapezoidal floor plan dominates the access, while the longest side comes in contact with the yard.) There are two options for access to the house,

**57-64** Villa dall'Ava,
St.Cloud, Paris, 1985–1991

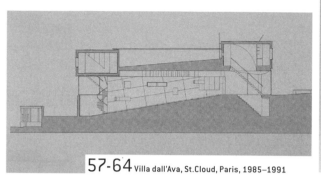

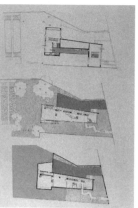

**57-64** Villa dall'Ava, St.Cloud, Paris, 1985–1991

one pedestrian and the other vehicular. The pedestrian access is protected by the slanting forest of the *pilotis* amongst which a path winds: the Corbusian grid transformed into a forest of slender steel columns painted in many colors. All this becomes a frame from which to contemplate the surrounding world in a different light. As for the garage, it is like a cut in a natural slope. At the point where the two accesses converge a ramp and a helicoidal staircase appear leading upstairs, to either the living room or the dining room and kitchen area. This is the house's most public zone. The whole space is open and the fireplace and curve of the kitchen "float" in it, could actually be isolated and turned into autonomous volumes. The transparency of the spaces is so literal that it's the entire garden city that the residents inhabit. Privacy seems a prejudice. There is nothing to fear about a world in which the house poses so comfortably and confidently. We've already said that the architecture of this project was based on movement. The occupants gain access to the bedroom/studio through a private staircase near the living room; guests reach their room through a staircase situated at the opposite end. Yet another flight of stairs, an exterior one reachable from a gallery that horizontally connects the master bedroom to the guestroom, leads to the swimming pool area, where the Corbusian garden becomes an austere platform with a distant view of the city. This complex, sophisticated sequence of spaces can hardly be explained in functional terms. It takes on meaning only when seen as a tribute to architecture.

**57-64** Villa dall'Ava,
St. Cloud, Paris, France 1985–91

Earlier we talked about Kool-haas's cinematographic education. His cineast vision makes itself felt in his work, and the Villa dall'Ava is a good example. The linking of spaces seems dictated by the movement of a camera, which is why there is no room for any global or synthetic reading of the house. In Koolhaas, spaces are the result of assembling areas of activity, and the viewpoints that complete a take are framed from there. This Koolhaas way of looking at architecture becomes patent in the way his architecture is photographed. The images of the house when lit artificially are very interesting. The artificial pigments, rendered rather flat under natural light, take on relief under electric light.

Again, a word about materials and language. The syncretic nature of Koolhaas's architecture, which we have dared to call "cocktail architecture," is evident here. Natural and artificial materials, stones and metal sheets, glass and concrete, all these flavors help create a special and unique atmosphere in which modernity is based on tolerance and nonexclusivity. As for stylistic features, Le Corbusier always appears as the ultimate reference, but is manipulated in a personal and malevolent way. The *pilotis*, the *fenêtre*

*en longueur*, the *toit-jardin* are now the property of Koolhaas. In the course of translation, he has appropriated them completely. Neither the *pilotis*, which oozes critical irony, nor the *fenêtre en longueur*, which indulges more in its industrial production than in its form, nor the *toit-jardin* on the roof, which speaks more of textures and surfaces than of volumes, has much to do with Le Corbusier. No matter how controlled and sophisticated the materials and language, they are not what count. At the heart of it all, what counts in this house is its occupant. It's a house designed to be consumed visually, to speak of how its owner wishes to be perceived. This house cannot detach itself from its owner. We saw what Siza's houses suffered in the hands of their users, making us think of them as objects invented by the architect and transformed into toys by their occupants. In contrast the Villa dall'Ava is daughter at once to the architect and the client, verifying Koolhaas's claim that he always pays attention to program.

**65-69** The Kunsthal in Rotterdam (1987–1992) is not very different, as a project, from the National Dance Theater in The Hague. In the Kunsthal Koolhaas seems willing to waste not a single square meter, to build over the whole area of the lot, and to use the full volume established by the guidelines. The building is an occupied volume, a container. But of course that's not the end of it. Koolhaas's strategy of activating the neutral volume that defines the perimeter is carried out on two fronts. On one hand, the prism is transformed by means of a series of slanted planes that help consolidate the program while fostering movement. On the other hand, a series of fissures and cuts illuminates the spaces dramatically while facilitating vertical communications. If we look at the floor plans, we recognize procedures Koolhaas has used in his urbanistic projects. The rectangle base is broken into a series of transverse bands associated with functions, uses, and services. Koolhaas skillfully introduces a ramp, which is associated with movement and allows us to speak once again of Le Corbusier's influence on his work. Also see how skillfully he handles the structure. The slanting structure, which helps give shape to the entrance hall and auditorium and

**65-69** Kunsthal, Rotterdam, 1987–1992

allows him to build one of the slanting planes mentioned before, is one of the most notable features of this building, where once again we appreciate the architect's capacity to avoid the simplistic formulas to which his followers have so often succumbed.

65-69 Kunsthal, Rotterdam, 1987-92

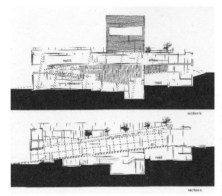

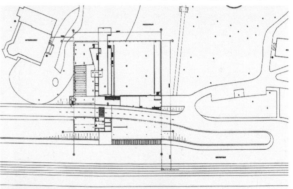

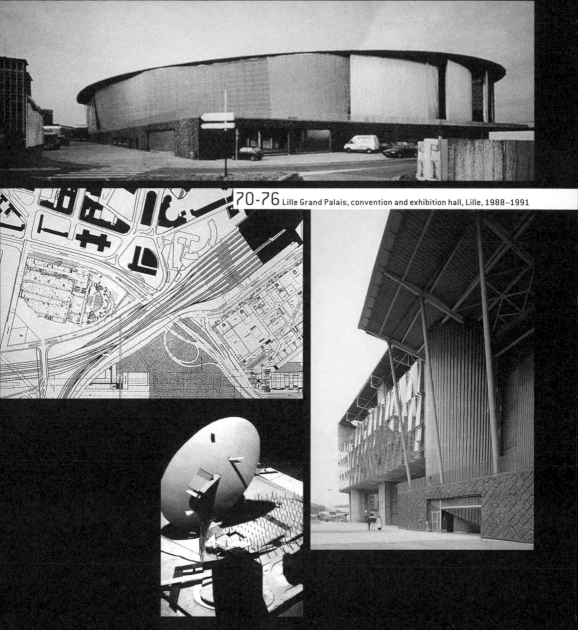

**70-76** Lille Grand Palais, convention and exhibition hall, Lille, 1988–1991

**70-76** Any discussion of the project for a convention and exhibition hall in Lille (1988–1991) must be preceded by an examination of the site plan. The place was awkward: broad and spacious, but the result of the encounter of railway and road systems; in other words, a huge and not easily accessible residual space. Koolhaas acknowledges the potent geometry established by the railway tracks when he erects his building in the form of an ovoid. As on so many other occasions, he wholeheartedly accepts the scale of the contemporary metropolis and the impact of the infrastructure that characterizes it, and proceeds to propose an architecture of categorical forms. Shunning volumes that are fragmented or the result of a process of aggregation, Koolhaas considers that the new architectural programs of a mass society need unitary, synthetic forms that ensure them a presence in the chaotic everyday environment. So the Lille project must be associated with the ovoid that, on one hand, makes it possible for him to draw a floor plan that doesn't come in conflict with the perimeter in which it is inscribed, and on the other hand shapes the oval saucer like a paten that makes the construction of the roof possible. As on other occasions,

Koolhaas demonstrates the value of emphatic, categorical gestures. Whoever remembers the gorgeous model, whose precision of form brought to mind works of sculptors like Brancusi, will easily accept categoricalness of form as one of the most characteristic features of Koolhaas's architecture. We previously saw this in the project for the Agadir hotel and convention center. I would say that Koolhaas's basic intuition of form is the seed of these works.

But how to proceed once the form of the container has been established? Koolhaas applies the theory of bands with no prejudgments whatsoever. This is confirmed through highly efficient diagrams. In this way he seems to indulge in the contrast between geometries, while telling us that the perimeter is something abstracted from the interior it contains. Interior and exterior are taken as two separate worlds. There would be nothing to object to in these contrasts if the same attitude had prevailed during construction. But now the contrast becomes awkward. The paten-shaped roof that Koolhaas seduced us with when he presented the model is now supported by a conventional, ambiguous, confusing structure. I don't understand how the same architect who associated structure and slanting planes in the Kunsthal of Rotterdam can now proceed so carelessly. The roof in the model—so categorical, so beautiful—seemed to ask for a continuous and coherent vertical structure. Le Corbusier was well aware of these problems in his monumental projects, and would have expected Koolhaas to follow the lesson of one who had at so many points of his career been his master. Equally disappointing is the roof itself. The continuity promised by the model has been interrupted by a whole series of transverse structural elements, ruining the spatial promises Koolhaas had so energetically formulated. As for the building envelopes, they are applied so indiscriminately that we can't tell with what criteria they have been handled. At some points it's as if Koolhaas were indulging in industrial materials. At other points he appears focused on pseudo-natural textures. Finally, there are moments at which he seems inclined toward plastic and textural experiments, as in that segment where glass and concrete engage in an inconsistent dialogue.

The force of the plan is not manifested on the exterior. The surrounding free space is turned into an unexpected

70-76 Lille Grand Palais, convention and exhibition hall, Lille, 1988–1991

structural element that makes use of the building possible. The interiors are the mere result of occupying spaces and lack character. The Kunsthal of Rotterdam comes to mind again. How different are these spaces, these staircases! What lack of control over the interiors, giving one the impression that the only thing the architect cared to design was an elemental resistant structure! The radicality of the plan disappears, so does the energy that went into the zoning of the building. And, of course, the feeling of being covered and protected by the emblematic bowl of the ovoid also vanishes completely.

This project—which I would put beside others that ambitiously associate the new monumental scale with basic categorical forms, inevitably yielding architecture where the iconographic predominates—required the ultimate test of a solid and coher-

358

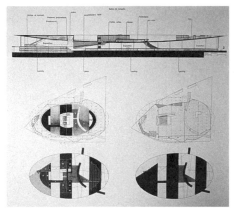

**70-76** Lille Grand Palais, convention and exhibition hall, Lille, 1988–1991

ent construction. What we see in Lille today confirms this. Primary, schematic, categorical, total architectures are impregnated with the iconography we admired in projects like the Agadir hotel and convention center. The Agadir model certainly justified our expectations of Koolhaas's work. But this commendable architectural agenda requires an adequate constructional response. Without one, there is nothing left in the end, not even that constructive violence that is often so attractive in an architect like Gehry. The sections of Lille do not in themselves have any formal value, nor do they solve the technical problems posed. The vulgar architecture that Koolhaas admired in New York City skyscrapers did solve problems, both constructionally and

formally. With Lille, we can't draw a parallel. Koolhaas's promise to resolve large-scale buildings with present-day architecture requires the skill he demonstrated in projects like the Bibliothèque de France. So let me end this lecture with the wish that Koolhaas will demonstrate that skill anew in the large-scale works awaiting him.

# HERZOG &
# DE MEURON

Jacques Herzog and Pierre de Meuron burst onto the contemporary architectural scene with a work that surprised friends and strangers alike, and which can be said to contain the seed of everything they would do in future. When at the close of the eighties they finished the Ricola warehouse, which magazines were quick to publish, suddenly they were architects whose careers were worth tracking, with both still under 40. After graduating from the Eidgenössische Technische Hochschule (the ETH) in Zurich, where they had had the opportunity to study under Aldo Rossi, they had carried out a handful of minor works in their native city of Basel, some of which we will look at later.

What exactly was surprising about the austere architecture of Ricola? At the end of a decade that had seen much excess, what critics and architects admired was its deliberate formal restraint that culminated in the canonical—a category that recent architecture, in the conviction that it was unreachable, seemed to have discarded. Despite reduced dimensions, the Ricola warehouse is a manifesto. Architecture need neither depend on externalities (function/program) nor find personal expression (language/style). It should be the formal result of its own logic. Hence, in Ricola, the space that the walls enclose—the simplest of rectangles—is neutral. There is not a single formal gesture of the kind that tends to constitute personal expression in architecture. The intelligent handling of a material, laminated wood, included applying formal aspects of traditional architecture to the light wall—aspects having to do with number, proportion and rhythm. At the same time, the solution of the specific—the cornice—gave rise to allusions to history: a certain flavor overwhelms us, at once archaic and modern, at the sight of this small but nevertheless intense work of contemporary architecture. The postmodern movement, with its absurd iconography, had worn itself out, and this Swiss architecture that seemed to ignore the academic discussions of the day by proposing new goals altogether was certainly very refreshing. The work of Herzog & de Meuron seems to be inspired and guided by a search for origins. This in fact was the objective insistently pursued by many artists of the second half of the twentieth century, who believed it would put them in line with an entire train of great thinkers, from Nietzsche to Heidegger. That a whole mode of going about architecture had worn itself out and we had come to the end of history was manifest in the senseless repetition of styles. Given the situation, there was room only for a return to origins: to start anew. Looking at Herzog & de Meuron's early buildings, especially Ricola, one thinks of Semper and initial moments like that of the very first builders. This is an architecture that arises from a construction where form is an expression of logic; it is architecture as the conspicuous structure. And so it is that the vibrating wall of Ricola, where the density of horizontal elements responds to simple gravity-related criteria, strikes us as something not too different from that used by the Cyclopean builders who would place the heaviest ashlars at the base, the point where the wall meets the ground. In this search for origins, unsurprisingly, Herzog & de Meuron renew in us a fascination for the archaic. And by doing so, they simply coincide with those who believe that culture needs new foundations. The history Foucault referred to as lord and master of the nineteenth century must be ignored. On one hand, the return to origins leads to the simplification of form, to extremes that leave no room for discussing expression. On the other hand, it leads to questions about the nature and potential of materials. The evolution of Herzog & de Meuron's career is a case in point. Some of their finest projects—the Dominus Winery in the Napa Valley naturally comes to mind—are architectures that explore the formal potential of materials, without such explorations necessarily calling for a structure. I would therefore say that their work is first and foremost a celebration of matter, where form is but the vehicle that makes this possible.

The importance given to matter and materials in their work—with the attendant importance of these in construction, through technique—comes with a deliberate suppression of image, a conscious abandonment of iconographic references. One could say that this is in open opposition to everything that involves stylistic caprice. For Herzog & de Meuron architecture appears, or is "deposited," in austere prismatic volumes, minimal units ready to be acted upon by the architect. If architecture offers the best it has by giving materials the capacity to show all they are capable of, then any subjection to form, whether dictated by language or by symbolic intentions, must be energetically rejected. We could therefore say that Herzog & de Meuron ignore iconography, renounce expression and communication, in order to win back for architecture the gravity of construction and bring about a joyful rediscovery of the fundamental nature of materials. Besides the first Ricola and Dominus buildings, suffice it to remember projects like the Stone House and the railway signal box in Basel. This is all contrary to what we saw in discussing some of Rem Koolhaas's projects, where we discerned an obsessive desire to find a synthetic form that could serve a program and place but also become a symbol, an icon with territorial value (for example, the Lille transportation hub). At least for a central part of their career, Herzog & de Meuron have seemed determined to resist the temptation of the iconographic: image does not exist. The essence of architecture lies in making materials talk, and for this it needs only the most elemental volumes. On these volumes the architects project the meshes and braidings that make the construction possible, and which can be considered the territory that architecture operates within. Iconographic references appear in only one or two of their latest projects, and only to be negated. As anyone familiar with their most recent works will guess, I am thinking of projects like the Rudin House.

The rejection of iconography also carried with it the rejection of any architecture that could be interpreted as a mere venting of the individual. Hence, we find no personal gestures in the work of Herzog & de Meuron. It does not have a formal stamp of the kind we saw in the work of Gehry, nor do its floor plans have the peculiar calligraphy of a Siza. Maybe Rossi taught them that an architect should distance himself from his works. Herzog & de Meuron's success—or, if you will, their synchronization with the sensibilities of the nineties—largely stems from this apparent renunciation of individuality, or from their relinquishing of the opportunity to manifest their individuality in their work. In times of democratic massification, architecture ceases to be a property of the individual, it ceases to be personal, to become instead a mere object of reflection and a harmless, inert frame for action. A similar thing has occurred in the aesthetics of the arts. The architecture of Herzog & de Meuron endeavors to work toward the specific from the universal. What matters is knowledge of the universal. The Ricola warehouse perfectly exemplifies this attitude. Its space is the direct consequence of its construction. Wall and roof, generated by a simple rectangle, are the primary and primordial architectural elements. The sophisticated wall is born of the architects' explicit desire to solve all problems in one stroke. Architecture, hence, as a synthetic expression of the problems posed by construction and use. Light, insulation, visual order, and so on serve as stimuli and motives for the work of the architect. By putting himself in the originary trance of construction, the architect comes up with what the ancients called architecture. It is candor when confronting a work, or confronting architecture, that allows the architect to discover the efficiency of numbers, series, and finally rhythms. By operating in this manner, like a builder ready to encounter an unknown reality, the architect discovers the territory we know as architecture.

To make architecture is to build. It is to give life to materials, which acquire in the built thing their true nature, their true selves. Herzog & de Meuron are well aware of this. They do everything in their power to make materials express themselves as what they are, and in doing so they chance upon new proposals, new ways of using the materials. Materials are what make forms emerge. In Ricola, the flat nature of the wooden panels is what ultimately brings about the texture of the wall, and it is here that the construction manifests itself as an architectural form. Their Orthodox church project anticipated the potential of traditional glass. In the Blue House of Oberwil, Switzerland, the concrete blocks are transformed when painted. The construction by way of panels calls for divisions, so it is the divisions that are made responsible for the character, the "drawing," of the surface. Herzog & de Meuron's sensibility for materials gives rise to the sophisticated experiment we find in the Stone House in Tavole. The role played by the different materials—concrete, blocks, stone—is crucial in defining the position of the windows, the connection of the ceilings to the walls, and so on. The materials help define the structure, which is exposed to view. Thus the importance of joints in the architecture of Herzog & de Meuron. The basic elements, often products of a manufacturing process, have to be put together with joints, so anyone interested in going deeper into the subject of their architecture must pay attention to these.

This interest in materials reaches a peak with the invention of materials. The Dominus Winery is a good example. Obviously Herzog & de Meuron admire those infrastructural works in which gabions (large blocks composed of loose rubble encased in steel cages) are used to build walls. But it's a surprising experience to see the gabions from inside the building, with the sun's rays filtering through the gaps. The architects have transformed the conventional gabions of Swiss highways into a new and inimitable material. The Dominus experience becomes a unique sensation that can in theory be transported to another place; but the invention of the new material addressed a specific architecture. It wouldn't be easy, therefore, to extrapolate the invention elsewhere.

It may be relevant to talk about archaism, a concept that seems neither far from nor alien to the desire to reencounter origins that we have been discussing. Let us say that the prize awaiting those who take such intricate paths is a reencounter with a reality that expresses the desire for permanence present in much of primitive architecture: the logic of construction is so evident that any temptation to let aesthetic parameters come into play is forgotten. Although the architecture of Herzog & de Meuron is rooted, as we shall shortly see, in modern tradition, their commitment to construction is so patent that it may rightly be described as elemental and primary. Hence its echoes of archaism. But their interest in materials is ecumenical; it does not exclude materials produced by industry. Side by side with architectures in which the materials seem to celebrate their natural or telluric origins are many others where Herzog & de Meuron reveal an interest in assimilating the artificial, what a world governed by industry can offer. (Among these materials, they have paid particular attention to glass. Indeed, I would like to stress the invaluable contribution that Herzog & de Meuron have made to the practice of the profession through their projects and constructions in glass.) Their interest in industrial materials rules out any temptation to assimilate their archaism to the manner of the romantic thinker or noble savage. On the contrary, in their architecture there is always a desire to cool the fire of the spontaneous, or extinguish it altogether, true to that renunciation of personal gesture we mentioned before.

One perceives in their work a puritanical attitude that recalls someone like Mies van der Rohe, who was obsessed with showing us that reality—that is, his buildings—couldn't be any other way. When the logic of construction becomes the physicality of the architecture, and this identity becomes the controlling condition of his work, the architect's freedom, his capacity to choose forms freely, begins to come into doubt. Nevertheless we have to draw a line between the two parties and situate the Swiss architects in time. Whereas Mies's obsession was to purify the means of construction he worked with in order to establish a universal and absolute language, Herzog & de Meuron take pleasure in the specific, the concrete. Their architecture responds to particular, precise, well-defined situations, to each of which they associate a material that has a meaning of its own, and the procedure has its supreme moment when a material is actually invented, as in the Dominus Winery. But the materials, the means of construction, are handled with a conscious effort not to trap them in the framework of a single and exclusive language. Quite a far cry from Mies.

The endeavor to return to origins is not far removed from some of the artistic tendencies of the times, and so it is that Herzog & de Meuron have often been presented as exemplifying minimalist architecture. The artists who worked their way from what was called conceptual art to the tendency known as minimalism emphasized the value of the simplest forms and aspired to bring out the energy of anything that was matter, eliminating all allusions to representation and personal expression. The minimalists proposed a reflexive understanding of artworks, leaving up to the spectator all possible judgments and establishing certain aesthetic criteria not too different from those that Herzog & de Meuron make use of for their architecture. The prisms with which Herzog & de Meuron began their architectural explorations are not unlike the formal proposals of artists like Carl Andre or Donald Judd. The admiration they have always professed for Helmut Federle would help us specify their affinities and tastes. Federle is not a minimalist to the letter, but the manner in which he takes up the territory of the canvas, forcing the spectator to feel included in its austere but absorbing formal world, is very close to the way Herzog & de Meuron make use of materials, turning them into the actual protagonists of a world that one cannot possibly feel excluded from.

It may not be possible to draw as close a parallel between Herzog & de Meuron and minimalism as the one drawn by earlier critics between Le Corbusier and cubism, but surely few architects nowadays are as responsive to the proposals of artists as Herzog & de Meuron, and this may be the moment to insinuate that, if there is any help from the outside world that can be useful to architects, it comes from the experiences of artists. The relation between architecture and painting has given rise to a broad field of study. That this relation can extend to our times is an attractive idea, and makes the work of Herzog &

de Meuron interesting in a way that transcends the purely disciplinary. Theirs is not a common attitude, and to affirm this one has only to compare them to Rem Koolhaas—the closest to Herzog & de Meuron chronologically of the architects discussed in these lectures. Although it is possible to trace ties between Koolhaas's architecture and some contemporary artists (as we did between Koolhaas and Andy Warhol or David Salle), the Dutch architect has never expressly proclaimed a connection to any aesthetic current, whereas Herzog & de Meuron frequently allude to their debt to contemporary art styles.

As a counterpoint to the aesthetic attitude of Herzog & de Meuron, something must be said about the importance they have always given to professional commitment—about the pure pragmatism of their work, if you will. The fact is that from the very start of their career, Herzog & de Meuron have put much weight on the practice of the profession. Their incursion into the international scene was not the outcome of a proselytizing activity carried out in an academic environment (the case of Venturi, Eisenman, Rossi), nor of the publication of an attractive or provocative manifesto (Koolhaas), but of widespread recognition of a bona fide professional practice, with all its attendant subjection to the conventional rules of the game. As we will see, the Ricola pavilion was hardly their first work, and those that preceded it are of a solidity and consistency that were a premonition of what was to come. Such consciousness of themselves as practicing architects, such pragmatism, proves that the work of Herzog & de Meuron is strongly rooted in the society they live in, that of Switzerland. From the very beginning, their works have reflected some of the virtues and attributes that have accompanied Swiss architecture in the past: respect for place, attention to scale, rigor, and careful handling of detail. Comparison to the seven other architects of these lectures is inevitable. On one hand we have Herzog & de Meuron's willing emphasis on professional practice. On the other, the more radical attitudes of those who proclaim themselves theoreticians (Eisenman, Rossi, Koolhaas), those who indulge in sophisticated provocation (Gehry, early Venturi), and those who followed a narrow path in professional work in order to make a name for themselves (Stirling, Siza).

In my opinion, it makes sense to place Herzog & de Meuron in the uninterrupted chain of modern Swiss architects that includes the likes of Karl Moser,

Hans Bernoulli, and O. R. Salvisberg, or even the heterodox and disturbing Hannes Meyer. Right measure, precision, and rigor are qualities that quickly come to mind when we think of the work of these architects, and it isn't difficult to recognize them in the architecture of Herzog & de Meuron as well. These qualities accompany an approach to architecture that is based on reason, and this, I believe, has always been the criterion of Herzog & de Meuron when setting strategies for their work. They pursue—or pursued—the minimal prism, stripped of all personal allusions, but this hasn't prevented them from delicately encrusting a window into a concrete wall (in the student residence, Dijon), or from superposing two grids with an exquisite geometry (in the SUVA office building, Basel). Such a deliberately professional mindset perhaps explains the continuous presence of technics in their work, yielding very unique buildings. Contemporary architects are preoccupied with other questions. Few pay attention to the importance of incorporating technics into architecture. Hence, Herzog & de Meuron deserve credit for their efforts in supplying a solution to a problem that is nowadays crucial for architecture: the construction of the curtain wall. Herzog & de Meuron's contribution to the development of glass technology is invaluable. And their professional pragmatism has also led them to explore and contribute generously to the architecture of housing, where they have worked on known types but added nuances that have occasionally transformed them.

Having said this much about their commitment to country and professional practice, it may be good to establish a continuity between the rationalism of interwar Swiss architecture and the architecture of Herzog & de Meuron. The premises of avant-garde architecture in the period between the wars, notwithstanding the critical positions taken against them, have been an obligatory reference in the course of the entire second half of the twentieth century. There is, however, a certain contradiction between advocating the rediscovery of the elemental on one hand—an attitude that calls for depth and brings the architectural work close to the condition of a trance—and professionalism on the other hand, which makes Herzog & de Meuron accept the most diverse commissions and compete in the crudest of markets. An architecture of high goals is by definition not compatible with a professional practice that is willing to accept the rules of the game and understand that repetition is sometimes inevitable. Herzog & de Meuron's architecture in the late eighties and after did not always have the intensity of their earlier works. Here and there we can find unnecessary details of outside influence that turn the buildings into communicating machines, deprived of the hermetic opacity that so enthralled us in their first works. I must say at this point (to anticipate the commentary on the illustrations) that their works did not in fact always merit a favorable judgment. I think of the SUVA building, the Pfaffenholz sports center, the new Ricola factory, the library in Eberswalde, the projects for the Jussieu campus of the University of Paris, and the cultural center in Blois. These works and projects leave no doubt about Herzog & de Meuron's professional capacities, but in each of them the architects' field of action is limited to control of the facades, the definition of the skin. The materials now only serve to do just that; gone is the structural condition of the solid that mesmerized us in the early works. Fortunately, works like the Dominus Winery are the happy, very happy, exception, and we will be giving them special attention. We will also be looking at other works that, in their search for new courses, reveal a clear capacity for self-criticism. Examples are the Rudin House, the Cottbus library, and the Centro Óscar Domínguez in Las Palmas. All this makes the future of Herzog & de Meuron as exciting as their beginnings. So, without further delay, let us examine their works.

**1-5** Plywood House, Bottmingen, Switzerland, 1984–1985

**1-5** The Plywood House in Bott-mingen (1984–1985) was an early work in which Herzog & de Meuron explored the most elemental aspects of construction. They discovered that constructing implies, first of all, the creation of a horizontal plane on which to move about, covered by another plane that, also horizontal, protects us and fosters the use of the space in between. Like Mies, Herzog & de Meuron understood that the lifting of the horizontal plane to separate us from the ground, the earth, is a true foundational gesture, the one moment that gives rise to a building process. The enclosing comes later and in an almost autonomous manner. There is a near-obsessive determination to make a clear and fundamental distinction between ground and building. The paneling and the ceiling, the positioning of the upper horizontal plane, become key elements of the materiality that engenders a building. The paneling is therefore responsible for the window and door openings. The interior space is a neutral and inert given, unfolding in a way we might call automatic.

But despite the endeavor to attain the generic or universal by associating the architecture of the house with what we have called "foundational gestures," Herzog & de Meuron are sensitive to conditions that are specific to each construction. Here they acknowl-

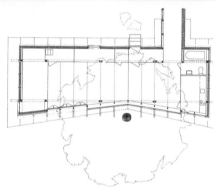

1-5 Plywood House, Bottmingen, Switzerland, 1984–1985

edge the presence of a tree and allow it to give rise to the inflection that moves the architecture. Not that the Plywood House owes its form to this circumstance. No one would consider the house a consequence of the tree. For the architects, the important thing is to define the construction, to establish a system that in the final analysis can embrace the specific. To think of this as an example of an architecture that makes circumstance its starting point would be to misinterpret the work of Herzog & de Meuron. Quite the contrary. It is the quest for the universal, the elemental, that seems to have been their concern from the very beginning of their career.

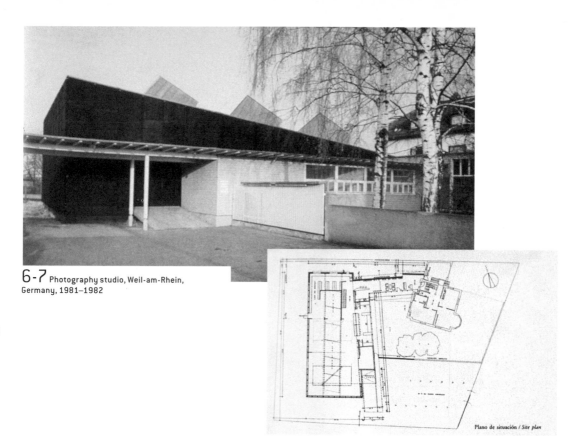

6-7 Photography studio, Weil-am-Rhein, Germany, 1981–1982

Plano de situación / *Site plan*

6-7 The penchant for the purest construction comes to the fore in the Weil-am-Rhein photography studio (1981–1982). Here, the architecture seems to want to find its essence in function. The building can be read as an enormous camera where the skylights play the role of the diaphragm. Pay attention to the floor plan and the painstaking exercise in articulation implied by the passage from the preexisting construction to the workshop. One can rightly speak of functionalist puritanism when contemplating a work like this.

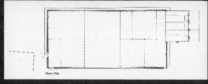

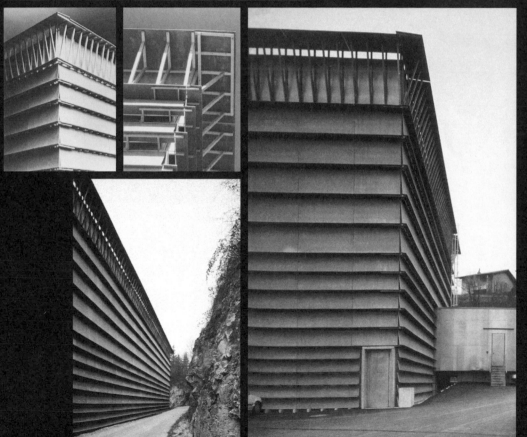

**8-13** The Ricola warehouse in Laufen (1986–1987), situated in an industrial complex, was an opportunity for Herzog & de Meuron to draw up a radical proposal: architecture as visual unfolding of the construction. Neither the floor plan nor the section nor any concept of space would be their referents here. The important thing was to make the construction visible and tangible. It is the skin of the void generated by a rectangle that the architect manipulates. Aware of this, and once it was accepted that the construction system would be based on wooden panels, Herzog & de Meuron set about to explore how a form could be generated. The strict volume is constructed through the artifice of exposing the panel joints, enhanced with horizontal pieces that have the effect of dotting the surfaces with numbers and proportions—parameters for design, the attributes that architecture always makes use of. The horizontal pieces may suggest a nostalgia for the thickness and magnitude of past stone walls. Manipulating the repeated form of the wooden panels creates three intervals defined by the breadth of the band with which each is worked out, and the use of these three different measurements creates an upward sense that allows us to talk about rhythm. The strict construction, the purest of tectonics, recuperates notions and concepts for us that seem always to have been present in architecture.

This observation is endorsed when we see that the three increasing intervals that have defined this upward rhythm are finished off with a cornice that, inevitably, calls to mind traditional wooden construction. The exploration of a possible new way of working with wooden panels seems to come in conflict with an ancient gesture. The shape of the building recalls those primitive constructions that all cultures have built to protect the food that has so laboriously been taken from the earth.

The sophisticated wall that seems to be the ultimate object of the project is born of the architects' explicit desire to solve all problems in one stroke. The construction thus acquires a degree of generality that makes it something abstract, not specific. Let us pay attention to a singular detail: the corner. Herzog & de Meuron do not waver: the corner does not give rise to reflections on how a solid is built. For them it is clear that the corner is simply the encounter of two different planes. So the two walls meet, and a beautiful, unexpected detail appears.

We are lured by the immediacy of the gesture, which becomes the emblem of an entire procedure. But the gesture is really not fortuitous. Just compare how the corner under the eave was solved in the model with the solution that was later adopted in the actual construction, and it is evident that the architects worked hard to refine it. So, curiously, their zeal for the elemental, their desire to attain the essential construction, gave rise to the singular, the unique. Also pay attention to the unsettling interstitial space between the warehouse and the hill slope. And finally, observe how the architects made the most of the encounter of an ordinary element—a door—and the episode that characterizes the architecture, the wall of light wooden panels.

**14-15** In the Stone House in Tavole, Italy (1982–1988), too, the architecture centers on the construction of the wall. Again, the architects made construction the substance of the architecture. In this case they concentrated on a question that would recur throughout their career. The infilling, the relation between structure and enclosure, is the protagonist of this architecture. The structure here is the concrete grid, a grid that guarantees the construction of interior spaces while contributing to the stability of the wall. The envelope is a stone wall that appears to be constructed dry, without mortar, a technique that has existed since the Neolithic. Stone predominates, and one would say that, anticipating what would occur in many future works of theirs, Herzog & de Meuron manage to make us see the architecture as a eulogy of the material it is constructed of. With an attitude I would call phenomenological, they make us perceive it as the purest manifestation of the petrous. The concrete frame practically disappears in the exterior walls, taking on an ambiguous double role. On one hand, it can be understood as a mere joint for the stone surfaces, which need it for stability. On the other hand, we know it serves another, very different purpose when we see it become a subtle cross, governing the vertical plane by establishing the quadrants that define the formal structure of the stone surface.

The cross, in turn, leads us to a discussion of the floor plan. Here we have a hermetic floor plan with no trace of movement and no distinctions dictated by use (questions that frequently determine the floor plan). The hermetic floor

**14-15** Stone House, Tavole, Italy, 1982–1988

plan is yet another proof of Herzog & de Meuron's desire that their works take on the nature of abstract objects. Hence, the Stone House is a silent object that gives few clues to its instrumental virtues.

As in the Ricola warehouse, where an opening is inserted in the wood-paneled wall and a canopy protects loading and unloading activities, so in the Stone House there are moments when the norms imposed by the architects themselves are violated. The band of horizontal windows of the top floor is one such anomaly, to be understood as a breather from the rigidity that otherwise acccompanies strict compliance with puritanical norms. For Herzog & de Meuron, the anomalies are transgressions of the norms that anchor their constructions to the world around them.

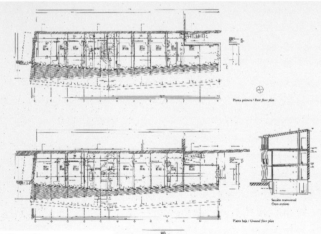

Planta primera / First floor plan

Planta baja / Ground floor plan

Sección transversal
Cross sections

80

**16-18** Apartment building, Hebelstrasse, Basel, 1987–1988

**16-18** Though it may strike us as less radical and at some point ambiguous, this apartment building on Hebelstrasse in Basel (1987–1988) is in my opinion one of Herzog & de Meuron's best works. Let us start with the floor plan. No one should be surprised when I say that it follows an innovative strategy. The idea of occupying an inner courtyard on ground that still maintains the memory of medieval property division made the architects insist on a longitudinal structure attached to one of the party walls. The floor plan of the apartments respects this primary and primordial decision. The key element of the bourgeois dwelling is the room. It accommodates either a use/activity (dining room, living room) or the individual (bedroom). Here the bourgeois dwelling takes on its most direct expression by dispensing with spatial articulation and connecting the rooms through the simplest mechanism, the corridor. Parallel to the corridor, an uninterrupted balcony seems to stress the formal elementality of the planimetric proposal. The floor plan is laconic, minimal. No one would say that it generates the architecture. Only an inflection in the facade introduces the accident that comes into dialectical conflict with the alignment of the roof. Like the Plywood House, the house on Hebelstrasse stresses the structural value of the system of horizontal planes, made manifest in the lightweight edge that is drawn with precision in the front of the balconies. Once again, the choice of material is crucial. It determines not only the character but also the appearance, the physicality that gives life to a building. Then, consider to what extent the mode of construction resolves solids and voids, partitions and windows, all at the same time. In this particular case, wood—of the kind more linked to the past, in a craft tradition—is used for the pillars, elegantly shaped pillars that become key iconographic elements. The house on Hebelstrasse owes its image to these pillars, ambiguous elements if ever there were. They are perhaps also responsible for giving the house a certain archaic, timeless look—certainly a far cry from the styles and manners we have decided to call modern. Like other works of Herzog & de Meuron, the house offers us a generic, universal lesson on how to build, but it is precisely through its generic condition that there is an encounter with the past and we are able to talk about archaism. Of course this archaic flavor is then neutralized by the way the higher horizontal plane, the roof, is manipulated. Herzog & de Meuron apparently went about it very freely, in a way that has little to do with the puritanical exhibition of an immaculate construction that the rest of the house is. Perhaps in such inconsistency lies the charm of the building.

**19-21** Herzog & de Meuron's professional mindset comes to the fore again in the Schwitter Apartments in Basel (1985–1988), which had to address a larger market than those on Hebelstrasse. As we have seen, their early works had put emphasis on the construction of the horizontal plane. They now used this experience, conceiving the new building as a simple superposition of horizontal planes. Once again they entrusted the definition of the building to its envelope, which in this case, anticipating future projects, would be in glass. As in Hebelstrasse, the contrast between two profiles—here the perimeters of the balconies and the apartment units—determines the shape of the building. Hence what we call architecture takes shape through the meeting of opposites. This dialectic is the instrument through which architecture becomes a conspicuous reality. Le Corbusier was one of the masters in the handling of this efficient instrument for creating architectural forms.

**22-24** Here is another sample of Herzog & de Meuron's professional versatility. But whereas we might describe the floor plan of the Schwitter Apartments as simply correct, the elongated unit plan of this other apartment building in Basel (1984–1993) is more subtle, complex. This is in my opinion the best thing about the building, is the control of the floor plans at different levels, carried out with admirable precision, gives rise to a very interesting public interior space. The building's presence on the street is made to depend on the window blinds, which cease to be traditional elements because they are manufactured in metal. But despite the architects' good intentions of recuperating ornament, such liberty does not echo positively in the design, and one can't help yearning for the lightness and efficiency of traditional blinds. Herzog & de Meuron's assertion of non-dependence on context does not in this case yield anything of particular value. The building dispenses with a perhaps desirable continuity with its neighbors, but, given the narrowness of the lot, without assuming the protagonism that would have warranted discontinuity.

**19-21** Schwitter Apartments, Basel, 1985–1988

**22-24** Apartment building, Basel, 1984–1993

25-28 The idea of formally modifying a known floor plan—an exercise that stems from typological considerations and calls to mind the rationalist *Siedlungen*—led Herzog & de Meuron to explore the reach of their principles in an architecture of greater scales. The sketch of the project for the dwellings on Pilotengasse in Vienna (1987–1992)—a drawing that aspires to have a figurative value in itself and evokes artists like Lucio Fontana—shows how aware the architects were of the ground they were operating on. Their intervention makes use of geometry, and a simple rupture of the orthogonal order can have a huge bearing on the result. Hence, what was subjected in the original orthogonal scheme to the tyranny of the perspective view becomes a unitary image, thanks to the insertion of the dwellings within an arc, which makes them elements shaping a higher-order element. This reading of the complex as a unitary gesture, in which orthogonality is implicitly forgotten, makes the space resist the perspective view, and this undoubtedly means a substantial shift from the models the architects began from. In this way, Herzog & de Meuron prove how efficient interventions we would describe as "minimal" can be in visual terms, thereby again invoking the aesthetic sphere they like to situate themselves in.

But having made these observations, I would like to point out the subtle presence of transverse cuts that introduce a capillary network of paths, raising doubts about the categorical gesture of the arched strokes. We must also mention the degree to which an urban scheme like that of Pilotengasse gives importance to interstitial spaces. Possibly the most potent of these is the space that defines the convex condition of the last arched row of houses, or the one that reinstates the perimeter of the parcel. In my opinion, these images endorse such an affirmation. But leaving aside all these reflections that draw attention to the scheme, Pilotengasse was also an opportunity to make interesting linguistic proposals. Herzog & de Meuron indulged in strictly linguistic epithelial transformations of the walls, in search of a diversity that would make the district lose that utopian vision of a future society that had stimulated the builders of the *Siedlungen*. Maybe we should consider this architectural experience a symptom of times in which socialist ideals tend to give way to a new social democratic credo.

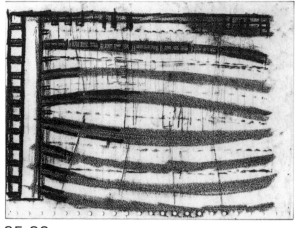

**25-28** Housing on Pilotengasse,
Vienna, 1987–1992

**29-30** Railway depot,
Basel, 1989–1995

**29-30** Chronologically close to Pilotengasse is the railway depot in Basel (1989–1995), another opportunity for Herzog & de Meuron to operate on a large scale. Serialization, repetition, and continuity are the inevitable questions surrounding the construction and the architecture. A desire to associate form with construction is evident in the monumental structural elements of the roof span. These huge elements, which seem to want to exalt the dimensions that befit an infrastructural architecture, resolve the illumination problem of the monumental roof, thereby becoming abstract grids in space that remind us of the aesthetic principles on which Herzog & de Meuron's architecture is based. The general look recalls the architecture of the *Siedlungen*. Whether for persons or locomotives, the question of storage would ordinarily call for one same form; but here there is no more need for that quest for diversity which in Pilotengasse made the buildings seem camouflaged, and the architects indulge in transforming a space's usefulness into an aesthetic experience, at least for the initiated.

**31-34** The project for an Orthodox church in Zurich (1989) is another well-worked proposal of Herzog & de Meuron, and what a pity it was never carried out. Start by observing how intelligently the existing difference in street levels is used to inscribe a dihedral. The two planes of the dihedral form the facades of the volumes of the church's ancillary services, while on a third plane—the dihedral's horizontal—rises the prism of the actual church, which presents itself as a solid freed of any obligation to conform with

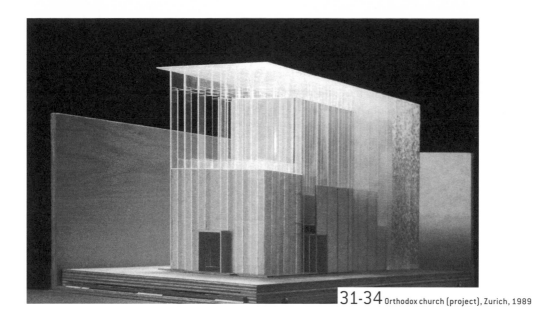

**31-34** Orthodox church (project), Zurich, 1989

the lot's alignments. The result is that the church appears as something loose or exempt, enjoying a volumetric autonomy that Herzog & de Meuron go on to exploit. In its enigmatic transparencies, the austere solid anticipates a complex and evocative interior space.

With a lot of talent, Herzog & de Meuron make the most of the spaces transpiring between the translucent solid and the walls of the dihedral. These walls can be understood as a background or frame for the edges defining the volume of the church, which in its reduced scale comes across majestically from the lower

plane and can hardly be seen from the higher street. The minimal solid containing the sacred space is constructed with a double wall of glass that leads to the proposal for a beautiful facade. It could be said that the Orthodox church assumes at once the thickness of Romanesque walls and the light transparency of the Gothic. It is hence not difficult to imagine an aerial interior where religious sentiments are associated with the fantasy of a levitating architectural space. But if we have mentioned the Gothic and the Romanesque in speaking of the construction and the atmosphere of the church, we

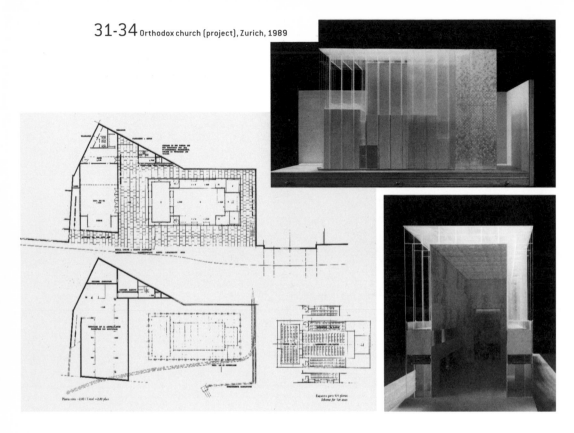

**31-34** Orthodox church (project), Zurich, 1989

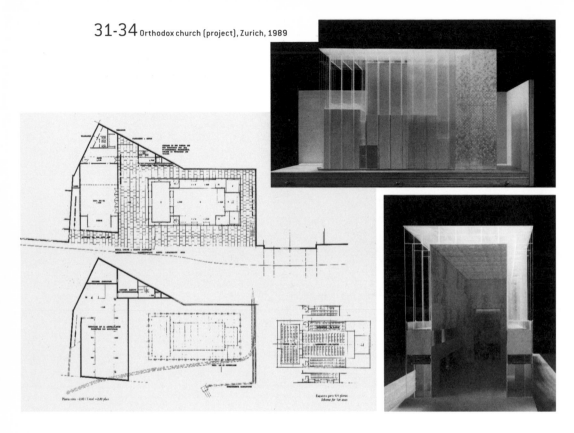

must also recognize the Byzantine. The images on the glass inevitably bring to mind old mosaics, and the verticality of the space recalls the churches of Ravenna. Everything is light, and matter dissolves in the luminous experience. Herzog & de Meuron were among the first to discover the importance of translucent glass for nineties architecture. The diffuse light emanating from the wall itself would have been the protagonist of this architecture, had it been carried out. Was it modeled after Koolhaas's Bibliothèque de France? Chronology justifies the drawing of a connection to that project.

35-36 Cultural center (project), Blois, 1991

LA REGARDANT. SI JE POUVAIS LIRE DANS TA TETE...

JEAN PAUL SARTRE

LES MAINS SALES   JE

387

35-36 It would seem correct to refer to Koolhaas, and an architecture full of activity, when we talk about the cultural center for Blois of 1991. In this case, consistency in the floor plans does not yield an attractive volume: the conventional design of the facade is not compensated for by the messages à la Jenny Holzer that the parapets of the floor slabs promise. The use, and later abuse, of a building as a broadcaster of images is such that the messages themselves lose their character as provocative urban elements.

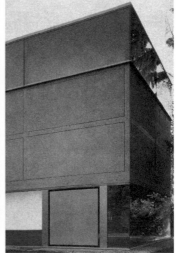

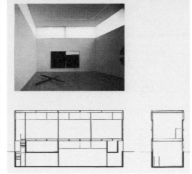

**37-41** Goetz Art Gallery, Munich, 1989–1992

**37-41** The connection between minimalism and the work of Herzog & de Meuron is evident in works like the Goetz Art Gallery in Munich (1992). For this project, it could be said that the architects pursued no other goal than to isolate a piece of pure abstract space. Here a work of art could offer itself to us in all its splendor—an inert, neutral atmosphere with the capacity to display art of the late twentieth century. But what did such an atmosphere look like? How to present or represent it? These questions led to another: what does the solid that contains it look like? From the very start of their career, Herzog & de Meuron had diligently pursued the goal of transforming the abstract, generic solid into a building. Because of the eternal question of architecture, which leads one to think of interior and exterior at the same time, the minimal solids that Herzog & de Meuron work with are not impenetrable solid masses. Their masses rely on a system of voids inside them, in this case created by the superposition of two nearly identical floor levels, judging from the dimensions and positions of the windows, though they fragment differently to define the spaces occupied by the Goetz collection. Once again proportion, measurement, and the construction of the wall are what count, and the architects' presence is reduced to these. As for the uninterrupted window, we call it a window only out of force of habit, because the architects' real intention was to transform a portion of the walls defining the public space into a continuous band from which light emanates. The continuity of the luminous band makes us overlook the corner, a mechanism that accounts for the disturbing alternation of glass and concrete. Herzog & de Meuron here also show us the degree to which they want materials to express their identities regardless of the structural functions that have been assigned them.

Again the floor plan, opaque and hermetic, excludes movement. The passages that connect the spaces must be understood as inevitable perforations that make it possible for us to move from one to another, in a way not too unlike the passage through a diaphragm that physicists call osmosis. This has nothing to do with traditional corridors. We have before us an architectural object that in a way could be described as organic. The sections clarify these points and help us appreciate the way space is used: the mechanisms are almost always closer to subdivision than to grouping. Two more observations are in order. One has to do with the floor plan: as in the Stone House, the division of spaces is not carried out through known elements, and there is a constant effort to eliminate any possible references to elements. Hence the walls that materialize the different spaces, or rooms, hardly have thickness, and they can be identified neither as jambs nor as doors. The other observation is about the importance Herzog & de Meuron give to the way materials meet, and this leads us to an architect who may seem a far cry from them in sensibilities, yet is present in an important aspect of their work. Needless to say, I am thinking of Louis Kahn's use of materials.

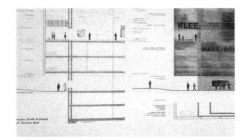

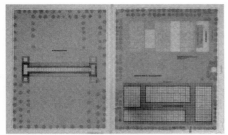

**42-43** Museum complex (project), Munich, 1992

**42-43** In a way, this 1992 proposal for a museum complex in Munich can be interpreted as an extension of the previous project. We will therefore not dwell on it. Suffice it to point out the elementality of the floor plan. The Alte Pinakothek by Leo von Klenze is a building that gives value to masses, according to compositional criteria we can rightly call classical, and ignores the perimeter of the lot it stands on. Here, in contrast, Herzog & de Meuron propose a set of buildings that emphasize the boundaries of the lot they stand on and decompose the area inside according to a series of rectan-

gular forms, whose autonomy makes itself felt from interstitial spaces that would certainly have played a definitive role in the architectural experience of this project had it been carried out.

**44-45** Herzog & de Meuron's professionalism stands out again in the SUVA office building in Basel (1988–1993). All their attention went to developing the glass facade, which this time had to assume the features of a conventional program. The result is an efficient building where the exposure of built elements determines aesthetic content, which in turn indulges in a minimalism dictated by an obligatory submission to certain well-defined conditions (insulation, solar protection, etc.).

**44-45** SUVA office building, Basel, 1988–1993

46-49 Ricola, the client that had given Herzog & de Meuron their big break in the mid-eighties, summoned them again ten years later for a building with a similar program: an industrial pavilion in Mulhouse (1992–93). There are similarities with the first job as far as attitude is concerned: the same pragmatism in the floor plans and the same lack of prejudgments in assigning new uses to materials. But there are greater differences. If the first Ricola building lent itself to discussions of provocative archaism, based on making construction the substance of the form, in the second the architects seem to have been preoccupied with discovering the potential of materials and procedures of conventional construction. The new Ricola pavilion served them as a laboratory for testing the degree to which industrial serialization could be a mechanism for reincorporating image and iconography in architecture. When the architects used industrial materials in the construction, the architecture gained an unexpected iconographic component. So it is that a common curtain wall here acquires a new status. The serigraphed glass panes allude unreservedly to lost ornamentation. The insistent repetition of a figure, though also replete with architectural resonances, recalls an artist like Warhol and his search for artistic expression in a mass culture. Is this sudden interference of the figurative related to the architects' apparent interest in ensuring that industrialized architecture doesn't lose all the attributes of traditional architecture? Is Warhol the inspiration for this

46-49 Ricola industrial building, Mulhouse, France, 1992–1993

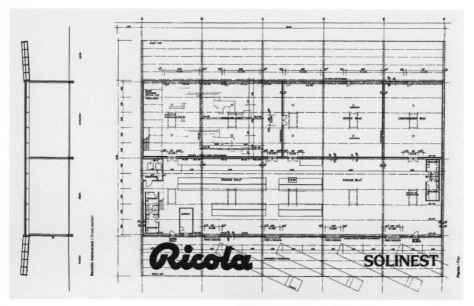

**46-49** Ricola industrial building, Mulhouse, France, 1992–1993

proposal? The answers are in the air. In the meantime, let's say that the serigraphy
satisfies a desire for an architectural work that testifies to "artistic intentions."
Never mind that the architects do nothing to hide the commonness of the industrialized construction systems used.

**50-52** Student residence, University of Burgundy, Dijon, 1990–1992

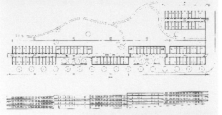

**50-52** Yet another sample of Herzog & de Meuron's professional capacity. The student residence in Dijon (1990–1992) brings to mind that illustrious constellation of Swiss professionals of the first half of the twentieth century composed of Salvisberg, Moser, Bernoulli. But unlike the SUVA building, where efficiency ended up overshadowing the architectural achievements, Dijon shows how far Herzog & de Meuron's aesthetic minimalism—when it reaches its goals, and without losing sight of its radical proposal—yields unexpected results that have to be taken as bona fide contributions to professional knowledge. In Dijon, the concrete frame's radical encounter with the metal elements of the windows results in an architecture that is a clear manifestation of pragmatism. The student bedrooms are halfway between institutional and private architecture. By making its function apparent, Herzog & de Meuron come up with an eloquent construction. No one can doubt that it is a university building, where both the solitude of the individual and the communality of social life are addressed. All this in an architectural exercise where the architects seem to have resorted only to the syntax of the construction and the concrete volume activated by the windows.

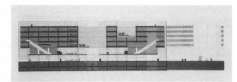

**53-54** Library (project), Jussieu campus, University of Paris, 1993

**53-54** It is easy to connect this competition project for a library for Jussieu (1993) with the cultural center in Blois. But although the floor plan has interesting aspects—curiously with echoes of El Escorial in Spain—I feel no enthusiasm for these cluttered facades that to me bear the stamp of an architect I understand Herzog & de Meuron much admired in those years, Rem Koolhaas.

**55-58** The commission for a control center of a railway station—by definition a hermetic building—was an optimal opportunity to design a solid in all its splendor. That is how Herzog & de Meuron took it. The signal box of the Basel railway station (1994–1998) is a giant artifact evoking those electrical transformers that are always amazing on account of their dimensions. How exactly did the architects arrive at such a potent result? First they accepted a given: the volume of a conventional building meant to contain railway equipment. This they then wrapped with a copper skin: a clear packaging operation not so different from that used for ordinary household appliances. The signal box is thus an exaltation of copper. A material that architects have used to build roofs now took on an identity of its own. Applying a copper skin to a whole solid is not a literal operation, nor is it predictable or anticipated. On the contrary, there were no precedents. Herzog & de Meuron went about this work with their usual sophistication. The slats at first sight seem to follow a uniform scheme of parallels but soon reveal an anomaly, a subtle skew. The solid dressed with fins of copper vibrates, producing an optical illusion that brings to mind reflections on silk. Once again, a minimalist aesthetic made it possible for them to explore new looks for built solids, and this in turn led them to open up a territory they had previously shunned, the territory of architectural iconography. Herzog & de Meuron's debt to minimal-

55-58 Signal box, Basel railway station, 1994–1998

ism is evident. The basic solid here endeavors to lose its character as a solid and show only the material condition of one of its elements. Can architecture bring out the attributes of copper? Herzog & de Meuron try to make it do so. Unfortunately, at nightfall, lights go on inside and the slats don't hide the gleam of the conventional windows. The solid loses its enigma and just has to wait for the dawn of a new day, when it becomes its true self again. In any case, the iconographic force of this unexpected volume remains engraved in our retinas.

59-65 Surely the Dominus Winery (1995–1997) should serve as the ultimate endorsement of affirming materials as architecture's vehicle of expression. Herzog & de Meuron's elemental solid, the simplest parallelepiped, more distant than it is arrogant, more silent than outspoken, is now a Cyclopean wall made of gabions of rough stone. Like the railway signal box that we have just seen, this work of architecture is a true exaltation and celebration of material. To be sure, a material that does not need a form—the observation about iconography that we made when examining the signal box doesn't apply here. This is tantamount to saying that the form can be absent and mute, removed from context. Only the material is present; only the material has a right to express itself. This is what happens in Dominus, whose most characteristic feature is certainly its actual invention of a material. For Herzog & de Meuron, this invention marks a culminating point of their career. The gabions here are really gabions only at first sight. We are used to seeing gabions as opaque elements consolidated into an incline, not as translucent elements. By intuiting the translucence of the gabions, Herzog & de Meuron discovered a new building material, and deserve to be called inventors.

Were Herzog & de Meuron paying tribute to the primary material, earth, and its importance to the growth of life? Do the rocks in captivity speak nostalgically of the caves and caverns that were the first wine cellars? Were they trying to tell us that a building breathes? Or that caged, jailed stones ensure protection against the elements but also the healthy air needed for fine wine to be produced? All these questions have to do with the gabions and the material they contain.

But while we recognize the importance of material in this project, we

**59-65** Dominus Winery,
Yountville, California, 1995–1997

shouldn't overlook the dialogue with the environment or landscape. This dialogue is what gives meaning to the construction. The landscape is none other
than the geometry of the vineyard on the gentle slopes of the Napa Valley. The
built solid doesn't alter it. An old path stretches through the vineyard, creating
an amazing void where the Californian concepts of interior and exterior are confused. It is in this void that the literal "transparency" of the wall of caged rocks
is first appreciated. The walls acquire their full formal dimension when sunlight
filters in, producing a vivid and changing plane of shadows. The building is a
cosmic clock inside which we witness the passage of time and learn to appreciate the moment. That this was the intention of Herzog & de Meuron becomes
evident when we observe that larger stones are used in the gabions defining

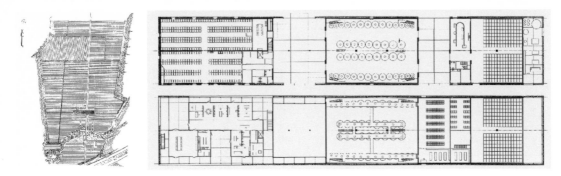

**59-65** Dominus Winery,
Yountville, California, 1995–1997

the corridors. With the changing world of shadows, this produces the light effect desired in that area.

It would be simplifying matters to say that the charm of the project lies entirely in the dialectic that takes place between the stone solid and the light structure defining it. But indeed, it is there that the architecture exhausts itself and acquires its fullness. Herzog & de Meuron are aware of this when they indulge in the procedure of confronting the horizontal plane of the wine-tasting room's wooden table with the casks, or when they have us walk through the corridors, where the lightness of the glass and steel admits the aleatoriness of the caged stones.

**66-67** The solid that contains the library of Eberswalde, Germany (1994–1997), doesn't have as attractive a skin. The aleatoriness we find in Dominus, at once efficient and beautiful, here becomes a mechanical repetition of glass panes serigraphed with images literally alluding to books and culture. Whatever radicality there is in the definition of the solid—whether in its encounter with the horizontal plane, in the nature of the last panel that borders it, or in the openings that are made to have the same dimensions as one of the panels—doesn't compensate for a certain triviality or lack of inspiration that renders Eberswalde less admirable than the Dominus Winery. Despite the radicality, the underlying structure of the building is conventional. I hesitate to approve of an architecture that is only in control of the skin, fundamentally epithelial, and which therefore does not have that transcendental character we find in other works of Herzog & de Meuron.

**68-69** Institut für Spitalpharmazie, Basel, 1995–1998

**68-69** And likewise for the Institut für Spitalpharmazie (ISP) in Basel (1995–1998), where only some subtlety in the arrangement of the openings is worth looking at. I would say that with this project, Herzog & de Meuron's efforts to find significant skins for solids came to an end. The mine was exhausted. At the start of the lecture I mentioned Herzog & de Meuron's self-criticism. Happily, this would reemerge in subsequent projects.

**70-71** That Herzog & de Meuron wished for a way out of the formula is evident in this small private house, the Rudin House in Leymen, France (1996–1997). The architects opted for the "canonical representation of a house," the most direct and literal image of what people hold to be a house. Pitched roof, chimney, windows, everything seems to serve the nonurban resident's canonical idea of a house. This was a radical turn for the architects. If they had previously treated material as the depository of architectural expression, they now seemed keen to recuperate the notion of type, the premise being that image is all that remains in the end, not structure. Hence an architecture where what prevails is an iconography stripped of attributes, empty. It may be pertinent to recall how Rem Koolhaas used the concept of iconography in the Lille convention center. For the Dutch architect, it was still possible to come up with synthetic architectures with a capacity for the figurative, and thus to speak again of iconography. In some of his projects it was form, being responsible for image, that integrated functions, addressed circulations,

70-71 Rudin House, Leymen, France, 1996–1997

401

and resolved structures. For Herzog & de Meuron in this project, iconography made sense only as memory. And with the reappearance of iconography, a dissociation of form and content was inevitable as well, manifest in all the imbalances and anomalies for which the architects seem to congratulate themselves.

That this was the architects' intention from the start is evident when we compare the initial project with the built work. There are differences (chimneys, roofs, windows, etc.), but the similarities are more important. They are manifested where they count most, in the intentions. To the point that the projects can be taken as identical. But what were the architects trying to tell us? Was this a mere academic gesture? Might they have been trying to be ironic about the way people look at architecture? Or did this small project contain a hidden desire to bury a whole manner of making architecture, the one Rossi had recuperated? Herzog & de Meuron's future architecture might answer these questions.

**72-73** In Herzog & de Meuron's search for new roads, the perfect prism was altogether abandoned in the building for Ricola's marketing offices (1997–1999). The alternative was to exploit the perimeter created by a complex floor plan where the oblique prevails and inflections are omnipresent. Orthogonality is deliberately discarded, and the job of materializing the solid generated by the perimeter is entrusted to glass. Anyone who studies the images perceives the importance of the reflective property of glass, thanks to which we forget about the building's solid condition. Also note that the glass comes in large pieces that serve to emphasize the geometry of the interior spaces and, in minimalist manner, show the elemental superposition of the two horizontal planes that shape the inhabitable space. On the other hand, the plane of the roof engages in an immediate and efficient dialectic, with a projecting finish that recalls the starting conditions, namely the irregular contour of the ground plan, multiplying the reflections. The volume virtually dissolves with the superposition of images in an infinite play of reflections, rendering impossible any reading that might understand the building as a static reality. The image multiplies and

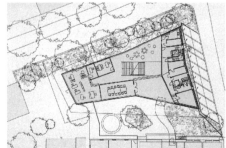

**72-73** Ricola marketing offices, Laufen, Switzerland, 1997–1999

dissolves, and the architects seem to be interested not so much in the values accompanying a world of presumably impenetrable solids, as in the values that are present in the virtual and atmospheric spaces to which the systems of voids have accustomed us.

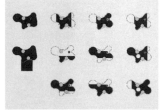

**74-76** Library (project), Technical University, Cottbus, Germany, 1993

**74-76** Herzog & de Meuron's abandonment of the prism seems necessarily to lead to a counterpoint: a formal world about which it seems obligatory to speak in terms of biology. A case in point is the 1993 competition project for the university library of Cottbus. The architects explain it in this manner: **"Our competition scheme was based on the juxtaposition of two rectangular buildings. Once we were commissioned to start with the final design of the building, the programme had changed and one of the two juxtaposed buildings had been omitted."** [1] Was this the ultimate reason? Herzog & de Meuron seem to deny this: **"Also we were convinced that the city of Cottbus needed a different kind of building which would be more sculptural and more of a landmark building within the very generic urban pattern built after the war."** [2] The change cannot therefore be attributed only to functional reasons. Perhaps the architects saw an opportunity to experiment with new languages. The image that shows the transformation of the original prisms is so eloquent that it needs no commentary. The curving perimeter arrives at a final situation, as if a system of superficial tensions had made it arrive at a situation of equilibrium.

The open form seems to be the leitmotiv of a perimeter that encloses a volume with the capacity to absorb multiple uses and divisions. The architects' objective is not so much the skin, the envelope of the solid, but a formal exploration that leads to our understanding the form as the boundary of a rich inner life. Note how the curtain wall exposes a system of bands of windows that clearly comes from Corbusian tradition. Everything is continuous! Projects of this kind maintain the linguistic exploration that Herzog & de Meuron have so accustomed us to, making us expect much in future from a tandem of architects we can still consider young.

**1** *El Croquis* 109–110, double issue, "Herzog & de Meuron 1998–2002. La naturaleza del artificio" (Madrid, 2002), p. 210.

**2** Ibid.

403

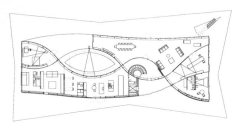

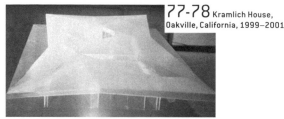

77-78 Kramlich House,
Oakville, California, 1999–2001

77-78 In the Kramlich House in California (1999–2001), a residence for a collector of video art, the floor plan is defined by an irregular rectangle, one where the two long sides are curved and the other two are straight and parallel to one another. Herzog & de Meuron seemed inclined to explore how a pattern of interlaced curves could become the substance of a floor plan. That is, they were testing their capacity to turn any formal pretext into a plan: once again, the phantom of the arbitrary form as the seed of an architecture. But this plan, which permits a certain regularity in the pieces and gives rise to unique spaces wherever the projection of videos requires them, comes into play as much with the roof as with the floor, once again provoking a dialectical encounter of disparate formal systems. The intimate relation between the three levels results in a series of fluid spaces and systems of voids that give the house a continuity

we architects of the turn of the century have been able to learn as much from Le Corbusier and Mies van der Rohe as from Wright and Neutra. Hence the fluidity of the ground-floor plan contrasts with the orthogonal structure of the basement. And the generous roof insists the polygonal condition of the perimeter it defines, as becomes more evident when it meets the curvilinear envelope of two sides of the house. The Kramlich House therefore seems to advocate a fluid architecture, in constant movement as befits our end-of-century culture, where change as a way of life is the rule. The interlacing curves seem inclined to guarantee permanent mobility, thereby denying that architecture is a paradigm of "radical immobility," as Juan Borchers would have liked—and the same could be said of some of the other works of Herzog & de Meuron, particularly one of the more successful ones, the Dominus Winery in the Napa Valley.

404

# Index

# Photo credits

JAMES STIRLING
1-9: CCA
10: James Stirling
11-16: CCA
30, 34: Richard Einzig
49: John Donat
62: Peter Walser
66: John Donat

ROBERT VENTURI AND
DENISE SCOTT BROWN
1, 2, 5: Rollin R. La France
7: Mark Cohn
8: William Watkins
9, 10: Courtesy VSBA
11, 12: George Pohl
13: Rollin R. La France
14-18, 20-27: Courtesy VSBA
28, 29: Tom Bernard
30: Courtesy VSBA
31-33: Tom Bernard
34, 35: Courtesy VSBA
36: Tom Bernard
37: Courtesy VSBA
38-41: Tom Bernard
42: Matt Wargo
43: Courtesy VSBA
44: Matt Wargo
45, 46: Courtesy VSBA
47: © Susan Dirk/ Under The Light
48, 49: Matt Wargo
50: Courtesy VSBA
51: Matt Wargo
52: Phil Starling
53, 54: Courtesy VSBA
55: Matt Wargo
56: Courtesy VSBA
57: Matt Wargo
58-61: Courtesy VSBA
62: Panoptic Imaging
63-65: Courtesy VSBA

ALDO ROSSI
11: Robert Freno
19: Heinrich Helfenstein
20, 22-24: Roberto Schezen/Esto
25: Studio Aldo Rossi
26: Maria Ida Biggi
27: Peter Arnell
28: Studio Aldo Rossi
29: Roberto Schezen/Esto
32-35: Studio Aldo Rossi
41: José Charters
42: Robert Freno
43-45: Gianni Braghieri
46: Heinrich Helfenstein
47, 48: Robert Freno
49: George Tice
50: Robert Freno
51: Edouard Stackpole
52-54: Antonio Martinelli
56, 57: Roberto Schezen/Esto
67, 70-81: Studio Aldo Rossi

PETER EISENMAN
1-6, 7-13: Richard Frank (Five
Architects)
23: Norman McGrath
24: Judith Turner
43-48: Courtesy Eisenman Architects
54: Jeff Goldberg/Esto
55-59: Courtesy Eisenman Architects
64: Jeff Goldberg/Esto
66: Dick Frank Studio
67: Jeff Goldberg/Esto
71, 72: Courtesy
Eisenman Architects
76: Dick Frank Studio

ALVARO SIZA
2: Giovanni Chiaramonte
3, 7: Roberto Collovà
12: Giovanni Chiaramonte

17: Roberto Collovà
24: Luis Ferreiro Alves
34: Roberto Collovà
35, 37: Hisao Suzuki
41: Roberto Collovà
46: Luis Ferreiro Alves
47: Giovanni Chiaramonte
52: Roberto Collovà
53, 56: Hisao Suzuki
62, 64: Roberto Collovà
65: Giovanni Chiaramonte
66, 68: Von der Vlugt & Claus
71, 73, 74: Luis Ferreiro Alves
76-80, 82-84, 85, 86, 89, 90: Hisao
Suzuki

FRANK GEHRY
3: Yukio Futagawa
7: Gehry Partners, LLP.
9, 16, 22: Tim Street-Porter/Esto
24, 26, 27: Gehry Partners, LLP.
40-42, 44, 45: Michael Moran
46, 47: Jeff Goldberg/Esto
48, 49, 51: Mark Darley/Esto
52, 54, 55: Grant Mudford
59: Gehry Partners, LLP.
60: Grant Mudford
61: Gehry Partners, LLP.
62: Grant Mudford
63, 65: Gehry Partners, LLP.
66: Scott Frances/Esto
68: Don Wong
70, 71: Richard Bryant/ Arcaid
72: Peter Mauss/Esto
76: Jeff Goldberg/Esto

REM KOOLHAAS
16, 18: Hans Werlemann
51-53: Richard Barnes
57-59: Hans Werlemann
62, 63: Peter Aaron/Esto
65: Hisao Suzuki
66, 69: Hans Werlemann
70: Christian Richter
71: Hisao Suzuki
74: Hans Werlemann
76: Arnaud Carpentier
Page 316:
© Andy Warhol, VEGAP,
Barcelona 2004
© David Salle, VEGAP,
Barcelona 2004

HERZOG & DE MEURON
1: Margherita Spiluttini
2: Hisao Suzuki
3: Margherita Spiluttini
6, 12, 13, 16, 19, 21, 23: Hisao Suzuki
25- 27: Margherita Spiluttini
29-32, 34, 37: Hisao Suzuki
38: Margherita Spiluttini
39-41, 44, 45, 50, 52: Hisao Suzuki
59-63: Timothy Hursley
68-70, 73: Margherita Spiluttini
74: Hisao Suzuki

Photographs by Hisao Suzuki used
in the Álvaro Siza and Herzog & de
Meuron chapters have been published
with the permission of *El Croquis*.

We apologize for any possible omission
of the sources of images used in the
book. We have done everything possible to locate and obtain the rights to
their reproduction.